D0065024

Expanding U.S.-Asian Trade and Investment

Expanding U.S.-Asian Trade and Investment

New Challenges and Policy Options

Claude E. Barfield, editor

The AEI Press

Publisher for the American Enterprise Institute
WASHINGTON, D.C.

1997

The American Enterprise Institute would like to thank the American Express Foundation and the Sasakawa Peace Foundation for support for this project. Partial funding for this volume was provided by the Korea Foundation.

Available in the United States from the AEI Press, c/o Publisher Resources Inc., 1224 Heil Quaker Blvd., P.O. Box 7001, La Vergne, TN 37086-7001. Distributed outside the United States by arrangement with Eurospan, 3 Henrietta Street, London WC2E 8LU England.

Library of Congress Cataloging-in-Publication Data

Expanding U.S.-Asian trade and investment : new challenges and
   policy options / Claude E. Barfield, editor.
      p.   cm.
   Includes bibliographical references.
   ISBN 0-8447-3934-0 (cloth : alk. paper)
      1. United States—Foreign economic relations—East Asia.   2.
Asia—Foreign economic relations—United States.   3. United States—
Commercial policy.   I. Barfield, Claude E.
HF1456.5.E18E95   1997
337.7305—dc20   96-41171
                                                              CIP

Printed in the United States of America

Contents

1997

TABLES

FIGURES

Contributors

CLAUDE E. BARFIELD is a resident scholar at the American Enterprise Institute and the director of Trade and Technology Policy Studies. As a consultant with the Office of the U.S. Trade Representative, he wrote the Reagan administration's Statement of Trade Policy in 1983. He was the staff codirector of the President's Commission for a National Agenda for the Eighties. Mr. Barfield has taught at Yale University and the University of Munich. He is the author and editor of several books.

TAEHO BARK is the vice-president of the Korea Institute for International Economic Policy. Before joining KIEP in 1989, he was a research fellow at the Korea Development Institute. In 1993–1994, Mr. Bark was the senior economist in the trade and industry division, Office of the Secretary for Economic Affairs, Korea. He was an assistant professor of economics at Georgetown University from 1983 to 1987 and had been a consultant to the World Bank. Mr. Bark is a member of the Advisory Committee on International Trade Policy of the Ministry of Trade and Industry and is the chairman of the Advisory Committee on WTO Trade Policy Review Mechanism.

GUOCANG HUAN is the managing director of BZW Asia Ltd. He is the coeditor of *The Chinese View of the World* and has written articles for *Foreign Affairs, Foreign Policy, Asian Wall Street Journal, Far Eastern Economic Review, New York Times,* and *Far Eastern Executive Review.* Mr. Huan was a vice-president and senior economist at J. P. Morgan Co. Inc.

LINDA Y. C. LIM is an associate professor of international business and the director of the Southeast Asia Business Program at the University of Michigan. She also teaches MBA and executive education courses on international and Asian business at the University of Michigan Business School and the Wharton School, University of Pennsylvania. Ms. Lim has taught at Swarthmore College and the National University of Singapore. She founded and was the first director of the University of Michigan's Center for International Business Education. Ms. Lim has been a consultant for the United Nations, World Bank, Organization for Economic Cooperation and Development, and AEI. She is a member of the UN Committee for Development Planning, the Program for International Studies in Asia, and the Advisory Board of the Korea Economic Institute of America.

IL SAKONG is the chairman and CEO of the Institute for Global Economics, Seoul. He has been a special consultant to the International Monetary Fund since 1989. He is a member of the Korea-U.S. Wisemen Council. From 1979 to 1988, Mr. SaKong was Korean minister of finance, senior secretary to the president for economic affairs, senior counselor to the minister of economic planning board, and senior economist of the Presidential Council on Economics and Scientific Affairs. He had been senior fellow, research director, and vice-president of the Korea Development Institute and president of the Korea Institute for Industrial Economics and Trade.

YU-SHAN WU has been an associate professor in the Political Science Department, National Taiwan University since 1991. He was a visiting scholar at the Institute of East Asian Studies, University of California at Berkeley, and a research fellow in foreign policy studies, Brookings Institution. The author of four books, Mr. Wu has contributed to *Asian Survey, Pacific Review, Political Science Review,* and several books.

MASARU YOSHITOMI has, since 1992, been the visiting executive professor of finance and chairman of the U.S.-Japan Management Studies Center at the Wharton School, University of Pennsylvania. He is also the vice-chairman of the Long-Term Credit Bank Institute of Research. Mr. Yoshitomi had been director-general of the Coordination Bureau and director-general of the Economic Research Institute, Japan's Economic Planning Agency. He was the director of the General Economics Branch of the Organization for Economic Cooperation and Development, an economist at the International Monetary Fund, and a lecturer at the United Nations Asian Institute for Economic Development and Planning, Bangkok.

1
Introduction

Claude E. Barfield

The purpose of this volume is to analyze current and potential trends in the trade and investment flows between the United States and the East Asian economies and to describe the evolving policy challenges for both U.S. and East Asian political leaders. In attempting to achieve a greater understanding of the economic and political changes sweeping the region, the American Enterprise Institute recruited scholars from the United States, Japan, the People's Republic of China, Korea, and Taiwan to contribute studies of their respective countries and of the members of the Association of South East Asian Nations (ASEAN) as a group.

Whether described as an economic miracle or as the result of a more mundane process of human and physical capital accumulation still subject to the laws of diminishing returns (as Paul Krugman has recently argued), the growth of East Asian economies over the past two decades has dramatically changed the structure and the dynamics of the world trade and investment system. Since 1980, East Asian economies have grown at rates between 1 percent and 6 percent greater than other major economies. By mid-1996, East Asia accounted for more than 20 percent of world gross domestic product and almost 20 percent of total world trade. According to projections by the World Bank, for the balance of the 1990s East Asian economies will create 40 percent of new world purchasing power and take in at least one-third of all additional imports.

East Asia has also become a major recipient of foreign direct investment (FDI). In 1994, 66 percent of total world investment flows to developing countries ($53 billion) went to this region. Both the United States and Japan have established strong investment portfolios in East Asia, with total Japanese investment reaching $81 billion in 1992 and total U.S. investment, $76 billion (including $26 billion in Japan itself). The most important recent development regarding East Asian FDI, however, has been the emergence of the Four Tigers (Korea, Taiwan, Singapore, and Hong Kong) as major investors in the lower-income East Asian economies. The tigers now account for about half of all

1

FDI in the less-developed East Asian economies, including the People's Republic of China.

In the past several decades of extraordinary East Asian economic growth and increased prosperity, two underlying conditions are striking: one, that growth has been essentially market driven and not dependent on regional trading bloc institutions or preferential rules; and two, that growth has also been heavily dependent on an open world trading system, especially the assurance of a relatively open U.S. market. Even though East Asian intraregional trade has risen steeply in the past decade, East Asia as a whole still ships two-thirds of its exports outside of the region. While the situation is changing, until the early 1990s the United States ranked as the first or second leading export market for most East Asian countries.

Although the United States has been the single most important economic influence (as well as the guarantor of political stability) in East Asia over the past few decades, U.S. trade and investment policy, until quite recently, eschewed special regional arrangements. Multilateralism—with bilateral pressure in special situations, such as those presented by Japan after 1970—was the hallmark of U.S. trade and investment policy.

In the late 1980s, however, important new strands appeared in U.S. trade and investment policy. Regional trade initiatives, first with Canada and Mexico and later with the transpacific region, assumed a high priority among U.S. trade objectives. Established in 1989, the Asia Pacific Economic Cooperation forum became a real force only after it was adopted—some might say highjacked—by the Clinton administration in 1993.

For two reasons, APEC fit neatly into the goals of Clinton trade policy. First, the distinctly mercantilist, export-oriented trade policy adopted by the Clintonites was naturally attracted to the substantial opportunities afforded by burgeoning East Asian markets. Seven of the ten nations heading the administration's list of big emerging markets were from Asia. And, second, APEC had the political virtue of being virgin territory—that is, unlike the North American Free Trade Agreement (NAFTA) and the Uruguay Round negotiations, East Asia and APEC were not initiatives inherited from earlier Republican administrations. APEC could be hailed as an original Clinton initiative and policy.

Thus, while the Clinton administration maintained that multilateralism remained the top venue for the achievement of U.S. trade goals, it gave increasing attention to regional initiatives—first with APEC and then with the extension of NAFTA to Central and South America. The 1995 Economic Report of the President stated candidly that the "most distinctive legacy" of the Clinton administration in trade policy will be the "foundation it has laid for the development of overlapping plurilateral trade agreements as stepping stones to global free trade."

President Clinton's strong personal interest in and the attendance of other heads of state at APEC summit meetings raised the profile and importance of the nascent Asia-Pacific regional trade forum. And the forum produced concrete actions: in 1993 in Seattle, APEC nations agreed to adopt a volunteer investment code, and then in 1994 in the Bogor Declaration, APEC members pledged to achieve free trade in the region by 2020 (2010 for the developed countries).

From the outset, however, two visions regarding the structure and future of APEC competed against one another. The United States, strongly backed by Australia and New Zealand (the Anglo-Saxons), in effect envisioned the creation, over time, of a mini–World Trade Organization (WTO) for the Pacific, complete with legally binding rules, timetables, and mechanisms for dispute settlement. Most of the Asian members, however, wanted to move forward through a much less legalistic consensus process that would give great freedom to each country to proceed toward liberalization at its own pace—"concerted unilateralism" was the name given to this process. In general, the authors of the chapters in this volume subscribe to this view of the future of APEC.

At Osaka in November 1995, the "Asian way" seemed to have won the day, but many issues regarding the future directions and shape of APEC were left undecided. For instance, a consensus on a definition of *open regionalism* was unrealized—Should liberalization within APEC be open to the rest of the trading world, or should liberalization be granted to outside countries only on a reciprocal basis? And although the United States did not oppose steps toward unilateral liberalization within APEC, it served notice that it would not grant most-favored-nation (MFN) status to free riders. Thus, the triumph of the Asian way at Osaka may be deceptive, for after the 1996 presidential election, when U.S. trade officials feel freer to express strong opinions, U.S. negotiators will likely press to reopen the contentious questions relating to open regionalism and concerted unilateralism.

The Design of This Volume

The authors of the chapters in this volume were asked to undertake two assignments: first, to describe the economic development of the country they were analyzing, as well as the increased complexity and diversity of its trade and investment relations; and second, to assess from the prism of that country's perspective the implications these current and future international economic developments have for trade

3

and investment relations with the United States, with neighbors in East Asia, and finally, with non-Asian nations and regions.

In chapter 2, which deals with the United States, the author's initial economic point is that the United States, alone among the triad (European Union, Japan, and United States), enjoys a balanced worldwide trade and investment portfolio. Europe is in a weaker position in East Asia than the United States is, and East Asia is much less represented in Europe than the United States is.

In absolute terms, U.S.-East Asia trade is projected to be double that of U.S.-European Union (EU) trade within the next few years. EU trade with East Asia accounts for only about 14 percent of that region's total trade, and, conversely, East Asia accounts for only about 7 percent of total EU trade. Further, in the area of foreign direct investment, the United States and the EU are closely intertwined, with EU companies accounting for almost two-thirds of all FDI in the United States, while 44 percent of all U.S. FDI is concentrated in Europe. Japan, the leading East Asia investor, has less than $100 billion committed to the EU, while U.S. investment tops $250 billion.

These facts form the basis for the major trade policy conclusion that U.S. "trade and investment policy is best achieved through the multilateral trading system, embodied in the new World Trade Organization." While regional arrangements have a place in U.S. trade and investment policy, U.S. international economic interests can be fully realized only through multilateral means.

Chapter 2 traces the recent tilt in U.S. trade policy toward regionalism and comes down strongly on the side of the dissenters from this policy, agreeing with their emphasis on the dangers of trade diversion, the protectionist effects of strict rules of origin regulations, and the potential high transaction costs and concomitant inefficiency of a trading world "dotted with separate bilateral and plurilateral FTAs, each with different interim timetables, tariff levels, and nontariff barriers and liberalization rules."

Regarding APEC, the author supports the views of many Asian leaders that the path to regional liberalization is through maximum unilateral moves, with each nation fulfilling its commitment to trade barrier reduction at its own pace. *Open regionalism* in APEC should be defined as liberalization on an MFN basis to members and nonmembers alike. Finally, the chapter argues that future APEC meetings should provide a forum for discussion and planning for a new multilateral trade round. Together, the members of APEC represent a potentially formidable force within the WTO; they should use this clout to advance the cause of further worldwide trade and investment liberalization.

U.S.-Japan Relations. In chapter 3, "Building a New U.S.–Japan Relationship in Asia," Masuru Yoshitomi first describes Japan's changing trade and investment patterns in Asia, particularly since 1985. He presents details on the evolution of the "flying-geese" pattern in trade and investment, with Japan leading the way followed first by the new industrialized economies (Korea, Taiwan, Hong Kong, and Singapore) and later by the less-developed economies of the ASEAN countries. For the NIEs, the older pattern of interindustry trade, characterized by Japan's importing food, minerals, and apparel, has been supplanted largely by increased intra-industry trade, in which the NIEs provide components and, more recently, even entire low- and medium-technology goods, and Japan increasingly provides the capital and manufacturing equipment needed to produce these components.

The ASEAN countries, though evolving rapidly, retain the older interindustry patterns. Currently, some 70 percent of Japan's imports from the ASEAN countries consists of fuels, crude materials, and food. Yoshitomi predicts that intra-industry trade between Japan and the ASEAN countries will rise steeply, particularly in the home electronics, home appliances, and motorcycles sectors. Thus, like the NIEs before them, the ASEAN countries are set to move up toward the front of the flying-geese pattern.

Yoshitomi next traces the evolution of Japan's FDI in East Asia and the role of Japanese FDI in the integration of East Asian production and trade. As he demonstrates, globalization—through the activities of multinational corporations—has strengthened the complementarity of trade and investment.

Using the electrical machinery industry as an example, Yoshitomi presents the history of Japanese FDI in Asia over the past three decades. During the 1960s and early 1970s, Japanese companies invested in host countries to evade high tariffs by getting inside the perimeter and targeting these domestic markets by import substitution. Japanese FDI concentrated on the production of less sophisticated products such as radios, fans, electric frying pans, and small black-and-white television sets.

During the 1970s and early 1980s, political motives provided an additional incentive for Japanese East Asian FDI, as Japanese companies shifted production abroad in an attempt to reduce the trade deficit with the United States and the EU and avoid trade friction. This move particularly affected consumer electronics products such as small and medium-sized television sets, VCRs, and window air conditioners.

Finally, over the past decade, while the political factor in substituting overseas for Japanese production in exporting to other regions has remained important, the rise of the yen and the general increase in

5

production costs in Japan have given even stronger impetus to the movement of Japanese manufacturing overseas. Thus, Asian affiliates of Japanese companies are now producing entire product lines for export back to Japan, particularly consumer electronics such as compact disc players, VCRs, videotape recorders, video cameras, and standard television sets.

In the last analytic section, Yoshitomi turns to doubts about Japan's import absorption capacity. Using export and import data since 1985, he shows that while the nominal value of Japanese exports (measured in dollars) increased by 100 percent, the actual volume of Japanese exports went up only 20 percent. The performance of imports has been just the opposite, with volume increasing by 67 percent, three times as fast as exports. This has meant that from 1985 to 1993, on a volume basis Japan lost 36 percent of market share. Yoshitomi thus doubts about Japan's import capacity are "unfounded."

Yoshitomi makes two recommendations regarding the future of APEC and of the negotiating framework. Liberalization, he argues should proceed "incrementally" because of the diversity of APEC nations not only in language, religion, and culture but also in their various stages of economic development. "APEC countries," he writes, "recognize that APEC is not a place for negotiations but a place for regional cooperation and development of consensus." He recommends that each country formulate a basic plan for liberalization for the next five to ten years and then confront its own vested interests with this "international promise of liberalization as an established fact." Through an APEC review process, peer pressure can also be exerted to ensure that each country is proceeding on schedule. Finally, he argues that liberalization should be on an unconditional MFN basis to nonmember countries.

Yoshitomi's second recommendation is for the formation, under the aegis of APEC, of a non-NAFTA Pacific caucus (NNPC); its main purpose would be to exert strong pressure against any drift of the EU or NAFTA toward discriminatory or protectionist action. He sees the NNPC as a middle ground between no organization of the Asian countries and the distinctly anti-Western premises behind the East Asian Economic Caucus (EAEC) pushed by Malaysian Prime Minister Mahatir. Unlike the EAEC, which excludes Australia and New Zealand on racial grounds, the NNPC would include these countries as fully qualified members of the APEC Asian community.

U.S.-China Trade. Guacang Huan, in his chapter on the People's Republic of China, carefully traces the intricate connection between political and economic issues in the often roller-coaster relations between the United States and the PRC—right down to the summer of 1996 (as this volume went to press) when, after a great deal of threat and bluster on each side, the two nations reached an agreement on intellectual property and piracy issues and the United States renewed the PRC's most-favored-nation status.

Huan begins the main body of his study with a historical survey of the major changes in U.S.-PRC trade and investment flows since 1979, when commercial relations were normalized. Bilateral trade between the two countries grew from $6.3 billion in 1981 to more than $40 billion in 1993.

At the outset, the main items sold by the United States to the PRC were grain, chemical products, industrial machinery, and telecommunications equipment. U.S. imports were primarily labor-intensive products, such as textiles, simple machine tools, and such primary goods as mining products.

Until the mid-1980s, U.S. corporations were heavily dependent on Hong Kong middlemen in their approach to the PRC market—and, similarly, PRC businessmen had little direct experience in the U.S. market. Thus, early on many of the PRC's exports were channeled through Hong Kong—more than 40 percent through the late 1980s. Over the past several years, however, this situation has changed, and by 1994 only about one-quarter of China's exports went through Hong Kong. Huan cites two reasons for this shift: first, Chinese companies have become more competitive and experienced in the international market; and second, as U.S. and other foreign corporations have increased their direct investment in the PRC, they have developed their own distribution networks and now import and export directly.

The development of U.S.-China trade was also strongly affected by developments in East Asia itself. By the late 1970s, land and labor costs in the Four Tigers had risen to such heights that these countries were becoming increasingly uncompetitive in labor-intensive industries. In turn, they began to upgrade their industrial structures, moving up the scale to medium- and, in some cases, high-technology sectors. Led by Hong Kong, all the tigers have dramatically increased their economic activities in mainland China. Huan identifies three phases of PRC–Four Tigers trade and investment relations: first came subcontracting in low-technology manufacturing and consumer goods; next came actual relocation of the more labor-intensive manufacturing to the mainland, with the high value-added processes remaining in the home business; and finally, multinationals relocated all their production facilities to the PRC (and other less-developed East Asian economies) and exported finished products from the host country.

Huan identifies five major challenges to continued high economic growth in the PRC. First, China must overcome the increasing bottle-necks and inefficiencies associated with its underdeveloped infrastructure, including major deficiencies in its road, air, and railway systems. In addition, its ability to improve both its power generation and its telecommunications sectors will be a powerful determinant in the PRC's continued economic progress.

Second, a more stable and consistent central macroeconomic management system must be adopted and sustained. Here, reform of the banking and financial markets systems is crucial, as well as the creation of a more wide-based and efficient system of taxation.

Third, the government must maintain a balanced but steady policy of privatization. Forty percent of state sector companies lose money, but too rapid privatization, Huan argues, could produce a political backlash if millions of workers were thrown out of work—particularly before the PRC develops a stronger social safety net.

The fourth challenge is the high population growth rate. Currently, the PRC's net birthrate is about 1.2 percent per year, meaning that there are 14 million new mouths to feed each year.

Fifth, Huan posits that balancing China's foreign accounts is essential. By that he means achieving an economically stable balance of foreign capital inflow and importing machinery and consumer items against internally generated exports. Huan predicts that although this will be a difficult balancing act, China's rapid economic growth will continue and will translate into "a huge potential market" that will require "more financial resources, technology, and capital goods imported from overseas."

Turning to the evolution of Chinese international economic policies, Huan points out that only over the past decade has China emerged from a strategy of self-reliance and internal autarchy. As late as 1978, foreign trade accounted for less than 5 percent of its gross domestic product. Over the past decade and a half, however, the Chinese government has developed strong and active trade and investment policies that contain bilateral, regional, and multilateral elements.

According to Huan, for the PRC, APEC serves as a forum for discussion of common regional international economic issues, including important trade and investment questions, and as a forum in which its growing international power and status can be confirmed and advanced. The PRC, Huan argues, would resist turning APEC into a formal regional trading bloc.

The WTO is the center of China's focus and priorities. Negotiations, particularly those with the United States, for China to reenter the WTO are by far the most important issues on China's trade agenda.

Huan makes a strong case for compromise on both sides and argues that Chinese membership in the WTO is a key to achieving future stability in U.S.-PRC trade relations. He states:

> There is . . . a middle ground whereby both nations can solve their dispute. . . . While the Chinese side will insist on joining the trade organization as a developing nation, it is likely to make further concessions concerning intellectual property rights. China will also concede greater access to its domestic manufactured goods market and accept the reduction of disparities in the treatment of Chinese and foreign companies in China. Reduction of tariff and nontariff trade barriers will also be conceded by China.
>
> For the United States, the key issue is not whether China is treated as a developing nation, but rather how to work out the compromises on the issues listed above—what level of tariff, which nontariff barrier to remove, and just where are Chinese intellectual property laws the weakest.

In a concluding point, Huan argues that "Washington's economic policies toward China should continue to be separate from its political and security concerns." The strongest reason for this separation, according to Huan, is that "solid U.S.-China economic relations will support Washington's long-term political objectives in China: democracy, internal stability, regional stability, and peace."

Korea-U.S. Economics. In their chapter on Korea, Il SaKong and Tae Ho Bark take note at the outset of four factors that have contributed to the emergence of a new international economic order and environment: the end of the cold war, the relative decline of the economic position of the United States compared with its trading partners, the rapid advance of information technologies, and the conclusion of the Uruguay Round and the formation of the WTO.

Both Korea and the United States are in the process of adopting policies and strategies to cope with the new environment. Korea is attempting to speed up liberalization and the abolition of government regulations that inhibit internal economic reform as well as increased trade. President Kim Young Sam's "globalization" initiative is symbolic of the changed government attitude, particularly its emphasis on encouraging foreign industrial alliances and facilitating foreign direct investment in the Korean economy.

Regarding the United States, SaKong and Bark argue that there has been a decided shift away from a primary focus on multilateral trade leadership and toward the increased use of bilateral and unilateral measures to force open foreign markets. This shift has been accompanied by a heavy mercantilist-tinged emphasis on increasing U.S. exports, especially to the so-called big emerging markets of the developing countries.

SaKong and Bark trace the history of postwar U.S.-Korean trade and investment relations, beginning with the period of the 1950s and 1960s, when security issues were predominant. During the 1960s and 1970s, as Korea undertook to develop its economy, the United States acted as a major supplier of industrial equipment and technology and was as well the most important market for Korean goods. During the 1980s, a fundamental change took place, as Korea emerged as one of the newly industrialized economies, with a stronger position in some basic industries such as automobiles, steel, and textiles. Korea also began to run a growing trade surplus with the United States, thereby provoking a negative response from the United States, which pressed Korea to open its own market and to allow its currency to appreciate against the U.S. dollar. The high—or low—point in this period of tension came in 1988 when the U.S. Congress passed a trade act that included Super 301, the addition to U.S. trade law, which mandated retaliation against unfair trading partners if they did not change their practices. Korea, through a series of strategically timed market-opening steps, avoided a major confrontation with the United States, and today, while there remain areas of substantial trade friction between the two countries, no major trade crises are looming on the horizon.

Before turning to policy questions, the authors briefly survey recent trends in Korea's trade and investment position. While the United States remains the most important market for Korea's exports, dependence on the United States—and on other developed country markets—is declining. Conversely, Korea's exports to developing countries are rising rapidly, reaching almost 50 percent by 1994. A large part of this increase is going to the burgeoning ASEAN and Chinese economies. Japan and the United States are still the largest importers into Korea, but since 1988 the level of imported goods from other Asian economies has more than tripled.

Korea, along with the other NIEs, has also emerged as an important investor in less-developed Asian economies, particularly China, which received almost one-quarter of Korea's outward flow of investment in 1994. Inward FDI in Korea remains small—a newly perceived concern for the Korean government—with Japan and the United States providing half of the total.

Regarding future Korean and East Asian trade and investment policy options, the authors endorse the recent decisions in APEC to proceed toward greater liberalization through flexibility and volunteer means, though they warn that flexibility cannot become a permanent shield against meaningful market-opening moves by APEC members. In that light, they state that both the United States and South Korea were derelict in their initial trade-opening offerings at the 1995 Osaka meeting. They praise the comprehensive intent of President Kim's "globalization" effort but argue that Korea must take stronger leadership in the next few years by offering a "plausible, but visionary liberalization package."

SaKong and Bark also suggest two additional roles for Korea: as a mediator between advanced economies and less-developed countries in Asia, through its own recent experience in rapid development, and as the bridge for technology transfer, particularly in manufacturing technology.

They urge the United States to continue to take a strong leadership role in APEC but warn that "it would be counterproductive if the trade liberalization agenda of the United States is perceived as being designed mainly to extract new trade concessions or to attack internal practices of some economies." In light of this danger, they suggest that the United States place more emphasis on trade facilitation measures, such as standardization, and they specifically recommend that the United States and Korea consider the possibility of establishing a Northeast Asian Development Bank to provide much-needed infrastructure funds for the joint development of Russian, Chinese, and, ultimately, North Korean lands in this sector.

Finally, they state that, as a medium-sized country striving to complete globally, Korea should ensure that it continue to be a strong, forward-looking multilateral system. And they urge the United States to retain leadership in the WTO as its top priority, because "any visible diminished U.S. commitment to multilateralism is bound to weaken the very foundations of multilateralism."

Changes in Taiwan. In chapter 6, covering Taiwan, Yu-Shan Wu traces the "shifting dependency" of the Taiwanese economy on international trade and investment since the 1940s, arguing that during that time Taiwan passed through two periods in which import substitution was the dominant policy and two periods in which the government and the private sector concentrated on export expansion.

The 1950s represented the first period of import substitution, as Taiwan instituted high tariffs and import and currency exchange controls in order, states Wu, to nurture the domestic food processing and textile industries. From this base, during the 1960s, the Taiwanese government shifted its focus toward export-expanding policies, including financial reform and the construction of a system of export incentives. There were several results from these policy initiatives. First, Taiwan's

11

exports climbed rapidly, particularly to the United States, which, by the end of the 1960s, had surpassed Japan as the most important export market for the island. Almost 40 percent of Taiwan's exports were going to the United States by the year 1970. Second, textiles and food were supplemented by other light industrial exports such as wood products, sporting goods, and footwear. And by the beginning of the 1970s, there was also an infant electronics industry, based largely on foreign companies—Ford, Motorola, RCA, and Admiral—from the United States. At the same time, Japan became the dominant source for the importation of capital goods and machinery, and Taiwan began to run what has become a permanent deficit with Japan (in the early 1970s Japan accounted for just under half of all Taiwan's manufacturing imports).

Political and economic changes in the 1970s produced a reversion to the import substitution policies of the 1950s. The death of Chiang Kai-shek and the succession of his son, combined with the oil crisis and the economic stagnation in the developed world, ushered in new efforts to establish infant industries in key sectors such as shipbuilding, steel, and petrochemicals. Heavy subsidies of state-controlled firms led to a two-tiered industrial structure, for small and medium-sized firms still predominated in the exporting sectors. Taiwan's economic relations with its two main partners, the United States and Japan, remained essentially unchanged. Taiwan benefited greatly from the U.S. generalized system of preferences (GSP), which lowered duties for many developing countries: at the end of the 1970s, almost 40 percent of Taiwan's exports to the United States were covered by this program. In turn, the government adopted a clearly pro-U.S. investment and import policy. Despite the pro-U.S. import tilt, Japan remained the most important supplier of capital, capital goods, and machinery.

By the mid-1980s, Taiwan had become one of the so-called Little Tigers and a minor exporting power. Foreign investment poured in, and exports reached 21 percent of the island's GDP. By 1987, almost half of Taiwan's exports were going to the United States, and Taiwan ranked just behind Japan as the most important source of the U.S. trade deficit. This, in turn, generated great political pressure from the United States, in the form of bilateral demands for voluntary export restraints and currency appreciation. In 1989, Taiwan lost its GSP status.

By the end of the 1980s, however, a new phenomenon was overshadowing all other factors in Taiwan's international economic position: the role of the PRC as the island's most important trade and investment partner. The opening of the Chinese market came at a crucial point for Taiwan. On the push side, rising labor and land costs, a surging Taiwan dollar, development opposition from environmental groups, and increased competition from lower-wage Asian countries all impelled Taiwanese corporations and investors to look outward to the PRC. On the pull side, geographic proximity, cultural affinity, huge market potential, low wages, lower production costs, and access to the United States through the GSP exerted strong effects. Thus, from a few projects in 1987, Taiwanese investment grew to $10 billion by the end of 1993, making it second only to Hong Kong in FDI in the PRC.

Wu describes in some detail the current investment-driven trade patterns between Taiwan and the PRC. The cross-strait investment boom has had a major impact on Taiwan's industrial structure. For instance, Wu points out that 80 percent of the island's shoe industry has been transferred to the mainland; in turn, the Taiwanese-dominated PRC companies have captured a large portion of the U.S. shoe market.

The cross-strait trade between the two economies is also highly unbalanced, with Taiwan's trade surplus with China reaching a level of $14.2 billion in 1994. This has increased Taiwan's dependence on the Chinese market as an outlet for its total exports: in 1988, the PRC accounted for about 4 percent of Taiwan's exports, but by 1994 this had risen to more than 16 percent. Much of such exports consist of the transfer of machinery and parts for new factories or, in some cases, intermediate components, which Taiwanese firms must supply themselves for ultimate reexport as finished goods from the mainland. The government of Taiwan has recently begun to worry about the heavy dependence on the mainland market—for both economic and political reasons—and has taken steps to encourage more diverse investment in developing Southeast Asian countries such as Malaysia, Indonesia, and Thailand.

Finally, regarding Taiwan's trade and investment policy goals, Wu states that achievement of some status in the WTO remains the top priority, though the Taiwanese government is aware that this goal depends on the PRC's reentering the WTO. Taiwan has unilaterally begun changing its trade and investment rules to comply with the new multilateral rules adopted during the Uruguay Round. On APEC, Taiwan generally supports the Osaka decisions to move forward voluntarily, but it views the annual APEC meetings more in political than in economic terms and hopes, through persuasion with APEC hosts, to use them as a means to break out of the island's PRC-enforced isolation.

U.S.-ASEAN Trade. In the final chapter of the book, Linda Lim presents an analysis of economic developments among the ASEAN nations (Brunei, Malaysia, Indonesia, the Philippines, Singapore, and Thailand), em-

13

phasizing the increasing complexity and diversity of the trade and investment patterns exhibited by individual countries as well as the group as a whole. Collectively, the ASEAN nations constitute one of the largest and most dynamic regions of the developing world. They have a combined population of 330 million, and most have maintained growth rates of more than 6 percent annually for the past thirty years.

Lim begins her chapter with a detailed analysis of the triangular trade pattern among the ASEAN nations, Japan, and the United States. Using evidence from recent trade and investment statistics, she challenges the claim by some trade experts that the United States is losing out to Japan in economic importance in the ASEAN region. The real picture of what is happening, she argues, is much more complex—and less daunting for U.S. corporations.

Lim concedes that Japan, because the ASEAN region is in its backyard geographically, is the single most important outside economic factor in the region. She points out, however, that from 1980 through 1994, U.S.-ASEAN trade increased more rapidly than Japan-ASEAN trade (4.2 times larger for U.S.-ASEAN; 2.6 times larger for Japan-ASEAN), reducing the "excess" of Japan's total ASEAN trade over U.S. total ASEAN trade from 84 percent in 1980 to a mere 14 percent in 1994. The U.S. share of total ASEAN trade also increased slightly during these years, from 15.2 percent in 1980 to 16.4 percent in 1994, while Japan's share fell from 28 percent in 1980 to 18.8 in 1994.

Lim also challenges the conventional wisdom regarding the flying-geese pattern of East Asian trade and investment. Although this model may have been accurate in the past, the current and prospective trade and investment situation in East Asia and among the ASEAN countries is more complicated. The persistence of the high yen, expensive land and labor costs, and a stagnant home market have induced major shifts of production in a number of manufacturing sectors from Japan to the ASEAN economies.

ASEAN leaders and economists point out that though the technological ladder still exists in some sectors, increasingly the NIEs and the ASEAN corporations are not only overtaking Japanese companies but also carving out niches where they are supplanting Japanese (and U.S.) companies. Examples cited by Lim include shipbuilding and DRAMs (Korea), computer parts and peripherals (Taiwan), financial services (Hong Kong and Singapore), and computer disk product design (Malaysia and Singapore). And she notes that increasingly the target markets both of Japanese factories in the NIEs and ASEAN and of NIE and ASEAN corporations are less than those of the United States and the EU and more likely to be of Asia itself, including, particularly, China, Japan, and the growing markets of Southeast Asia (especially India).

14

This leads Lim to devote a section of the chapter to a more detailed description of the increasing integration of the ASEAN economies with China and the NIEs. During the late 1980s, ASEAN trade with the NIEs grew rapidly, increasing almost sixfold between 1983 and 1994. By 1993, the collective share of NIE trade with ASEAN equaled 80 percent of Japan's trade with these nations. Primary commodities still dominate ASEAN exports to the NIEs; but their imports increasingly are concentrated in manufacturing machinery and equipment. This change reflects the shift of low-tech and components manufacturing from the NIEs to ASEAN economies, as corporations in these countries faced ever rising labor costs and, in some cases, substantial currency appreciation.

After a brief slowdown of NIE-ASEAN investment after 1990, caused by slackening world demand and diversion of some investment to China and Vietnam, in the past two years NIE-ASEAN investment has again picked up, particularly in Indonesia and the late-blooming Philippines.

Until recently, formal trade arrangements among the ASEAN nations have carried little weight and had little influence. This changed in January 1993, when the ASEAN group of nations entered into an ASEAN free trade agreement (AFTA). The original target date for the complete eradication of barriers was 2008, but in late 1995 this date was advanced to the year 2000. Lim points out that because of the relatively low level of intra-ASEAN trade and the already substantial level of ASEAN integration with other East Asian economies, the AFTA is unlikely to change existing trade patterns very much. The most important effect, she states, will be increased competitiveness over time as a result of more efficient national economies and some scale effects.

In addition, in the past several years, the PRC has emerged as a major player in ASEAN trade and investment. In the ASEAN countries, a number of overseas Chinese companies have taken the lead in investment in China, in areas such as agribusiness, services, real estate, and even manufacturing. Indeed, the largest single foreign investor in the PRC is a Thai-based overseas Chinese company; second to it is a Malaysian tycoon, followed in turn by large groups in Indonesia and the Philippines.

After surveying the economic activity among the ASEAN countries, the NIEs, and China, Lim concludes that "the emerging division of labor is likely both to be more complex than the 'neo-colonial' pattern observed with United States and Japan" and to portend future integration of the diverse elements of East Asia.

Unlike AFTA, any movement in APEC toward free trade would

15

have an enormous effect on the ASEAN economies—because three-quarters of ASEAN total trade is with APEC nations. Both trade creation and trade diversion would occur on a large scale, according to Lim. For this reason, the ASEAN countries will opt for a slow pace in APEC trade liberalization, and they will resist U.S. attempts to speed the process or to turn APEC into a formal preferential trading arrangement with negotiated liberalization timetables or a dispute settlement system. For ASEAN countries, she writes, "both multilateral free trade under the WTO and regional free trade under AFTA are . . . more important . . . than APEC-wide free trade."

Malaysia's proposal for an East Asian Economic Caucus (EAEC) within APEC, composed of Asian members only, may become attractive for ASEAN countries in the future if the United States begins to push more aggressively for moving up APEC liberalization timetables. Such a caucus would be seen by ASEAN leaders as a means of increasing their clout within APEC and, in alliance with other Asian members such as China and Japan, slowing down any U.S. initiatives. Thus far, however, Japan and Korea in particular have been cool to the idea of an EAEC, partly out of a desire not to offend the United States. Lim notes, however, that Japan may be shifting its position somewhat as a result of recent bilateral confrontations (over automobiles) with the United States.

Whether an EAEC emerges or not, ASEAN nations will continue to prefer a path of unilateral liberalization on a step-by-step basis. The increased efficiencies to be realized under their own AFTA agreement will place them in a better position later to adjust to the more wrenching adjustment that will accompany APEC liberalization.

Regarding the future prospects for U.S. trade and investment involvement with the ASEAN countries, Lim concludes:

> For the ASEAN countries, the recent spurt in U.S. trade and investment is very welcome, not only for the stimulus it gives to regional growth but also for the opportunities it presents for a more diversified dependence on external sources of capital, technology, and markets even as the region itself develops greater technological and market self-sufficiency. . . . In short, U.S. fears that growing ASEAN trade and investment linkages with other Asian countries, especially Japan, will result in the progressive exclusion of U.S. companies from this large and dynamic regional growth market appear to be overstated.

Linda Lim's conclusions regarding the future of U.S.-ASEAN trade and investment relations could be expanded to cover all East Asia. As these studies have demonstrated, two trends are likely to become even stronger: a deepening of intra-East Asian economic ties and, concomitantly, an increasing role in the world trading system.

16

2
Trade, Investment, and Emerging U.S. Policies for Asia

Claude E. Barfield

The astonishing growth and development of the East Asian economies over the past two decades have continually revised models for trade and development. Early leaders such as Korea and Japan developed a mercantilist, export-driven strategy for high growth, but a second wave of exporters—Malaysia, southern China, and Thailand—has more recently pursued a quite different strategy of investment-led growth combined with relatively open trading regimes. Concurrently, pressure from the world trading community has caused Japan and Korea to move toward less restrictive trade and investment regimes.

U.S.–East Asian Trade and Investment Profile

In a recent analysis of the "East Asian miracle," the World Bank concluded that "in large measure [these economies] achieved high economic growth by getting the basics right." The World Bank described these fundamentals as follows:

> Macroeconomic management was unusually good and macroeconomic performance unusually stable, providing the essential framework for private investment. Policies to increase the integrity of the banking system and to make it more accessible to nontraditional savers raised the levels of financial savings. Education policies that focused on primary and secondary schools generated rapid increases in labor force skills. Agricultural policies stressed productivity and did not tax the rural economy excessively. All [the economies] kept price distortions within reasonable bounds and were open to foreign ideas and technology. (World Bank 1993, p. 5)

The World Bank also discovered that, in some cases, direct government intervention aimed at fostering specific sectors was successful (they also document spectacular failures) but the fundamentals produced

17

the major positive results for these countries. The results are evident in the record of the past decade and in the current economic and demographic profile of the East Asian economies and illustrate the extraordinary growth and continuing diversity of endowment and national income of the region.

During the 1980s, East Asian economies (with the exception of the Philippines) outstripped growth rates in all major economies by 1–6 percent (table 2–1). Incomes in Asia grew twice as fast as in the rest of the world. By 1990, East Asia's share of world gross domestic product (GDP) and of world trade was just under 20 percent (Panagariya 1993). From 1990 through 1992, East Asia increased its total output and export growth despite a worldwide recession, largely through an expansion of intraregional trade. Though this expansion slowed in 1993–1994, current projections by the World Bank predict that the region will account for 40 percent of increased world purchasing power and for at least one-third of additional imports for the balance of the decade (table 2–2).

Diversity, Japan, and a New Place for China. Because of the implications for any policy alternatives, the diversity of the Asian economies should be underscored. The most accurate indicator of a nation's resource endowment is per capita income. Generally, a high per capita gross national product (GNP) implies a high per capita stock of physical and human capital and natural resource endowment. By this measure of a nation's development, the relative resource endowments of the Asian economies vary tremendously. Japan remains the predominant economy, with an income more than twice that of all the rest of Asia combined. On the basis of this measure, the newly industrialized economies (NIEs) of Asia are not "four little tigers" in the least, since they embody a combined income equal to China and South Asia (India, Pakistan, and Bangladesh). Of the NIEs, Singapore and Hong Kong enjoy substantially higher incomes than Taiwan and Korea. Though expected to grow substantially over the next decade, the economies of the Association of South East Asian Nations (ASEAN) have much lower incomes than the NIEs—and a combined income of only 7 percent of Japan (figure 2–1; see also Noland [1995]).

A number of other disparities complicate the whole economic profile of East Asia. The first is Japan, which is by far the largest economy and accounts for 70 percent of the region's GDP. If Japan is excluded, East Asia's share of world GDP drops from one-fifth to one-twentieth.

Furthermore, there is the vexatious question of China's real GDP and per capita income. On the traditional exchange rate basis, the World Bank calculated in 1992 that China's GDP per head in 1990 was

TABLE 2-1
GROWTH RATES OF GDP, SELECTED COUNTRIES, 1988–1995
(percent per annum)

	Base Year	Average, 1971–80	Average, 1980–90	1988	1989	1990	1991	1992	1993	1994	1995
Indonesia	1983	7.7	5.5	5.8	7.5	7.2	6.9	6.4	6.5	6.7	7.0
Malaysia	1978	7.8	5.2	8.9	9.2	9.7	8.7	7.8	8.0	8.6	8.4
Philippines	1985	6.0	0.9	6.3	6.1	2.7	-0.5	0.1	1.7	4.0	5.5
Thailand	1988	7.9	7.6	13.3	12.3	11.6	8.1	7.6	7.8	8.2	8.5
Singapore	1985	7.9	6.4	11.1	9.2	8.3	6.7	5.8	9.9	7.0	6.0
Hong Kong	1980	9.3	7.1	8.3	2.8	3.2	4.1	5.3	5.5	5.7	5.9
Korea	1985	9.0	9.7	11.5	6.2	9.2	8.5	4.8	4.7	6.7	6.9
Japan			4.1	6.2	4.7	4.8	4.0	1.3	-0.5	0.5	2.3
China	1978	7.9	9.5	11.8	4.4	3.9	8.0	13.2	13.4	10.0	9.0
Industrial market economies			3.1								
United States			3.4								
Germany			2.1								
Middle-income economies			3.2								
India			5.3								
Brazil			2.7								
Mexico			1.0								

SOURCES: *World Development Reports* (1982, 1987, 1992), *Asian Development Outlook 1994*, and *Statistical Abstract of the United States 1994*; U.N. System of National Accounts (GDP) and U.N. COMTRADE data supplemented by World Bank Estimates (exports and imports); (Panagariya 1993).

TABLE 2–2
INCREASE IN IMPORTS, SELECTED REGIONS, 1992–2000

	Imports (billions of dollars)			% share of total increase
Region	1992	2000 (estimate)	Increase	
East Asia[a]	792	1,443	651	33
European Union	1,525	1,997	472	24
United States	553	922	369	19
Rest of the world	973	1,448	475	24

a. Based on conservative estimates.
SOURCE: World Bank staff estimates (World Bank 1994).

FIGURE 2–1
PER CAPITA GROSS DOMESTIC PRODUCT, SELECTED
ASIAN COUNTRIES, 1993
(thousands of U.S. dollars)

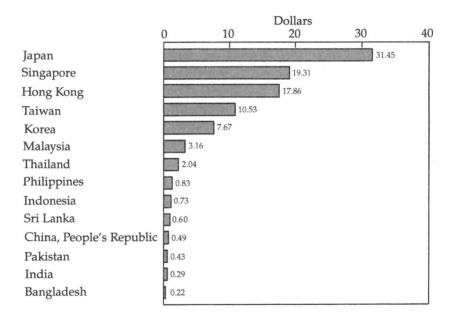

SOURCE: Asia Development Bank, *Asia Development Outlook*, 1994.

$370. When the bank substituted "purchasing power of parity" figures, however, it found that China's GDP per head rose to almost $2,000 in 1990, while other studies of that same year raised the figure to almost $2,600. More recent research undertaken by Nicholas Lardy, an economist and specialist on the People's Republic of China (PRC), and others points to a figure between the extremes—about $2,000 in 1995—that extrapolates to a total national economy about the size of Germany but still ranks China among the poorest nations as ranked by GDP per head (see Lardy [1994] and the March 18, 1995, *Economist*).

Various growth scenarios have been published for the individual East Asian nations taking into account economic, political, and social factors. While most foresee some convergence among Asian national economies, the most notable characteristic of the region, for the next several decades at least, will be diversity, with countries remaining at different levels of development, productivity, and income. Under such circumstances, as this chapter argues, any kind of "one size fits all" trade or investment policy for the region seems unlikely to succeed.

East Asian Trade and Development Patterns. East Asian trade increased substantially during the 1980s, especially after 1985. In 1991, total East Asian exports and imports both more than tripled their 1980 dollar values, resulting in an increase in the region's share of total world trade from 7.5 percent to almost 14 percent (figure 2–2).

Certain internal anomalies are worth noting regarding East Asian regional trade developments. First, excluding Japan, within East Asia the four NIEs accounted for more than 60 percent of total trade in 1991 (ITC 1993). But this figure can be misleading unless the China–Hong Kong–Taiwan relationship is fully understood. China funnels a substantial portion of its exports through Hong Kong (and to a less extent Taiwan). In 1990, China exported 43 percent of its goods to Hong Kong, of which about 32 percent was reexported (Panagariya 1993, p. 9; Barfield 1994). Thus, while the four tigers will remain important players in regional trade, China increasingly will become the most important trader in the region, behind Japan.

The strong growth of East Asian trade has been heavily dependent on exports to non–East Asian regions. In 1990, two-thirds of total East Asian trade (exports and imports) was conducted with non–East Asian economies, about half with trans-Pacific countries and about one-quarter with the European Union (EU).

This heavy dependence on nonregional sources of trade results from a distinctive pattern of internal development, the so-called flying-geese pattern. The flying-geese pattern describes an interconnected trade and investment synergy that has developed over the past three

21

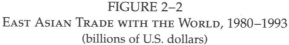

FIGURE 2–2
EAST ASIAN TRADE WITH THE WORLD, 1980–1993
(billions of U.S. dollars)

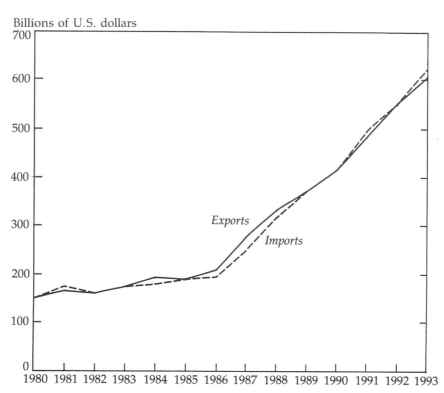

Billions of U.S. dollars

SOURCE: U.S. International Trade Commission, *East Asia Regional Economic Integration and Implications for the United States.* USITC Publication 2631. (Washington, D.C.: Government Printing Office, 1993); DOT 1994.

decades in East Asia. The NIEs emerged in the 1960s as leaders in labor-intensive manufacturing products through direct foreign investment and technology transfer largely from Japan and the United States. The specialization of production became more complex during the 1970s and 1980s as the NIEs moved up the manufacturing ladder toward more skill-intensive goods, while a new wave of lower-tier East Asian countries moved out of resource-based production into labor-intensive manufacturing.

Japan increasingly specialized in higher-technology goods and services, while utilizing upper-tier NIEs as sources for intermediate parts and services. Thus, trade and investment were directly linked, as

22

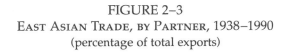

FIGURE 2–3
EAST ASIAN TRADE, BY PARTNER, 1938–1990
(percentage of total exports)

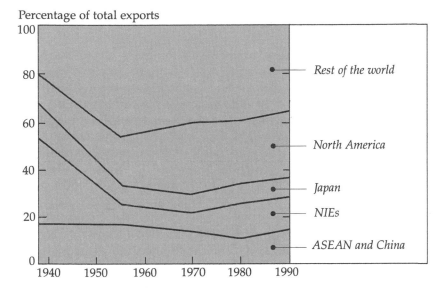

SOURCE: World Bank, *East Asia's Trade and Investment* (Washington, D.C.: World Bank, 1994).

regional investment flows promoted both intra-industry and intrafirm flows of capital and intermediate goods (Young 1994, 1993; Lee 1994).

Two other results stemming from the flying-geese pattern are relevant. First, the development strategy has produced East Asian economies that are competitive—not complementary—with each other, a reality that will complicate efforts to liberalize regional trade. Second, the flying-geese pattern has placed great pressure on the adjustment process for the rest of the trading world, particularly for the United States and Europe in the past decade as the NIEs have accelerated their climb up the technological ladder and broadened the scope of products in which they compete internationally. Though the recent rapid growth of intraregional East Asian markets has lessened the trade imbalances somewhat, East Asia remains vulnerable to a protectionist backlash from the Western economies.

Turning inward? In the early decades of the twentieth century, East Asian economies were highly interdependent, but after World War II this interdependence declined at least until the 1970s (figure 2–3). Di-

23

versification of the East Asian trade relationship stemmed from several sources, including the increasing integration of the world economy after 1945, the growing acceptance of East Asian products by the developed countries, and the similarity of East Asian development patterns, which meant that they became competitors rather than customers.

Since the 1970s, the interdependence of the East Asian economies has been on the rise again and, partly because of the huge growth in individual internal markets, accompanied by more liberal trade and investment policies. In addition, a number of special trade networks have developed and tightened, including the already discussed shift of industries from Japan and the NIEs to less developed countries within the region because of lower labor costs, and the rise of the special relationships such as those between China, Hong Kong, and Taiwan.

Questions have arisen as to whether East Asia is evolving into a trading bloc, either as a reaction to events in Europe and North America or as a result of a drive by Japan to assume a leadership role in the region. Recent research provides little evidence of a concerted effort by Japan to create a trade bloc. And the evidence as to whether the "natural" course of events will produce a definable East Asia trading bloc in the near future is inconclusive and subject to differing interpretations.

An excellent summary of research on this issue is found in the recent World Bank study of East Asian trade and investment (World Bank 1994). Citing work done by Peter Petri, Kim Anderson, Peter Drysdale, Jeffrey Frankel, and the U.S. International Trade Commission, the study notes ways of measuring regional trade relationships: absolute measures, relative measures, and the so-called double-relative measure.

As table 2–3 shows, in absolute terms East Asian intraregional trade increased almost fourfold between the mid-1950s and 1990, though it still remains below its pre–World War II level. In relative terms—that is, comparing the region's internal trade with its total trade—East Asia dropped from a prewar high of 67 percent to a low of 29.3 percent in 1969 and then increased to 40.7 percent in 1990. This level remains well below the degree of internal integration reached by nations of the European Community over the past decades.

Finally, there is the more technical economist's double-relative or gravity coefficient measure. This compares the share of a region in its own market with its share in world trade and results in a judgment regarding a region's trade "bias" or tendency to trade with its regional partners over nations outside the region. Thus, a lack of bias would be defined as a situation in which a country's exports to a given region are equal to the share of world exports going to that region. (For exam-

TABLE 2–3

MEASURES OF REGIONAL INTERDEPENDENCE THROUGH TWO-WAY TRADE,
SELECTED REGIONS, SELECTED YEARS, 1938–1990

Region	1938	1955	1969	1979	1985	1990
Absolute measure[a]						
East Asia	10.0	2.2	2.9	4.2	6.4	7.9
North America	3.0	6.7	6.9	4.2	6.4	5.3
Pacific region	18.0	13.5	16.9	15.6	24.8	24.6
Western Europe	18.2	19.6	28.7	29.3	27.1	33.8
Relative measure[b]						
East Asia	67.1	31.3	29.3	33.2	36.3	40.7
North America	22.7	33.4	37.9	28.7	33.0	31.3
Pacific region	58.3	45.0	56.6	54.5	64.3	64.9
Western Europe	46.1	49.1	64.7	66.4	65.4	71.2
Double-relative measure[c]						
East Asia	4.5	4.5	3.0	2.6	2.1	2.1
North America	1.7	1.7	2.1	2.0	1.7	1.8
Pacific region	1.9	1.5	1.9	1.9	1.7	1.7
Western Europe	1.2	1.2	1.5	1.5	1.6	1.5

a. Intraregional trade as a percentage of total world trade.
b. Intraregional trade as a percentage of regional trade.
c. Gravity coefficient.
SOURCE: Adapted from the World Bank 1994.

ple, if East Asia received 10 percent of world exports and 10 percent of Japan's exports, the trade intensity ratio would be 1.0, meaning that no bias existed in Japanese exports to East Asia.)

Recent studies using this methodology essentially find that there is a substantial bias toward regional trading partners but it has been lower since 1980 than in previous years—actually the trend has been flat or inconclusive since the mid-1980s (table 2–4) (Anderson and Blackhurst 1994; Noland 1995).

Two points regarding postwar East Asian growth and development should be underscored: (1) it was market driven and not dependent on regional trading bloc institutions or preferential rules and (2) it was highly dependent on the prospects of an increasingly open world trading system, particularly on the relative openness of the U.S. market. As Arvind Panagariya recently argued:

> The paramount objective of East Asia's regional trade policy has to be to ensure an open world trading system. Despite the

TABLE 2–4
FDI Inflows to Low- and Middle-Income East Asia, by Source, 1993

Source	China Millions of U.S.$	%	Indonesia Millions of U.S.$	%	Malaysia Millions of U.S.$	%	Philippines Millions of U.S.$	%	Thailand Millions of U.S.$	%	Total Millions of U.S.$	%
ASEAN	238	0.8	33	0.5	750	5.4	18	0.5	46	0.5	1,085	1.7
Europe	1,316	4.4	1,009	16.1	2,711	19.6	378	11.7	1,108	11.0	6,522	10.3
Japan	3,042	10.2	1,102	17.6	3,065	22.2	855	26.4	3,586	35.6	11,650	18.4
NIES	21,123	70.9	1,573	25.2	4,123	29.8	580	17.9	3,565	35.4	30,964	49.0
United States	2,390	8.0	428	6.8	1,499	10.8	1,193	36.9	1,373	13.6	6,884	10.9
Rest of the world	1,676	5.6	2,105	33.7	1,674	12.1	211	6.5	393	3.9	6,058	9.6
All countries	29,785	100.0	6,250	100.0	13,822	100.0	3,235	100.0	10,071	100.0	63,163	100.0

SOURCE: World Bank 1994.

redirection of trade towards itself in recent years, East Asia ships two-thirds of its exports to the rest of the world. There is little doubt that the phenomenal growth of East Asia during the past three decades has been facilitated greatly by relatively open world markets. (Panagariya 1994)

Foreign direct investment in East Asia. East Asia has become the predominant recipient of foreign investment for industrialized countries. According to a recently published report from the UN Conference on Trade and Development (UNCTAD), 66 percent ($53 billion) of total world investment flows of $80 billion went to East Asian economies in 1994. Eighty percent of all investment inflows to developing nations went to ten nations, of which seven were East Asian (the top ten included the PRC, Singapore, Argentina, Mexico, Malaysia, Indonesia, Thailand, Hong Kong, Taiwan, and Nigeria, as reported in the March 9, 1995, *Journal of Commerce*).

Both the United States and Japan strengthened their investment positions in Eastern Asia during the 1980s, with Europe falling slightly behind. Total U.S. investment (on a historical basis) in the region reached about $76.4 billion in 1992 (of which Japan received $26.2 billion compared with a Japanese total investment of $81 billion) (Noland 1995). Japanese foreign direct investment (FDI) in East Asia—as with the rest of the world—peaked in 1989 and then fell back (40 percent) as a result of the crash of the Japanese financial markets and the ensuing recession (figure 2–4). In 1992, U.S. FDI exceeded the stock of Japanese FDI in five of nine East Asian host countries (Hong Kong, Singapore, Taiwan, the Philippines, and China), and U.S. FDI was increasing in three countries where Japan had historically been dominant (Korea, Indonesia, and Malaysia) (ITC 1993, p. 73).

The most important recent change in FDI in East Asia, however, has been the emergence of the NIEs as the major source of investment in low- and middle-income Asian economies. Taiwan particularly has been aggressive in outward investment, becoming the top source of FDI in Malaysia and Indonesia and the second leading source in China. According to World Bank calculations, the NIEs accounted for about half of all foreign investment in the low- and middle-income East Asian economies (table 2–4). Indeed, as some of the scholars have pointed out, the NIEs are themselves becoming lead geese in smaller flying-geese patterns of trade and investment in Asia (see Linda Lim's work, chapter 6, in this volume).

The United States, World Trader and Investor. In assessing the comparative positions of the three leading world trading regions—Asia, the United States, and the European Community (EC)—there are two paradoxical circumstances to keep in mind regarding the United States. First, U.S. trade and investment patterns position it as a major

FIGURE 2-4
JAPANESE FDI OUTFLOWS TO ASIA, 1985–1995

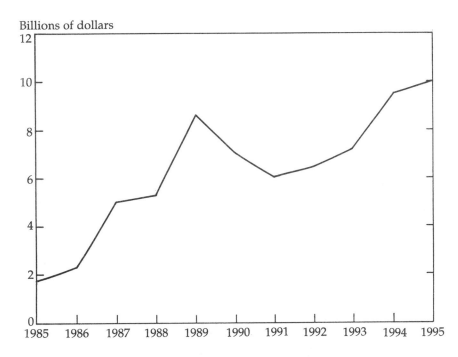

SOURCE: Organization for Economic Cooperation and Development, *International Direct Investment Yearbook* (Paris: OECD, 1995).

player in all regions while Europe is much less involved in Japan and Asia than the United States is and the Asian economies, in turn, are much less involved in Europe than is the United States. Added to the equation is the historical and current dominance of the United States in Central and South America, a fact that underscores the position of the United States as the only worldwide economic power at this time, with strong ties in each region.

Also, paradoxically, the huge internal U.S. market and the abundant U.S. natural resources leave the country much less dependent on trade than either of its major rivals. Exports and imports have accounted for only 11–18 percent of U.S. GDP during the 1980s, while the comparable figures for the EC were 45–47 percent and for Asia, 26–29 percent (developing Asia, 37–47 percent [Anderson and Norheim 1994]).

World trade and investment ties. Table 2–5 sets out the trade patterns of the EC, North America, and East Asia from 1980 to 1991. Clearly,

TABLE 2-5
TRADE PATTERNS OF EC, NAFTA, AND ASIA, 1983–1993
(percent)

	1983	1984	1985	1986	1987	1988	1989	1990	1991	1992	1993
EC											
EC[a]	52.9	52.5	53.5	56.8	58.2	58.6	58.5	59.2	59.7	60.2	54.7
NAFTA[b]	9.4	10.3	10.5	9.6	9.1	8.9	8.9	8.4	8.3	8.1	8.9
Asia[c]	3.8	3.9	4.1	4.3	4.6	4.9	5.0	4.9	5.4	5.7	7.1
NAFTA											
EC	18.0	16.9	17.7	18.7	19.4	18.3	17.8	19.3	18.8	18.0	15.9
NAFTA	36.6	37.5	38.0	35.6	35.6	35.8	36.2	36.9	37.2	37.9	40.2
Asia	12.7	12.6	12.0	12.9	14.5	15.4	15.5	15.3	16.2	17.0	17.4
Asia											
EC	12.7	12.0	12.4	14.1	14.2	14.1	13.8	14.9	14.4	14.1	13.9
NAFTA	21.4	22.8	22.0	22.9	22.7	22.1	21.6	20.2	19.1	18.9	19.0
Asia	24.2	24.7	25.6	25.3	27.1	28.7	30.1	31.9	34.6	36.7	36.5

a. The European Community includes the twelve member-countries.
b. NAFTA includes Canada, Mexico, and the United States.
c. Asia includes thirty-five countries.
SOURCE: International Monetary Fund, *Direction of Trade Statistics* (Washington, D.C.: IMF, 1990 and 1994).

TABLE 2–6
IMPORT PATTERNS OF MAJOR EMERGING MARKETS, 1993 AND 2010
(billions of U.S. dollars)

Major Emerging Markets	1993 Total Imports	U.S. Market Share, 1993 (%)	Projected Total Imports, 2010
Chinese economic area	320	11	577
Indonesia	29	14	97
India	24	12	79
South Korea	84	18	236
Mexico	49	85	119
Argentina	17	22	28
Brazil	26	23	69
South Africa	20	14	36
Poland	16	6	18
Turkey	29	11	67

SOURCE: U.S. Department of Commerce, "National Export Survey," *Business America,* October 1994.

the trade relations between North America and East Asia are much stronger than those between the EC and the other two regions. Furthermore, only North America demonstrated reasonably strong relations with both of the other regions. In 1991, for instance, the EC and East Asia, respectively, accounted for 17.3 and 22.7 percent of total North American trade. The EC, however, accounted for only 14.2 percent of East Asia trade; conversely, East Asia accounted for only 7 percent of EC trade. A recent projection suggests that, by the year 2003, U.S. trade with East Asia will be twice that with Europe (Noland 1995).

In absolute terms, U.S.–East Asia trade has exceeded U.S.-EC trade since the early 1980s: in 1993, total U.S.-European trade was $235 billion while total U.S.–East Asian trade was $347 billion (U.S. Department of Commerce 1993). Furthermore, as table 2–6 indicates, East Asian countries remain highly dependent on the United States as a market for their exports. The United States ranks either first or second as an export outlet for each of them, except China (with data including Hong Kong's reexports as Chinese exports, Chinese exports jumped to $21 billion, or more than 28 percent of China's global exports [Korea Economic Institute of America 1994, p. 205]).

U.S.-European investment ties. In a world where interdependence is increasingly defined by investment and not trade flows, the enduring strong ties between the United States and Europe must be factored into any analysis of regional economic relations. And here the picture is quite the reverse of developing trade patterns. Jointly, the United States and Europe control more than two-thirds of all foreign direct investment, with total cross-investment of $488 billion in each other's economies.

In 1990, European companies accounted for 64 percent of all foreign direct investment in the United States, while 44 percent of total U.S. foreign direct investment was in Europe. In contrast, Asia accounts for about 20 percent of foreign investment in the United States and about 16 percent of U.S. foreign direct investment (Barfield 1992a). In 1993, the total value of Japan's investment in Europe slightly exceeded $75 billion—this contrasted with a total U.S. cumulative investment of almost $240 million (Noland 1995).

U.S. Trade and Investment Policy for East Asia

It is the thesis of this chapter that the United States alone among the major trading powers holds a strong, balanced trade and investment position in each of the major regional economic areas. In light of U.S. economic interests that span the global trading world, its trade and investment policy are best achieved through the multilateral trading system, embodied in the new World Trade Organization (WTO). Of equal importance, by historical tradition (at least since 1945), the United States has been the chief guarantor and patron of the multilateral system. Despite some internal questioning of this role in the 1980s, multilateralism should remain the central focus of U.S. trade and investment policies.

The following analysis of U.S.-East Asian regional trade policy focuses on its implications for the new WTO and on policies that will strengthen rather than weaken the new multilateral system that was adopted in the Uruguay Round. The chapter also argues that, contrary to the views of U.S. policy makers, the Asian-Pacific Economic Council (APEC) should not become a reciprocity-based preferential trade arrangement and that the so-called Asian way of unilateral liberalization—with continued adherence to an unconditional most-favored-nation (MFN) system—will ultimately produce larger economic gains for both Asian and non-Asian nations.

Rise of Regionalism in U.S. Trade Policy. From the 1930s to the early 1980s, the United States steadfastly opposed derogations from MFN obligations and, therefore, most regional trading arrangements (cold war exigencies account for the exception regarding the formation and growth of the European Community). The United States essentially followed a two-track trade policy: (1) multilateralism, embodied in its leadership in the General Agreement on Tariffs and Trade (GATT), and (2) bilateralism-unilateralism, dictated by the political reality that GATT did not cover key trading sectors and by internal political demands that directed the United States to pursue bilateral negotiations—particularly with Japan and the EC—to achieve its trade policy goals. Unilateralism was linked directly to bilateral negotiations, since the United States also reserved the right to act on its own by enforcing its will should bilateral negotiations be unsuccessful.

In retrospect, in the early 1980s the United States clearly drifted into the regional alternative through a combination of unlinked events and diverse forces. Ambassador William Brock's call in 1982 for a GATT-plus negotiation if efforts for a new multilateral trade negotiation failed was based on the inability to achieve a consensus for a new trade round, not on a desire to change the fundamental priorities of U.S. trade diplomacy. (Similarly, the decision to sign a bilateral free trade treaty with Israel was motivated almost entirely by political and security concerns, not trade policy considerations.)

The initiative for the U.S.-Canadian and the subsequent U.S.-Canadian-Mexican (NAFTA) free trade agreements came from Canada and Mexico, respectively, and not from the United States. The most important reason behind both nations' desire for stronger ties to the United States was a fear of growing protectionism in the United States in the form of unfair trade laws (ironically neither country escaped the harassment of these laws under the free trade agreements [FTAs]).

By the late 1980s, however, other forces coming into play would impel the United States toward raising the priority of regional agreements. In Europe the EC was finally moving toward significant economic union, as evidenced by the campaign for EC 1992 and later the signing of the Maastricht Treaty. The United States, thus, for the first time faced a trading partner with economic power equal to its own. Second, beginning with the Bush administration but continuing in a more urgent fashion in the Clinton administration, voices for a regional priority assumed a greater significance within the U.S. executive. Bush's secretary of state, James Baker, who in the tradition of former U.S. Trade Representative Robert Strauss was an inveterate deal maker, chafed at the inability to conclude the Uruguay Round and became attracted to the opportunities for smaller regional trading deals. In addition, Baker, as the architect of U.S. policy regarding the 1980s Latin American debt crisis, viewed FTAs with Latin American countries as complementary inducements for them to pursue more rational macroeconomic policies. Baker was largely responsible for President Bush's espousal of the Enterprise for the Americas initiative in 1990 to extend the NAFTA to all Latin America (part of the motivation of the Bush administration in advancing these regional initiatives was to force a conclusion to the Uruguay Round of GATT negotiations by threatening a regional alternative if multilateral negotiations failed) (Barfield 1992b).

A somewhat different economic and political calculus has propelled the Clinton administration much further down the regional path. First, despite great divisions in his own party, President Clinton staked a great deal of his presidential authority on the passage of NAFTA through Congress and along with his advisers viewed this victory as their greatest political triumph (in an administration that has had few such triumphs). In December 1994, the Clinton administration built on its NAFTA success by convening the Summit of the Americas in Miami. The major decision produced there was the negotiation of a hemispheric free trade agreement by 2005.

Although the completion of the Uruguay Round and the NAFTA and Miami Declaration are counted as major triumphs by Clinton administration officials, they see Asia as the greatest opportunity to place a Clinton stamp on U.S. trade policy. Politically and economically, Asia is the region holding the greatest attraction for the Clinton administration. Politically, Asia and the APEC initiatives are wholly Clinton initiatives, not hand-me-down policies from the Republicans. President Clinton's advisers correctly have told him that Asia is the area that he can claim as his own. Second, because of the rapidly increasing economic power of these East Asian nations, these countries represent an area of highest priority for an administration committed as none before it to increasing U.S. exports. In the mercantilist framework that identifies and shapes Clinton trade policy, it is not surprising that more than half (assuming Taiwan and Hong Kong counted separately) of the ten most important emerging markets where U.S. trade initiatives should be concentrated are in Asia (table 2–7).

To sum up, in 1995 the United States was projecting to the world a set of mixed, and not altogether integrated, trade policy goals. On the one hand, the Clinton administration continues to assert formally that multilateralism and the new WTO stand at the apex of U.S. trade policy priorities; on the other hand, much of the energy and resources of the administration's top trade officials are increasingly devoted to regional trade initiatives in Asia and Latin America.

Some trade analysts (Saxonhouse 1996) think that the United States is proceeding from a calculated design to create a series of hub-and-spoke systems, with the U.S. economy as the central hub for each of these systems. I find little evidence that the United States is proceeding from any grand design—trade policy making in the United States

TABLE 2–7
EAST ASIAN EXPORTS TO THE UNITED STATES, 1991
(millions of U.S. dollars)

	Total Exports	Exports to U.S.	U.S. Share of Total Exports (%)	U.S. Rank among Export Markets
Japan	314,832	92,200	29.3	1
NIEs				
South Korea	69,489	18,311	26.4	1
Taiwan	76,161	22,317	29.3	1
Hong Kong	98,579	22,239	22.6	2
Singapore	59,188	11,674	19.7	1
ASEAN-4				
Indonesia	29,142	3,509	12.0	2
Thailand	27,562	6,020	21.8	1
Philippines	8,839	3,151	35.6	1
Malaysia	34,405	5,808	16.9	2
China	71,986	6,193	8.6	3

SOURCE: IMF, *Direction of Trade Statistics Yearbook* 1992 and CCNAA; Ow-Taylor, 1994.

is too erratic and chaotic to support such an interpretation. But it is true that if the piecemeal approach now being pursued by the Clinton administration is successful, the United States will wind up as the major beneficiary of at least two hub-and-spoke systems, one extending down through Latin America and one extending across the vast Pacific region (recent calls for a transatlantic FTA [TAFTA] could add yet a third wheel to this mix). Thus, the United States would enjoy favored access to most of the markets in Latin America and East Asia—and potentially Europe—while no other country would enjoy a similar status.

For this reason, this essay argues that the economic interests and welfare of both Latin American and East Asian countries will be best served by avoiding strict, reciprocity-based preferential trade pacts such as the United States clearly hopes to create in APEC and the extension of NAFTA. Before analyzing in detail, however, the evolution and future of APEC, the chapter reviews the growing debate among economists regarding the pros and cons of regional FTAs—or, more accurately, regional preferential trade agreements.

Reconciling Multilateral Leadership and Aggressive Regionalism.
Despite the apparent determination of the Clinton administration to
push aggressively for the expansion of NAFTA and for the creation of
a free trade area in the Pacific, there is a growing debate in the United
States over the wisdom of this course of action, both from the perspective of U.S. national interest and from the perspective of world economic welfare. The reaction against a regional priority to U.S. trade
policy stems from three sources. First, among trade economists, the
dissent from the benign view of free trade agreements is growing, as
witnessed by powerful opposing arguments that have been advanced
recently by two leading U.S. trade economists, Jagdish Bhagwati and
Anne Krueger (Bhagwati and Krueger 1995). Second, the trade policy
community and business community has a heightened awareness of
the potential transaction costs associated with a complex world of multiple free trade agreements (the complexity arises both in front-end
negotiations to reconcile existing national commitments to the WTO
and to other bilateral and regional treaties and in back-end results
when corporations will face a maze of differential tariffs, barriers, and
rules of origin). Third, deep political divisions have emerged within
both political parties about the direction of U.S. trade policy. With the
election of a Republican Congress, the political climate is now such
that major new trade initiatives are off the agenda until after the 1996
presidential election.

Debate among economists. The 1995 *Economic Report of the President*
details the Clinton administration's goals and priorities for trade policy. The report distills the strongly held views of the administration's
principal economic spokespersons on trade, then Council of Economic
Advisors Chairperson Laura Tyson and Undersecretary of the Treasury
Lawrence Summers.

Summers, before joining the Clinton administration, had indeed
forcefully stated his "press on all fronts," pro–trade bloc philosophy.
He stated in 1991: "Economists should maintain a strong, but rebutta-
ble, presumption in favor of all lateral reductions in trade barriers,
whether they be multi, uni, bi, tri, plurilateral. Global liberalization
may be best, but regional liberalization is very likely to be good" (Panagariya 1994).

It should come as no surprise, then, that the 1995 *Economic Report*
states that the "most distinctive legacy" of the Clinton administration
in the trade policy arena will be the "foundation it has laid for the
development of overlapping plurilateral trade agreements as stepping
stones to global free trade." The administration is also candid about
the underlying mercantilist goals that drive the new thrust of U.S. trade

policy. In describing Clinton trade policy in the past year, the 1994 report stated, "The Administration's trade policy can be described as 'export activism.'" Export activism also is at the heart of the Clinton regional initiatives, as the 1995 report makes clear when it notes that "export and investment opportunities in emerging markets in Latin America and Asia will be a key engine of growth for the U.S. economy over the next decade."

Together, the 1994 and 1995 *Economic Reports of the President* set forth the case for regional trading arrangements serving as building blocks toward multilateral free trade. The administration argues that regional trade agreements allow some trading nations to move forward faster and achieve deeper economic integration than do cumbersome multilateral negotiations that include more than 120 nations.

Second, the administration predicts that a "self-reinforcing process" will be put in place and outsiders will clamor to become member-countries of expanding and increasingly attractive free trade areas. Finally, the administration sets out its own definition of open regionalism—a definition that largely tracks that of the APEC Eminent Persons Group. In committing itself to open regionalism, the Clinton administration states that it will negotiate only regional agreements that are nonexclusive and open to new members to join and that it will require that such agreements adhere to the GATT article 24 rule, which prohibits an increase in average external barriers (for comments on this rule, see the following section on WTO). Most important, though not stated explicitly, is the assumption in the *Economic Report* that regional agreements will extend benefits to outsiders only on a conditional MFN basis.

The dissenters. Economists critical of the Clinton administration's assumptions and assertions regarding the positive benefits of regional and bilateral free trade pacts begin by returning the argument to the fundamental fact that, in Bhagwati's words, it is "folly" to equate "free trade areas with free trade" because "they are inherently preferential and discriminatory."[1]

In building a case against a proliferation of free trade agreements,

---

1. In this chapter, I do not treat in detail the evolution of economic theory and empirical research regarding customs unions and free trade areas. Rather I refer the reader to the excellent collection of papers in Anderson and Blackhurst (1993) and de Melo and Panagariya (1994). This chapter only partially maps this terrain by explaining the particular points chosen by Bhagwati, Krueger, and other economists who have raised questions specifically about the Clinton administration's decision to give top priority to regional trading arrangements.

Krueger focuses on the potentially damaging political economy consequences of rules of origin (ROOs). (Rules of origin are border measures
in FTAs to ensure that trade diversion does not occur, allowing countries outside the FTA to tranship goods among FTA members. ROOs
consist of negotiated domestic content requirements.)

FTA negotiations allow producer groups among the member-
nations to lobby for increased protection as a payoff for their support
of the proposed agreement. ROOs negotiations result in a maze of regulations—in NAFTA 200 pages are devoted to ROOs—and often result
in increased protection. In NAFTA, increased protection clearly did
occur in textiles, apparel, and automobiles. And because ROOs must
be renegotiated each time an FTA expands to another nation, opportunities for protectionist producer political pressure are multiplied.

A world of increasing FTAs with numerous ROOs adds to the possibility that individual nations will begin to exploit the system with
little regard for logic or systemwide rules. A case in point is the wholly
contradictory U.S. positions regarding automobile transplants and
ROOs. The United States demanded that autos from Japanese transplants in the United States not be counted as U.S. exports to Japan,
while at the same time it vigorously protested an EU proposal that
aimed to define these same cars as Japanese under its quota for voluntary export restraints (VERs) with Japan.

FTAs also must be judged in light of the increased use of antidumping and other so-called unfair trade practice measures as instruments of protection. As Bhagwati has noted in several papers,
administered protection is highly selective; when FTA members face
major adjustment problems resulting from lowered barriers, they will
probably lash out against nonmember suppliers with antidumping
suits or other protectionist devices. Bhagwati's hypothetical case can
be strengthened with recent history—both Mexico and Canada are
pressing the United States to exclude them from administered protection actions. The Canadian trade minister has argued, for instance, that
North America should be considered as one market for steel and automobile parts, and therefore antidumping suits against Canadian companies in these sectors make no sense. The EU has eliminated
antidumping cases against countries in the European Free Trade Area
(EFTA) and the European Economic Area; other eastern European
countries are calling for the EU to adopt the same policy for this region
in future trade negotiations.

Moving beyond the problems related to ROOs, both Krueger and
Bhagwati point out that FTAs dominated by one economy (NAFTA
and its extension, for instance) allow the large economy to extract concessions that it could not get from full multilateral negotiations. Here

37

again recent events support the hypothetical case. The Clinton administration is determined to force the inclusion of environmental and labor standards in extensions of NAFTA—and, indeed, while it has never explicitly stated such a position regarding APEC, the White House has made clear that new presidential trade negotiating authority must include the power to conclude environmental and labor agreements. Those APEC nations fearful that the United States might well attempt to impose its labor and environmental views in a trade treaty have reason for disquiet.

Multiple FTAs and the Practical World of Negotiations. In moving from the analytical realm of economists to the practical world of trade negotiators, further reasons can be advanced for skepticism regarding the Clinton administration's enthusiasm for a world of multiple FTAs. First, though, it is necessary to challenge directly the premise that plurilateral negotiations are necessary because the WTO has become so large (120-plus nations) and unwieldy that multilateral negotiations are unmanageable and would go on forever without resolution. Here the example of the eight-year Uruguay Round negotiations is always invoked. But, in reality, the Uruguay Round demonstrated something different from this now conventional wisdom. The large majority of small and developing countries were ready for an agreement long before the two superpowers—the United States and the EU—could reconcile their differences. The clash between these two negotiating teams (on agriculture, entertainment, and telecommunications), not the need for consensus among more than 100 other nations, delayed the conclusion of the Uruguay Round.

Beyond the efficiency and equity of multilateral agreements, a move toward a world of multiple bilateral and plurilateral trading arrangements presents negative consequences. First, the effort and resources necessary for negotiating such agreements would inevitably divert attention and resources from the complicated task of substantively carrying out the mandates of the Uruguay Round and of administering the WTO efficiently and smoothly.

Second, a trading world dotted with separate bilateral and plurilateral FTAs, each with different interim timetables, tariff levels, and nontariff barrier liberalization rules, would become enormously inefficient. Assuming that most of the existing and proposed plurilateral agreements come into existence, a multinational corporation such as IBM or Siemens or Samsung would face a daunting task in sorting out trade rules that governed their simultaneous operations in APEC, NAFTA, MERCOSUR (Argentina, Brazil, Paraguay, and Uruguay), and the European Economic Area—not to mention individual countries such as Chile or Turkey, which had separate arrangements with regional groupings and individual nations.

Regional and Bilateral Developments. Until recently, the major focus of U.S. trade and investment policy toward East Asia was bilateral in nature, characterized by market-opening negotiations with Japan, Korea, Taiwan, and, in the last several years, with the PRC. With the arrival of the Clinton administration, however, U.S. policy has tilted sharply toward a regional focus. This change in priorities will likely be sustained, though bilateral negotiations on important trade and investment issues with Japan and the PRC will remain high on the U.S. trade agenda.

APEC and regional U.S. focus. Though the idea of a Pacific economic cooperation group has been around since the 1960s, not until 1989 was an institutional focus achieved, with the creation of the Asia-Pacific Economic Cooperation group, sparked by an initiative by then-Australian Prime Minister Bob Hawke.

At the first meeting in Canberra, the APEC trade ministers agreed to a set of principles to develop closer trade ties based on recognition of diversity within the region, on agreement by consensus, and on informal consultations rather than formal trade negotiations. As a corollary, representatives agreed that the organization would not evolve into a trading bloc.

As noted, the Clinton administration moved to change the focus and goals of APEC from an informal consultative mechanism to a more formal organization promoting trade liberalization within the Pacific region. At the fifth annual meeting in November 1993, President Clinton called for a strengthening of the organization and the formation of a Committee on Trade and Investment that would "create a coherent APEC perspective and voice on global trade and investment issues and increase cooperation among members on key issues." The most concrete trade liberalization step taken at Seattle was the commitment to develop a voluntary, nonbinding investment code for the region.

In November 1994, in Bogor, Indonesia, the APEC nations, after U.S. prodding but with crucial support from President Suharto of Indonesia, took a much larger step, agreeing to the goal of free trade and investment in the Asia Pacific region by the year 2020. The developed countries in APEC promised to attain the same goal by the year 2010. In addition, the Bogor Declaration committed the APEC nations to explore the creation of a voluntary dispute mediation service "to supplement the WTO dispute settlement mechanism, which should continue to be the primary channel for resolving disputes" (p. 7).

The 2020 (2010) APEC free trade goal was only that: a goal.

Though the APEC heads of state directed their ministers to "begin preparing detailed proposals for implementing [the] present decisions," no guidelines were established for such a blueprint. During 1995, in the planning and preparation for the Osaka summit, chaired by Japan, two different "visions" of the future of APEC emerged. The first, advanced by the United States with backing from Australia, New Zealand, and Canada (the "Anglo-Saxons"), envisions detailed negotiations to achieve strict comparability and then the creation of a binding preferential trade agreement among APEC nations. The second, or Asian way as it has been labeled, envisions dependence largely on unilateral liberalization, with each nation determining the pace and specifics of its market-opening policies. The multilateral principle of unconditional MFN would also be retained.

The U.S. view of APEC and EPG. Though an independent body composed of representatives of a number of APEC nations, the Eminent Persons Group, headed by U.S. economist C. Fred Bergsten, in its comprehensive vision and specific recommendations has actually laid out a blueprint for APEC that is a reasonable facsimile of what U.S. negotiators would like to see evolve. While the group states that it does not propose "an Asia Pacific Free Trade area," its specific recommendations seem inevitably to lead in that direction.

Thus, though the EPG in its 1994 report praises unilateral liberalization as "virtuous per se," it warns that APEC "would give away an enormous amount of leverage if its members—especially its largest members—were to liberalize unilaterally to any significant degree." The report also argues that "the largest members, including the United States, are unlikely to liberalize unilaterally when they can use the high value of access to their markets to obtain reciprocal liberalization from others" (APEC 1994).

Pursuant to its goal of a reciprocity-based preferential trade agreement by the year 2020 (2010), the EPG recommended a precise timetable for negotiations, beginning in 1995 and proceeding with actual implementation by the year 2000. In the months just after the Bogor meeting, the U.S. government unsuccessfully pressed for just such a commitment from APEC nations, according to the January 16, 1995, *Financial Times.*

Crucial to the EPG vision of APEC is a particular definition of *open regionalism,* a concept that virtually all nations claim to espouse but one that remains opaque in operation. The components of open regionalism for the EPG include maximum possible unilateral trade liberalization, a commitment to reduce barriers to non-APEC nations even as APEC liberalizes internally, a willingness to extend liberalization to nonmembers on a reciprocal basis, and recognition of the right of individual APEC members to extend APEC liberalization to other nations unilaterally and unconditionally. The key elements in the EPG assumptions about and definition of open regionalism are that (1) after Chile, APEC will not expand to include more members and (2) liberalization outside APEC will be extended only on a conditional MFN basis.

The EPG also recommended a series of actions, including adoption of a voluntary investment code, harmonization of standards, cooperation on environmental, financial, and macroeconomic issues, and the creation of a task force on the proliferation of antidumping practices. Finally, the EPG urged the creation of an APEC Dispute Mediation Service for the resolution of disputes among members (an early version of the 1994 EPG report contained a much more elaborate adjudicatory system that was scrapped because of opposition from some members). In effect, with the creation of a dispute settlement mechanism (even though voluntarily initially) on top of sweeping regional trading rules, the EPG was really advocating the creation of a mini-WTO for the transpacific region.

The Asian way. In the months leading up to the Osaka summit, it became clear that a second vision of the future of APEC—the so-called Asian way—would not only compete with the Anglo-Saxon vision but also, at least for the foreseeable future, triumph over it. Led cautiously (so as not to anger the United States) by Japan, at planning sessions to implement the Bogor Declaration the Asian APEC nations argued that, rather than by legalist rules and tight reciprocal concessions and timetables, APEC should proceed by a more loose consensus process that allows each nation to proceed toward the free trade goal at its own pace; *concerted unilateralism* is the term used to describe this negotiating system.

Against the U.S.-EPG contention that unilateral liberalization would not produce a substantial lowering of trade and investment barriers, the Asian countries pointed to the extraordinary changes that have occurred through acts of individual governments over the past decade. A recent paper by Gary Saxonhouse documents and supports the major thrust of the Asian leaders' arguments. As tables 2–8 and 2–9 (taken from Saxonhouse 1996) demonstrate, the major economies of East Asia have undertaken large-scale reduction in their tariff rates and the removal of many nontariff barriers. Indeed, at the Osaka meeting, though the United States offered little in a downpayment toward 2020, a number of Asian APEC countries, including Indonesia, the PRC, the Philippines, Malaysia, and Singapore, announced important

TABLE 2–8
EFFECTIVE RATES OF PROTECTION FOR MANUFACTURING IN
EAST ASIA, SELECTED YEARS, 1975–1992
(percent)

Country	Category	Year	Rate
Korea	Total manufacturing	1980	21.9
		1983	19.6
		1985	10.7
		1990	5.8
Thailand		1975	46.4
		1982	33.8
		1985	23.0
Malaysia	Textiles	1982	29.2
		1985	17.4
		1987	7.9
	Iron, steel	1982	24.6
		1985	10.7
		1987	2.2
Indonesia	Total manufacturing	1987	68
		1990	59
		1992	52
	Textiles	1987	102
		1990	35
		1992	34

SOURCE: Gary Saxonhouse, Sung-Duck Hong, "Myungmok mit silkyo bo-hoyul ui kujo byunwha," KDI Policy Monograph 92-01; Shujiro Urata and Ka-zuhiko Yokota, "Trade Liberalization and Productivity Growth in Thailand," *Developing Economies*, vol. 32, no. 4 (December 1994); Yumiko Okamoto, "Im-pact of Trade and Liberalization Policies on the Malaysian Economy," *Develop-ing Economies*, vol. 32, no. 4 (December 1994); P. G. Warr, "Comparative Advantage and Protection in Indonesia," *Bulletin of Indonesian Economic Stud-ies*, vol. 28, no. 3 (December 1992).

unilateral liberalization measures (as reported in the November 22, 1995, *International Trade Reporter*). In addition, as table 2–10, shows, since the late 1980s the ASEAN nations, which had been largely closed to foreign investment, have dramatically reversed course and drawn in ever increasing amounts of foreign funds (this according to the Octo-ber 18, 1995, *Financial Times*).

A crucial difference between the Anglo-Saxon view of APEC's fu-

TABLE 2–9

COVERAGE OF QUANTITATIVE RESTRAINTS ON IMPORTS AND
OTHER NONTARIFF BARRIERS IN KOREA AND INDONESIA,
SELECTED YEARS, 1961–1990

(percent)

Country	Year	Rate
Korea	1961	96
	1975	58
	1980	43
	1984	25
	1987	16
Indonesia	1986	43
	1987	25
	1988	21
	1989	15
	1990	13

SOURCES: Gary Saxonhouse, Kwang-suk Kim, *Suip jayuwha ui kyungjejeok hyokwa wa saneop jojeong jeongchaik* (Seoul: Korea Development Institute, 1988); General Agreements on Tariffs and Trade, *Trade Policy Review: Indonesia 1991* (Geneva: GATT 1991).

TABLE 2–10

FOREIGN DIRECT INVESTMENT, ASEAN NATIONS, 1988–1993

(millions of dollars)

	1988	1989	1990	1991	1992	1993
Indonesia	576	682	1,093	1,482	1,777	2,004
Malaysia	719	1,668	2,332	3,998	4,469	4,351
Philippines	936	563	530	544	228	763
Singapore	3,655	2,887	5,575	4,888	6,730	6,829
Thailand	1,105	1,775	2,444	2,014	2,116	1,621
Vietnam	n.a.	n.a.	n.a.	n.a.	n.a.	n.a.

SOURCE: *Asian Development Outlook*, 1995–1996.

ture evolution and that of most Asian nations revolves around the elusive definition of open regionalism. For the Asians, open regionalism means opening up on an unconditional MFN basis, unencumbered by the limitations of reciprocity. Thus far, Asian leaders have strongly resisted a commitment that would lead to preferential agreements that

43

would exclude other important trading nations in South Asia and Europe.

Osaka. At the Osaka meeting, for the most part the Asian way prevailed, though some issues will certainly be revisited. No strict timetables or deadlines were adopted, and each nation was left to construct the mix and timing of future market-opening policies. In place of the U.S. preference for a policy of strict comparability, the Osaka Action Agenda committed APEC members only "to endeavor to ensure the overall comparability of their trade and investment liberalization and facilitation." In explaining the rationale behind the mode of negotiations informally agreed to, Ryutaro Hashimoto, then Japanese minister of international trade and industry, stated, "The Asia-Pacific economies have pursued liberalization on their own without being pressured into it." And he further noted that attempts to forge strict, legalistic agreements were "not necessarily the best way to go when, like APEC, you have a collection of very diverse economies at different stages of development" (as reported in the November 22, 1995, *International Trade Reporter*). The APEC members also rejected at this time the EPG call for the immediate establishment of a Dispute Mediation Service, choosing rather to set up a study group to examine the potential for the evolution of such a service.

Thus, *consensus* and *flexibility* represent the major themes of the Osaka documents. "Given the diverse circumstances in the APEC economies, flexibility will be available in dealing with issues arising from such circumstances in the liberalization and facilitation process," the 1995 Action Agenda document stated.

The United States, however, did achieve one important goal: it stopped a retrograde move—led by Japan and Korea—to exempt certain "sensitive" sectors from the mandate of the goal of free trade by the Jakarta deadlines. (Even here there was not unanimity: in keeping with its previous positions, Malaysia defiantly argued that there is "no obligation on any APEC member to liberalize" by the year 2020 (according to the November 22, 1995, *International Trade Reporter*).

The crucial question of MFN. The APEC definition of open regionalism and the method of handling the underlying WTO principle of unconditional MFN were left undecided at Osaka. Clearly, by a substantial majority, for the Asian APEC members open regionalism is now framed on a WTO-consistent unconditional MFN basis—thus, liberalization does not depend on negotiated reciprocity but will be extended unilaterally. At this point, there is no intention—or necessity—to notify the WTO under article 24 that a preferential trade agreement is being negotiated. The informal consensus at Osaka is that the incremental liberalization plans to be announced in Manila (1997) and Canada (1998) will be framed as unconditional MFN. As Saxonhouse notes, Asian policy makers have concluded that they "may do better for the welfare of their economies by having the freedom to design liberalization packages facing only domestic constraints" and concomitantly "at Osaka nothing should be done that would in any way undercut the WTO's newly strengthened dispute settlement mechanism" (Saxonhouse 1996).

The United States made no definitive announcements about its general policy toward unilateral liberalization and MFN at the Osaka meeting. U.S. Trade Representative Mickey Kantor did warn, however, that the United States would not allow free riders to benefit without reciprocity from liberalization; he strongly implied that the United States in its own trade policy would adhere to conditional MFN and not open unilaterally beyond APEC. In effect, the issue remains hanging, to be fought out later in Manila or Canada. (For a view of the Osaka meeting by the chairman of the EPG, see C. Fred Bergsten [1996]; for a counter interpretation, see Saxonhouse [1996]).

One other central policy fact should be noted. The Clinton administration's commitment to institute free trade within APEC by the year 2010, while allowing China, with whom the United States now runs a $30 billion trade deficit, to delay full implementation until 2020, is politically unsalable to Congress—no matter which party is in control. Should APEC negotiations go forward, this portion of the Bogor Declaration would certainly have to be renegotiated.

Latin America and the European Union. Before turning to future policy recommendations regarding East Asia, it is important to understand U.S.–East Asian relations in the context of events and actors in other regions of the world, specifically the movement toward hemispheric free trade in North and South America and the role of the European Union in regional trade politics.

Latin America. Though the individual circumstances of key nations are different, the choices facing Latin American countries regarding multilateralism versus a hemispheric preferential trade agreement are strikingly similar to those facing Asian APEC nations. Separate from, though influenced by, the conclusion of first the U.S.-Canadian FTA and then NAFTA, a wave of intra-Latin American bilateral and subregional free trade agreements occurred over the past decade: MERCOSUR, the Andean Pact, CACM (Central American market), CARICOM (Caribbean nations), and a series of bilateral pacts including alliances between Mexico and Chile, Mexico and CACM, Chile and Venezuela,

Venezuela and CACM, and CARICOM with Colombia and Venezuela.

In 1990, President George Bush put forward the Enterprise for the Americas program, which envisioned a hemispheric free trade agreement. President Clinton endorsed the Bush proposal. In December 1994, the United States hosted the Summit of the Americas, at which the leaders of thirty-four Latin American governments committed their nations to the goal of free trade in the hemisphere by the year 2005.

MERCOSUR. By far, the most significant new subregional economic integration agreement is the Southern Common Market (MERCOSUR), which combines the economies of Brazil, Argentina, Uruguay, and Paraguay. The MERCOSUR nations have a combined GDP of more than $700 billion and represent more than 50 percent of the Latin American market. In 1994, global exports of MERCOSUR totaled $63 billion and global imports almost $59 billion.

As of January 1, 1995, 85 percent of the trade among the four nations became duty free; a common external tariff (CET) was established for about 85 percent of imports. Together, the MERCOSUR nations are in process of negotiating zero-tariff agreements with Bolivia, Peru, Ecuador, Colombia, Venezuela, and Chile. Finally, MERCOSUR has begun preliminary negotiations with the EU for an eventual free trade agreement; at a conference in December 1995 that brought together fifteen Latin American foreign ministers, the EU pledged to go forward with such negotiations on a continental basis. (The EU as a whole is a more important trading partner with MERCOSUR than is the United States.)

Alternative futures. As with the Bogor Declaration, the Miami summit agreed to the goal of free trade but left open the negotiating framework for achieving this end. Again—in striking similarity to APEC—two different approaches are being considered. The United States is pressing for expeditious negotiations to harmonize elements of existing bilateral and subregional agreements with the existing structure and substance of NAFTA. The Brazilians, supported by other Latin American countries, prefer a more deliberate process in which the immediate priority would be to deepen and expand (non-NAFTA) subregional agreements such as MERCOSUR and the Andean Pact. Only after this process had reached a certain point would direct negotiations leading to the more sweeping liberalization provision of NAFTA be undertaken (Ahearn 1995b).

Besides the historic desire of Brazil to be the leading power in South America, other Latin American countries are attracted to the second option for three additional reasons. First, they are aware that they will be in a stronger negotiating position if they consolidate subregional alliances before facing the United States. Second, in a number of so-called sensitive sectors, these nations prefer to delay change and liberalization: they think that adhering to NAFTA too quickly would force politically unacceptable adjustment problems. And, finally, for some countries—particularly Brazil and Argentina, which have strong cultural ties to the European continent—the EU, not the United States, is a more important trading partner; they are reluctant to adopt a discriminatory regime that would exclude Europe.

Ultimately, from the perspective of world economic welfare—and U.S. economic welfare—Brazil's second option is the better path for Latin American trade negotiations. Admittedly, the pace of liberalization would likely be slower, but this negative result would be counterbalanced by the potential for a more varied and flexible system of trade alliances (particularly if the EU presses forward with its Latin American initiatives). Such alliances would decrease the chance that entrenched regional trading blocs would become obstacles to further multilateral liberalization.

The European Union. The EU is the key to the outcome of future regional and multilateral trade initiatives. Until recently, most observers have assumed that Europe was incapable of further advancing trade liberalization through regional or new multilateral agreements (with the exception of preferential trade deals with nations in its backyard of eastern Europe). Difficult internal issues related to the far-reaching Maastricht Treaty and lingering recession and high unemployment seemed to have turned the EU inward for the foreseeable future.

Two eminent trade scholars, C. Fred Bergsten and C. Randall Henning, wrote in late 1993, "The Community is best conceptualized as an 'important secondary power,' one which possesses a veto over advancement of global economic cooperation but from which major initiatives and the bearing of the extra costs associated with global leadership cannot be expected over the medium term." And, in a statement aimed directly at East Asia, they added: "The rest of the world confronts . . . a choice between proceeding without the Community or abandoning further broadscale liberalization for a considerable period. If the U.S. and East Asia are able to do so . . . we think they should liberalize within the Pacific region."

Bergsten and Henning represented the prevailing view during 1993 and 1994, but over the past year the EU has rebutted this consensus by reversing course and signaling an increasing interest in exploring additional bilateral and regional free trade negotiations in North and South America and in East Asia. Calls for a North Atlantic free trade agreement first came from Canadian Prime Minister Chretien, but they were picked up during the spring of 1995 by both EU Trade Minister Sir Leon Brittan and British Prime Minister John Major. The U.S. response was mixed: then Commerce Under Secretary Jeffrey Garten was quite positive, but others, including representatives of the Office of the U.S. Trade Representative, were cautious or skeptical.

In the fall of 1995, two events moved the process forward somewhat. In mid-November, a conference of European and U.S. businessmen adopted a number of initiatives and recommendations to their respective governments, including calls for rapid harmonization of technical and product standards, acceleration of Uruguay Round tariff cuts, and completion of agreements on telecommunications and financial services (left over from the Uruguay Round). In early December 1995, political leaders from the United States and the EU formally agreed to the recommendations on standards and to an immediate lowering of tariffs on information technology, as reported in the November 15, 1995, *Financial Times.*

The EU has also moved vigorously to institute a new set of trade policies toward East Asia, based solidly on a growing—though belated—involvement with the region. Between 1987 and 1993, total trade between the EU and Asia more than doubled; EU exports and imports rose from $56.2 billion and $89.1 billion, respectively, in 1987 to $110.3 billion and $162.3 billion in 1993 (Olivier 1995). Japanese investment in EU reached almost $80 billion at the end of 1993.

Significantly, the EU has consistently criticized U.S. unilateralism toward East Asia, especially toward Japan; indeed, in 1991, with the Kaifu-Delors-Lubbers Declaration of Common Interests, the two trading partners moved to elevate EU-Japanese economic relations to equal status with U.S.-Japanese economic relations. Further, in 1994, the EU published an important white paper, "Toward a New Asia Strategy," which proposed "as a matter of urgency" that the EU strengthen its ties to the region. Subsequently, the EU established more formal relations with the ASEAN nations and in March 1996 held a trade and investment summit with a group of fifteen East Asian nations, as discussed in the December 18, 1995, *Korea Times.*

The reemergence of the EU as a counterweight to the United States has significant implications for both East Asia and Latin America. The nations of both regions must now recalculate the costs and benefits of entering into preferential trade arrangements that will discriminate against a third major trading partner that is actively seeking equal trade and investment advantages.

Regionalism with a Multilateral Framework

The conclusions and recommendations of this chapter are divided into three sections: the future of APEC; U.S.-Japanese relations; and the future of regionalism within a multilateral context.

APEC. Contrary to the views of many U.S. trade economists and analysts, this chapter argues that the paucity in new trade initiatives at least until mid-1997—caused by the U.S. presidential election—is fortunate. It will allow leaders among the major trading nations time to reassess more realistically the potential negative consequences of a "spaghetti bowl" world of overlapping bilateral and regional trade agreements.

For APEC, both in Manila and in Canada a year later, the situation will allow a testing of the Asian way of concerted unilateralism. To give credibility to their proposed liberalization mode, the APEC Asian nations must come forward with substantial and real liberalization proposals at each of these meetings. They will then be able to resist misguided U.S. proposals and pressure to turn APEC into a reciprocity-based preferential trade arrangement.

Continued progress in talks between the EU and the East Asian nations can reinforce the strength of the Asian way of liberalization. Increased EU-Asian trade and investment will deepen interdependence and will buttress resistance to trade rules that discriminate against the EU as a major trade and investment partner. Similarly, in Latin America the delay until 1997 will allow the MERCOSUR more time to develop ties with the EU—and to reevaluate whether an extension of NAFTA, which excludes the EU, is in its true economic interest. Finally, the reappearance of the EU as a major proponent of additional liberalization means that proponents of U.S.-centered regional hub-and-spoke systems can no longer argue that such suboptimal agreements are necessary because a multilateral negotiation is impossible in the near term.

The United States and Japan. The United States and Japan, by virtue of their economic power and position of leadership within the Asia-Pacific region, must exercise special caution and responsibility as they chart their separate trade and investment policy courses.

Even after the triumph at Osaka of the Asian way for APEC, Japan will remain under increased pressure and temptation to move toward leadership of an Asian bloc, as Malaysian Premier Mahathir continues to urge. Japan should resist such blandishments and retain her strong

49

commitment to the multilateral system. In this connection, Masuru Yoshitomi's recommendation that Japan take the lead in forming a Non-NAFTA Pacific Caucus within APEC deserves careful consideration (see Yoshitomi's work, chapter 3, in this volume).

Yoshitomi argues that even with APEC Asians must make an organized effort to prevent NAFTA and the EU from drifting toward protectionist and discriminatory actions. Japan alone, he contends, cannot exert strong and effective pressure, particularly in regard to abuses in antidumping and voluntary import expansions (VIEs).

More discussion of this proposal will be necessary, but two countering points should be noted. First, though Yoshitomi also believes strongly that U.S.-Japanese coordinated leadership is essential for further world trade liberalization, he underestimates the impact such an Asian caucus proposal would have in the United States. Unless carefully presented, it would certainly be seen as an act of bad faith, even duplicity, on the part of Japan—and a back-door means of agreeing to Mahathir's proposed East Asia Economic Caucus (EAEC). Second, with the new WTO, the Asian countries already have a ready means to counter U.S. or EU abuses of antidumping actions and VIEs. As Yoshitomi and other Japanese leaders and economists have argued for decades, Asian growth and development have depended on an open and functioning multilateral system. Asian nations should defend that system against protectionists' abuses, not turn to a problematic and untried regional caucus or incipient trading bloc.

Conversely, Japan should continue to resist U.S. demands for targeted import quotas. Japan was correct in its refusal to guarantee the United States a fixed percentage of its domestic automobile market and is correct in resisting the extension of a targeted import percentage in semiconductors. The spread of this type of managed trade would have a vitiating impact on the multilateral trading system, and the United States should be directed to take its complaints regarding closed markets to the newly strengthened WTO.

WTO and Regionalism. Despite the political weakness of the Clinton administration on trade issues and the divisions within the free trade coalition in the United States, steps can and should be taken to prepare for future trade liberalization. At a minimum, the Clinton administration should signal to major U.S. trading partners that the time has come to begin planning for multilateral negotiations, the timing of which will depend on political conditions in the United States and in the major trading nations around the world.

Quiet diplomacy is called for, particularly among the G-7 nations, the APEC leaders, and the largest economies in Latin America, such as

Brazil, Argentina, and Mexico. In 1994, the United States blundered by proposing a new multilateral trade round at the G-7 summit without first consulting with its trading partners. Predictably, the proposal received a cold reception and went nowhere. Despite this mistake, in the coming year the United States should prepare the groundwork for a new round after backstage consultations with its G-7 partners and the leading developing nations and should aim for an agreement on a tentative agenda. In light of its misstep, the United States must now proceed cautiously but might be able to get an agreement in 1996 for a G-7 study group to formulate a tentative agenda for a new round within the next few years. Once again, 1997 is a logical target for a decision regarding a new round; by that time, the U.S. presidential election will be over, and the EU will have concluded its seminal 1996 constitutional conference and will have reached major decisions regarding the federal state for Europe.

High on the agenda for new multilateral negotiations—along with competition policy, investment, and the environment—should be reform of the GATT article 24 rules regarding customs unions and FTAs. As noted, the trading world is experiencing a new wave of plurilateral trade treaties, and by common consent the existing article 24 rules are inadequate to protect the multilateral system from discriminatory trade diversion.

This chapter is not the place to make a single recommendation regarding reform of article 24, but among the suggestions already put forward the following are of particular note. First, nations entering into regional arrangements should be obligated to submit to full surveillance by WTO's new Trade Policy Review Mechanism. The WTO should have the authority to monitor and trace trade patterns by sector and industry both before and after a treaty is signed in order to assess trade diversion—and to issue rulings dictating changes in regional agreements or compensation for injured parties.

In addition, the WTO should consider prescribing that, for new FTAs or customs unions, the member-nations agree to adopt the lowest tariff or the most liberal trade or investment rule among their members as the baseline for the treaty (see Bhagwati 1994). Further, some mechanism should allow, after a certain period, the terms of the regional arrangement to be opened to all WTO members on an unconditional MFN basis. This suggestion represents a compromise between those who oppose additional FTAs and those who argue that the free-rider problem will make impossible an agreement by nations to extend their negotiated concessions to all nations immediately.

One final point regards a U.S.-led multilateral agenda. Assuming that after several years there is no consensus for a new WTO trade round, the United States, rather than proceeding with overlapping FTAs around the world as the Clinton administration intends, reverts to former U.S. Trade Representative William Brock's call for GATT-plus negotiations. This would be a call to any nation in any region to join in a multilateral negotiation for further liberalization (a similar proposal has been advanced by Canadian Trade Minister Roy McLaren, according to the March 7, 1995, *Journal of Commerce*).

Several years ago, when it seemed that the Uruguay Round might fail, the distinguished U.S. trade economist Robert Baldwin summed up the arguments for a GATT-plus alternative—they remain valid today. He stated:

> This initiative could take advantage of the desire to establish stricter trading rules that is leading some countries to pursue regional arrangements with other like-minded countries. The organization would be open to all GATT members at any time and would involve both greater responsibilities (e.g., an increased willingness to open domestic markets and accept GATT panel decisions) and additional privileges (e.g., great access to the markets of signatories and better safeguards against unilateral retaliation). (Anderson and Blackhurst 1993, p. 406)

References

Ahearn, Raymond J. "Andean Pact—U.S. Trade Relations: Evolution and Prospects." In *CRS Report to Congress*. Washington, D.C.: Congressional Research Service, 1995a.

————. "MERCOSUR-U.S. Trade Relations, Evolution and Prospects." In *CRS Report to Congress*. Washington, D.C.: Congressional Research Service, 1995b.

Anderson, Kim, and Richard Blackhurst, eds. *Regional Integration and the Global Trading System*. New York: St. Martin's Press, 1994.

Anderson, Kim, and Hege Norheim. "History, Geography, and Regional Economic Integration." In *Regional Interpretation and the Global Trading System*, edited by Kim Anderson and Richard Blackhurst. New York: St. Martin's Press, 1994.

Asian-Pacific Economic Cooperation. *Achieving the APEC Vision: Free and Open Trade in the Asia Pacific*. 2nd Report of the Eminent Persons Group, August 1994.

Barber, Lionel. "US-EU Accord Aims to Cement Transatlantic Ties." *Financial Times*, December 3, 1995.

Barfield, Claude. *The Ties That Bind: The United States and Europe*. Washington, D.C.: Trans Atlantic Partnership, 1992a.

————. "The Americas on World Trade." *American Enterprise*, July/ August 1992b, pp. 10–14.

————. "U.S.-China Trade and Investment in the 1990s." In *Beyond MFN*, edited by James Lilley and Wendell Willkie. Washington, D.C.: AEI Press, 1994.

Bergsten, C. Fred. "The Case for APEC." *Economist*, January 6, 1996.

————. "APEC: The Bogor Declaration and the Path Ahead." Institute for International Economics, Working Paper 95-1, Washington, D.C., 1995.

Bergsten, C. Fred, and C. Randall Henning. "Europe's Role in the World Economy: An American View." Washington, D.C.: Institute for International Economics, 1993.

Bergsten, C. Fred, and Marcus Noland., eds. *Pacific Dynamism and the International Economic System*. Washington, D.C.: Institute for International Economics, 1993.

Bhagwati, Jasgdish. "Departures from Multilateralism: Regionalism and Aggressive Unilateralism." *Economic Journal* 100 (1990): 1304–7.

————. *The World Trading System at Risk*. Princeton: Princeton University Press, 1991.

————. "Regionalism and Multilateralism: An Overview." In *New Dimensions in Regional Integration*, edited by J. de Melo and A. Panagariya. Cambridge: Cambridge University Press, 1994.

Bhagwati, Jagdish, and Anne Krueger. *The Dangerous Obsession with Free Trade Areas*. Washington, D.C.: American Enterprise Institute, 1995.

Commission of the European Communities. "Towards a New Asia Strategy." COM(94) 314, Brussels, 13.07. 1994, Luxembourg Office of the Official Publications of the European Communities, 1994.

Council of Economic Advisers. *Economic Report of the President*. Washington, D.C.: Government Printing Office, 1994, 1995.

de Jonquieres, Guy, and Lionel Barber. "Business Meets to Revive US-EU Ties." *Financial Times*, November 11, 1995.

Frankel, Jeffrey, Ernesto Stein, and Shang-jin Wei. *Trading Blocs and the Americas: The National, the Unnatural and the Supernatural*. Washington, D.C.: Institute for International Economics, 1995.

Graham, Edward. "Towards an Asia Pacific Investment Code." Working Paper Series, 94-2, Institute for International Economics, Washington, D.C., 1994.

Hufbauer, Gary C., and Jeffrey Schott. *Western Hemisphere Economic Integration*. Washington, D.C.: Institute for International Economics, 1994.

"Japan Conquers APEC." *Economist*, November 11, 1995.

Jensen-Moran, Jeri. "Trade Battles as Investment Wars: The Coming Rules of Origin Debate." *Washington Quarterly* 19, no. 1 (1995), pp. 239–53.

Khanna, Jane. "Asia-Pacific Economic Cooperation and Challenges for Political Leadership." *Washington Quarterly* 19, no. 1 (1995), pp. 257–75.

Kirkpatrick, Colin. "Regionalisation, Regionalism and East Asian Economic Cooperation." *World Economy*, March 1994.

Korea Economic Institute of America. *AFTA after NAFTA*. Joint Korea-U.S. Academic Symposium, vol. 4. Washington, D.C.: KEIA, 1994.

———. *Economic Cooperation and Challenges in the Pacific*. Washington, D.C.: Joint Korea-U.S. Academic Studies, vol. 5, 1994.

Lardy, Nicholas. *China and the World Economy*. Washington, D.C.: Institute for International Economy, 1994.

Lawrence, Robert. "Emerging Regional Arrangements: Building Blocks or Stumbling Blocks?" In *Finance and the International Economy*, edited by Richard O'Brien. Oxford: Oxford University Press, 1991.

Lee, Jae-Seong. "What Role Should the U.S., Japan, and Korea Play in Regional Economic Cooperation: Then Interests Clash." In *Economic Cooperation and Challenges in the Pacific*. Washington, D.C.: Korea Economic Institute of America, 1994.

Noland, Marcus. "Implications of Asian Economic Growth." Working Paper Series, No. 94-5, Institute for International Economics, Washington, D.C., 1995.

Olivier, Christian. "The European Union and the Challenge of 1995: Toward a New Asian Strategy." American Enterprise Institute, mimeo, 1995.

Ow-Taylor, Chwee Huang. "NAFTA: East Asian Perceptions." In Korea Economic Institute of America, *ARTA after NAFTA*, Washington, D.C., 1994.

Panagariya, Arvind. "Should East Asia Go Regional: No, No, and Maybe." World Bank, Policy Research Department, WPS 1209, Washington, D.C., 1993.

———. "East Asia and the New Regionalism." *World Economy* 17, no. 6 (1994), pp. 817–39.

———. "The Free Trade Area of the Americas: Good for Latin America." Mimeo, forthcoming.

Preeg, Ernest. *Trade Policy Ahead: Three Tracks and One Question*. Washington, D.C.: Center for Strategic and International Studies, 1995.

———. "Free Trade across the Atlantic." *Journal of Commerce*, November 15, 1995.

Riedel, James. "Intra-Asian Trade and Foreign Investment." *Asia Development Review* 9, no. 1 (1991).

Saxonhouse, Gary. "Regionalism and U.S. Trade Policy in Asia." In *The Economics of Preferential Trade Agreements*, edited by Jagdish Bhagwati and Arvind Panagariya. Washington, D.C.: AEI Press, 1996.

Schott, Jeffrey J., ed. *Free Trade Areas and U.S. Trade Policy.* Washington, D.C.: Institute for International Economics, 1989.

———. "From Bogor to Miami . . . and Beyond." Institute for International Economics, Working Paper Series, 95-2, Washington, D.C., 1995.

Sugawara, Sandra. "APEC Pact Forged the Asian Way." *Washington Post,* November 18, 1995.

Sung, Keuk-Je. "Post-NAFTA GATT: Whither Multilateralism." In Korea Economic Institute of America: *ARTA after NAFTA,* Washington, D.C., 1994.

Wolf, Martin. "Comments." In *Free Trade Areas and U.S. Trade Policy,* edited by J. Schott. Institute for International Economics, Washington, D.C., 1989.

World Bank. *The East Asian Miracle.* Washington, D.C.; World Bank, 1993.

———. *East Asia's Trade and Investment.* Washington, D.C.: World Bank, 1994.

U.S. Department of Commerce. *Business America,* "National Export Strategy," October 1994, U.S. Government Printing Office, 1994.

U.S. International Trade Commission. *East Asia: Regional Economic Integration and Implications for the United States,* USITC publication 2631. Washington, D.C., May 1993.

U.S. National Committee for Pacific Economic Cooperation. "APEC Economic Leaders' Declaration of Common Resolve," Bogor Indonesia, November 15, 1994. Washington, D.C., 1994.

Wonnacut, Paul, and Ron Wonnacut. "Liberalization in the Western Hemisphere: Challenges in the Design of a New Free Trade Agreement." Working Paper No. 95-1, Middleburg College, February 1995.

Yoshitomi, Masuru. "Building a New United States-Pacific Asia Economic Relationship for the Post-Uruguay Round Era." In *Economic Cooperation and Challenges in the Pacific,* Joint Korea-U.S. Academic Studies, Korea Economic Institute of America, Washington, D.C., 1995.

Young, Soogil. "Globalization and Regionalism: Compliance or Competition? In *Pacific Dynamism and the Infrastructure Economic System,* edited by C. Fred Bergsten and Marcus Noland. Institute for International Economics, Washington, D.C.: 1993.

———. "East Asia as a Regional Force for Globalization." In *Regional Integration and the General Trading System,* edited by Kim Anderson and Richard Blackhurst. New York: St. Martins Press, 1994.

3
Building a New U.S.–Japan Relationship in Asia

Masaru Yoshitomi

To highlight the global role of Pacific Asia in strengthening multilateralism, this chapter focuses on two recent fundamental trade issues: (1) the nature of the new trade and investment relationship between Japan and Asian developing countries since 1985; and (2) the global role of Pacific Asia in a post–Uruguay Round as well as in a post–Asian miracle era. Let me explain the main problems involved in these two international trade issues.

This chapter first analyzes how the "flying-geese" pattern of trade in Pacific Asia (that is, Japan, the newly industrializing economies, the ASEAN 4—Thailand, Malaysia, Indonesia, and the Philippines—and China) has been changing under the continued appreciation of the yen. What is the role of Japanese foreign direct investment (FDI) in the integration of Asian production and trade? Globalization through the activities of multinational corporations (MNCs) has strengthened the complementarity of trade and investment. How has the steep appreciation of the yen since 1985 strengthened the link between trade and investment in Pacific Asia?

The chapter then explores the role of Pacific Asia in maintaining and strengthening the free international trade and investment system in the post–Uruguay Round era. Because of the relative decline of U.S. hegemony, caused by the advance in technological capabilities and the growth of per capita income in other major industrialized countries, the United States is no longer willing to act as the sole guardian of the multilateral system. It even tends to drift into protectionism, while at the same time it has been pushing Pacific Asian countries toward liberalization and deregulation. Such drift is often supported by the perception that Japan is an outlier and by doubts about Japan's ability to absorb the large volume of imports. In fact, such perception and doubts were behind the U.S. support of the Framework Talks of 1993–1994. Therefore, the chapter starts with examining doubts about Japan's absorption capacity and the perception of Japan as an outlier and then proceeds to analyze the role of Pacific Asia in strengthening multilateralism.

The Changing International Trade Pattern in Pacific Asia

The development of the intra-industry trade can be measured as $1-|X-M|/(X+M)$ in percentage, where X and M refer to exports and imports, respectively, of particular products. The perfect intra-industry trade, namely, exporting and importing of a particular product in the equal amount of value (that is, $X = M$), indicates that the index is unity or 100 percent. In contrast, the perfect interindustry trade, namely, specializing in exports of a particular product by importing none (that is, $M=0$), shows up as the index of zero. Therefore, the greater the index, the greater the intra-industry trade. This index advanced from 1985 to 1993 for, say, audiovisuals (from 44 to 71), electric instruments (from 48 to 58), office machinery (from 47 to 96), and automobiles (from 7 to 26).

Japan's trade structure with ASEAN 4 naturally features a much more traditional interindustry trade pattern than its trade with the NIEs does. Japan's primary imports from ASEAN are mineral fuels, crude materials, and food, which together account for 70 percent of total Japanese imports from ASEAN (compared with 20 percent in the case of its trade with the NIEs). In contrast, Japan's exports to ASEAN are primarily composed of general, electrical, and transportation machinery, iron and steel, and chemicals, accounting for 70 percent (compared with 80 percent in the case of the NIEs). The position of Japan as a net exporter of iron and steel to the NIEs has sharply declined over the past fifteen years, whereas Japan has remained a large net exporter, although its position has gradually been declining.

What also strikes us is the rapid development of intra-industry trade between Japan and ASEAN in home electronics, home electrical appliances, and autobikes. This development is very similar to that between Japan and the NIEs.

Thus, the structure of trade between Southeast Asia and Japan was based on "traditional" comparative advantage. That is, Southeast Asia exported to Japan raw materials, fuel, and natural resource-based and simple labor-intensive manufactured products, while Asia imported from Japan capital-intensive and R&D-intensive products. Because of dynamic developments in domestic resource endowments through human as well as physical capital formation in both Southeast Asia and Japan, the trading patterns have moved away from such traditional ones toward interindustry trade within the manufacturing industries in the 1980s and further toward intra-industry trade since 1985, particularly in the broad categories of the electrical and the transportation machinery.

For the development of this intra-industry trade, Asian affiliates of Japanese parent firms have played an important role, particularly through the promotion of intrafirm and interprocess trade. Overseas production by Japanese firms in Asian host countries has been aimed at substituting for exports from Japan since 1985. In most recent years, however, the substitution for Japan's domestic production ("reverse imports") has become increasingly important.

Changing Features of Japanese FDI in Asia. Such intra-industry trade promoted by Japan's FDI in Asia can be clearly demonstrated by comparing the trade structure between Asian countries (the NIEs and ASEAN) and Asian affiliates of Japanese parent firms. In 1992, Asian affiliates' exports of electrical machinery to the world accounted for 49.5 percent of their total exports, compared with about 20 percent in the case of world exports of host Asian countries (table 3–1). Both these shares had been smaller in 1986, nearly 30 percent and 18 percent, respectively, suggesting that Asian affiliates of Japanese firms have much more rapidly concentrated their overseas production and exports into electrical machinery. More interesting, this concentration is even sharper for exports to Japan by Asian affiliates of Japanese firms. Corresponding to that concentration of exports in electrical machinery, imports of the same machinery by Asian affiliates of Japanese firms from the world that is mostly from Japan account for 44.5 percent, as compared with about 18 percent for Asian countries (table 3–1). The share of Asian affiliates' imports of electric machinery, however, did not increase much, unlike the case of Asian affiliates' exports of the same machinery, for reasons that will be explained later.

To illustrate the changing feature of Japan's FDI in Asia, let us look, for example, at the electrical machinery industry, whose overseas production alone accounted for nearly half the incremental in total overseas production by Japanese firms in Asia from 1985 to 1993.

Over the past three decades, the goals of Japan's FDI in Asia in this industry have changed considerably, undergoing three stages. First, in the 1960s and early 1970s, the goal was import substitution in host countries. Foreign subsidiaries of Japanese parent companies were established to evade high tariffs on imports imposed by Asian governments and to target their domestic markets. Japan's FDI in this period corresponded to import substitution policies of developing Asian countries in the production of less sophisticated electrical products

TABLE 3–1

TRADE STRUCTURE OF ASIAN COUNTRIES AND ASIAN AFFILIATES OF JAPANESE FIRMS, 1992

(percent)

Sector	Exports To world By Asia	By affiliates	Exports To Japan By Asia	By affiliates	Imports From world By Asia	By affiliates	Imports From Japan By Asia	By affiliates
Food	1.8	4.6	1.3	4.8	2.1	1.1	0.4	0
Textiles	8.4	7.3	3.2	5.1	6.6	4.4	3.9	2
Wood & pulp	1.8	0.2	5.8	0.5	2.7	0.1	1.3	0
Chemicals	5.3	5.5	3.8	1.6	9.9	3.4	9.2	2
Iron and steel	1.9	0.9	4.4	0.3	4.3	2.8	7.0	2
Nonferrous metals	3.6	10.7	3.5	13.4	4.2	6.0	3.7	2
General machinery	14.2	5.0	8.2	5.3	17.9	4.9	26.9	6
Electrical machinery	19.7	49.5	12.1	53.2	18.3	44.5	24.8	44
Transportation machinery	4.6	6.2	1.0	3.1	6.5	23.5	10.0	29
Precision machinery	3.2	4.3	2.5	7.5	4.1	3.5	5.8	4
Petroleum and coal products	6.9	0.3	28.8	0.0	9.7	0.0	1.0	0
Other	28.4	5.5	25.4	5.2	13.6	5.9	6.1	5
Total	100.0	100.0	100.0	100.0	100.0	100.0	100.0	100.0

NOTE: Percentages may not add to 100 because of rounding. Definition of Asia is as follows: Asian countries—South Korea, Taiwan, Hong Kong, Singapore, Indonesia, Malaysia, Philippines, and Thailand; Asian affiliates—South Korea, Hong Kong, Singapore, Indonesia, Malaysia, Philippines, and Thailand.
SOURCE: Computed from AIDXT, an international trade data base, Institute of Developing Economies, Tokyo and MITI. *A Comprehensive Survey of Foreign Direct Investment Statistics*, no. 5 (1994).

such as batteries, radios, fans, electric cookers, and small black-and-white TV sets.

Second, from the mid-1970s to the mid-1980s, Japan's FDI in Asia was aimed at avoiding trade friction with the United States and Europe, particularly in such standard electrical appliances as small and medium-sized color TV sets, video tape recorders, window-type air conditioners, and the like. They were produced under a mass production system for exports to the United States and Europe.

Third, after the mid-1980s Japan's FDI was aimed at substitution for exports from Japan and then, in the 1990s, substitution for domestic production in Japan, that is, export expansion from Asian affiliates of Japanese companies of host countries destined for the Japanese market. Many Asian countries have newly adopted policies that encourage inward FDI, permitting 100 percent ownership of subsidiaries for export-oriented production. Examples are separate air conditioners, standard video tape recorders, hand-held video cameras, compact disc players, and the like. As time has passed, increasingly sophisticated products have been "made in Asia by Japan."

Links between FDI and Intra-Industry Trade. Overseas activities of MNCs are explained as a firm's optimal response to the conjunction of the following three advantages (Dunning 1988). First, an ownership advantage gives the firm market power based on unique firm-specific intangible assets such as technology, management know-how, network capital, product designs, and an established reputation. The motivation behind expansion of overseas activities of MNCs is to maximize the returns to this intangible asset. Second is an internalization advantage. When the firm is unable to realize the full value of its unique asset through the market or arms-length transactions (because of transaction costs or other market failures), the firm attempts to internalize transactions through FDI and overseas production. This internalization advantage determines the choice between FDI on the one hand and licensing and exporting on the other. Third is a location advantage, that is, an advantage to location production across borders near consumers as well as production factors including low wages, rich natural resources, and good infrastructure. This location advantage makes overseas production more profitable in particular host countries than others.

Presuming that Japanese MNCs enjoy both ownership and internalization advantages, what determines location advantages? How are location advantages associated with the determinants of interindustry and intra-industry trade? More specifically, are the direct investment of Japanese MNCs in Asia, their overseas production, and their procurement and sales policies associated with differences or similarities of factor proportions between Japan and Asia? There are two types of intra-industry trade (IIT). One is horizontal IIT of differentiated goods in the same category, while the other is vertical IIT based on the division of labor in production processes of the same category of products. The latter type of IIT is interprocessed trade in the context of globalization of manufacturing activities of MNCs. Hence, this often takes place in the form of intrafirm IIT.

Development of the Vernon-Type of Horizontal IIT. The horizontal IIT is based on differences in national income and tastes. The product-cycle theory of Vernon (1966) provides a useful model of the horizontal IIT in the north-south context. The north creates a continuous flow of new products, exports the latest versions of technologically advanced, higher value-added products to the south, and imports older versions in the same category from the south. The south tends to be specialized in exporting the lower end of products (for example, small-screen versus large-screen TV sets, monophonic versus stereophonic audio sets). Hence, this horizontal IIT involves constant shifts in comparative advantage from the north to the south in the same broad category of industry, reflecting improvements in human capital formation in addition to relative cost changes in domestic resource endowments (labor, capital, R&D, and the like). The horizontal IIT in the context of north-south trade is thus different from IIT in the context of north-north trade in such a product category as automobiles. The rapid rise in the living standards in the south has provided ample opportunity for IIT in differentiated products by technology and quality.

The Vernon-type of horizontal IIT between Asia and Japan can be illustrated as follows. In 1985, overseas production by Asian affiliates of Japanese firms was already high for the following products whose overseas production accounted for more than 30 percent of the sum of domestic and overseas production. They were radios (55.2 percent), stereophonic sets (48.3 percent), color TV sets (38.8 percent), electric fans (32.9 percent), and hi-fi speakers (31.9 percent) (see table 3–2). For tape recorders (23.5 percent) and electric ranges (22.7 percent), the overseas production ratio was also nearly one-quarter. Since 1985, Japan's net exports (exports minus imports) in U.S. dollar value have declined very sharply for most of those products. The drastic appreciation of the yen, however, not only accelerated overseas production of these products up to more than 50 percent but also encouraged new production of more sophisticated products such as VTRs (from 6.3 percent in 1985 to 31.4 percent in 1992), tape recorders (from 23.5 percent to 50.8 percent), refrigerators (from 18.7 percent to 30.9 percent), car stereos (from 8.3 percent to 21.0 percent), tape decks (from 5.3 percent

61

TABLE 3–2

OVERSEAS PRODUCTION BY FOREIGN AFFILIATES OF JAPANESE FIRMS FOR EXPORT AND IMPORT SUBSTITUTION OF ELECTRICAL MACHINERY PRODUCTS, 1985 AND 1992

(percent)

	Ratio of Overseas Production[a]		Overseas Production/ Export Ratio		Import/ Overseas Production Ratio		Japan's Exports		Japan's Imports	
	1985	1992	1985	1992	1985	1992	1985	1992	1985	1992
Radios	55.2	61.1	153.1	649.0	30.1	37.7	5.6	1.6	2.6	4.0
Color TVs	38.8	65.9	89.4	341.0	0.3	9.8	13.4	6.8	0.0	2.3
Electric fans	32.9	59.1	121.2	111.0	15.7	57.5	2.1	0.0	0.4	3.0
Hi-fi speakers	31.9	77.0	45.0	144.0	12.7	64.8	4.4	4.7	0.3	4.7
Tape recorders	23.5	59.2	20.8	183.0	7.7	41.1	77.5	20.8	1.2	15.7
Electronic ranges	22.7	64.1	36.6	518.0	0.0	1.0	6.4	1.3	0.0	0.1
Refrigerators	18.7	40.8	64.6	680.0	0.8	11.3	1.9	0.4	0.0	0.3
Car stereos	8.3	28.3	9.0	46.5	8.7	7.7	16.3	15.6	0.0	0.6
VTRs	6.3	31.4	8.1	56.9	2.3	4.6	25.5	18.8	0.0	0.5
Washing machines	5.9	20.2	15.0	152.0	1.3	11.0	2.1	0.9	0.0	0.2
Hi-fi amplifiers	3.5	26.4	4.5	35.5	0.0	20.9	6.5	4.7	0.0	0.4
CD players	1.1	37.0	1.5	65.8	9.0	29.8	6.1	0.8	0.0	0.2

NOTE: Production, exports, and imports are all measured in units of products.

a. Overseas production divided by the sum of domestic and overseas production.

SOURCES: Japan Electronics Machinery Industrial Association, *Data for Home Electronics*, 1994, and Electrical Appliance Association, *Handbook of Electric Appliance Industry*, 1994.

to 30.1 percent), hi-fi amplifiers (from 3.5 percent to 20.7 percent), and CD players (from 1.1 percent to 37 percent) (see table 3–2).

The extent to which overseas production by foreign affiliates of Japanese parent firms substituted for exports from Japan can be seen from the ratio of overseas production to exports. The products whose overseas production was already high in 1985 also had high ratios of overseas production to exports, suggesting that their exports from Japan had been considerably replaced by overseas production. Such export substitution further advanced through 1992, and overseas production became two to seven times as great as exports (table 3–2). At the same time, increasingly larger portions of Japan's domestic production were replaced by overseas production as measured by increases in the ratios of imports from foreign affiliates ("reverse imports") to overseas production. Such domestic production substitution ratios were generally low in 1985 (except for radios), but in 1992 Japan's imports accounted for 40–65 percent of overseas production for less sophisticated home appliances and electronics.

A new development in the early 1990s was the participation of more sophisticated home appliances and home electronics in intra-industry trade through export substitution and reverse imports. In 1985, both the export substitution ratio (measured by the ratio of overseas production to exports) and the domestic production substitution ratio (measured by the ratio of reverse imports to overseas production) were low for car stereos, VTRs, hi-fi amplifiers, and CD players. In 1992, however, these ratios became as high as the 1985 ratios of less sophisticated home electronics and appliances. That suggests that further appreciation of the yen since 1992 (from 127 yen per dollar to about 100 yen per dollar in 1994) must be again a strong driving force for the increased overseas production of more sophisticated home electronics, causing greater export substitution and reverse imports in the same way as happened to less sophisticated electronics products between 1985 and 1992.

As a result, in 1992 all the home electronics and appliances listed in table 3–2 were engaged in intra-industry trade between Asia and Japan within the narrowly defined specific product category. This situation stands in sharp contrast to the trade pattern in 1985 when only four out of the listed twelve products registered intra-industry trade.

It is also interesting to observe that within the same narrowly defined product category such as color TV sets, the unit price (that is, the total value divided by total units) is much more expensive for Japanese exports and domestic production than for Japan's imports from overseas production, suggesting that Japanese firms have shifted abroad the production of less value-added products within the narrowly de-

63

fined same specific product categories. In sum, the Vernon-type of IIT involves not only IIT between low and high value-added products within the same specific product—say, between small- and larger-screen color TVs—but also IIT between the specific products within the broadly defined category of home electronics and appliances—say, IIT between radios (exported by Asia) and car stereos (exported by Japan).

Development of Vertical IIT between Asia and Japan. Vertical IIT is closely associated with the Vernon-type of horizontal IIT, although these two types are conceptually separable. To see the development of vertical IIT and its relations with horizontal IIT, let us look at sales and procurement policies of Asian affiliates, in comparison with those of other foreign affiliates of Japanese firms in host countries other than Asia. There are several interesting features of the destination of sales.

First, the ratio of exports to sales (overseas production) is high for Asian and EC affiliates, accounting for 34 percent and 46 percent, respectively, compared with only 8 percent for U.S. affiliates in 1992 (table 3–3). Those different ratios indicate that whereas the main motive behind Japanese overseas production in the United States is to capture the local market, Asian and European affiliates capture both the local market of hosting countries but also the export markets of neighboring countries. However, an important difference lies between Asian and EC affiliates. While EC affiliates export manufactured products mainly to other European markets (38 percent of total sales of foreign affiliates), Asian affiliates export not only to other neighboring Asian countries (10 percent) but also to distant Japan (16 percent).

Second, the share of exports to Japan in total sales has steadily increased from 9.8 percent in 1980 to 13.7 percent in 1988 and to 15.8 percent in 1992 (though the data are not necessarily consistent over time because of changes in samples).

Third, the geographical distribution of the ratio of exports to sales (overseas production) of Asian affiliates varies from one sector to another within the manufacturing industry. There are three different categories of sectors involved: (1) a high ratio of exports to sales, reflecting comparative advantage of Asia over Japan in such sectors as wood and pulp, food, textiles, nonferrous and petroleum and coal products; (2) a high ratio of exports to sales for electrical, general, and precision machinery, reflecting the adaption of host countries' policies to encourage both exports and inbound foreign direct investment in these sectors (the ratio in these sectors has been increasing over time); (3) an extremely low ratio of exports to sales for transportation machinery and iron and steel products, reflecting import protection policies by host countries (table 3–4).

TABLE 3-3
SALES AND PROCUREMENT OF FOREIGN AFFILIATES OF JAPANESE MANUFACTURING FIRMS, 1992
(percent)

	Local Market	Japan	Asia	North America	Europe	Others
Sales destinations						
Asian affiliates	66.1	15.8	10.0	3.3	1.8	2.9
NIEs	66.0	15.0	10.8	2.5	2.3	3.4
ASEAN 4	65.1	16.3	10.2	4.5	1.5	2.5
U.S. affiliates	92.4	2.7	0.6	1.8	1.8	0.7
EC affiliates	55.4	1.1	0.4	2.0	38.1	2.9
World	76.7	6.3	3.3	2.5	9.2	2.0
Procurement sources						
Intermediate goods						
Asian affiliates	48.5	37.9	8.1	1.6	0.4	3.5
NIEs	47.3	39.3	9.6	1.2	0.3	2.2
ASEAN 4	50.0	35.5	7.2	2.0	0.6	4.7
U.S. affiliates	51.7	42.1	3.7	0.4	0.4	1.8
EC affiliates	29.0	44.4	3.7	0.8	21.0	1.1
World	46.5	40.9	4.8	1.2	4.6	2.1
Capital equipments						
Asian affiliates	40.9	53.4	n.a.	n.a.	n.a.	5.7
NIEs	57.3	23.9	n.a.	n.a.	n.a.	18.7
ASEAN 4	36.4	61.3	n.a.	n.a.	n.a.	2.3
U.S. affiliates	80.6	19.1	n.a.	n.a.	n.a.	0.3
EC affiliates	71.8	21.0	n.a.	n.a.	n.a.	7.3
World	60.2	35.9	n.a.	n.a.	n.a.	3.9

n.a. = not available.
NOTE: ASEAN 4 = Indonesia, Malaysia, Philippines, and Thailand. Percentages may not add to 100 because of rounding.
SOURCE: MITI, *A Comprehensive Survey of Foreign Direct Investment Statistics*, no. 5 (1994).

TABLE 3–4
SALES AND PROCUREMENT OF ASIAN AFFILIATES OF JAPANESE FIRMS BY MANUFACTURING SECTOR, 1992
(percent)

Sector	Sales Destination				Procurement Sources			
	Local sales	Japan	Other Asia	Non-Asia	Local procurement	Japan	Other Asia	Non-Asia
			Exports to				Imports from	
Food	66.1	15.8	10.0	8.1	48.5	37.9	8.1	5.5
Textiles	46.0	26.5	4.9	22.5	72.0	4.5	22.9	0.6
Wood & pulp	56.1	14.2	9.5	20.2	40.7	22.4	10.6	26.3
Chemicals	50.2	47.2	0.3	2.4	83.7	13.2	0.1	3.0
Iron and steel	64.7	4.9	27.1	3.3	71.4	16.9	3.4	8.2
Nonferrous metals	85.5	2.1	2.3	10.1	29.0	47.3	15.7	8.0
General machinery	63.3	21.4	12.8	2.5	64.8	9.2	4.8	21.2
Electric machinery	53.0	23.6	11.3	12.1	49.0	47.8	0.7	2.5
Transportation machinery	45.7	27.2	17.7	9.4	36.6	46.7	15.2	1.5
Precision machinery	92.6	1.7	0.8	4.9	52.9	43.8	1.0	2.2
Petroleum and coal products	36.9	51.8	1.6	9.7	34.2	60.2	0.3	5.3
	55.9	0.0	0.2	43.9	92.6	3.8	2.5	1.1
Others	79.1	9.2	5.1	6.7	58.6	27.5	5.9	8.0

NOTE: Percentages may not add to 100 because of rounding.
SOURCE: MITI, *A Comprehensive Survey of Foreign Investment Statistics*, no. 5 (1994).

Turning to the procurement pattern of Asian affiliates, one can again find several interesting features. First, in 1992, the dependence of Asian affiliates on local markets for procurement of intermediate goods is as high as U.S. and European (EC and other) affiliates (at around 50 percent). In the mid-1980s, however, the local market dependence was rather low (at around 40 percent) for all foreign affiliates except NIE affiliates of Japanese firms. These varying local market dependences reflect differences in the history of Japan's outbound FDI between the NIEs, where that history is relatively long, and hence a procurement network has developed, on the one hand, and the United States, Europe, and ASEAN, where it is relatively short, on the other.

Second, the origin of procurement of capital goods differs in accordance with the development of the capital goods sector in host countries. In 1992, the local market dependence is highest for U.S. affiliates (81 percent), followed by the EC (72 percent), the NIEs (57 percent), and ASEAN (36 percent) (table 3–3).

Third, the geographical procurement patterns of Asian affiliates differ among subsectors within manufacturing. The dependence on local market is high (above 70 percent) for natural resource intensive sectors such as food, wood and pulp, and petroleum and coal products, whereas it is low (less than 50 percent) for electric, precision, and general machinery. The dependence on Japan is highest (more than 40 percent) for those machinery sectors and also for transportation machinery and iron and steel (table 3–4).

Fourth, Asian affiliates of Japanese firms appear to have been developing an international production network in Asia, particularly for electrical machinery, iron and steel, and textiles, for production of which the procurement of intermediate goods relies not only on Japan but also on other Asian countries.

Development of Intrafirm Trade and International Production Networks. This last observation in particular leads us to the issue of the new trade pattern of Asian affiliates of Japanese firms, namely, intrafirm trade, which is deeply engaged in interprocess and intra-industry trade.

In the case of electrical machinery, Japanese parent firms export electrical and electronic components to their Asian affiliates (203 billion yen in 1992) and import from them finished electrical and electronic products (223 billion yen). Those numbers reflect intra-industry trade within the same category of electrical machinery, which is, however, vertical or interprocess trade between Japan and Asia based on the differences in factor endowments or technological development. This vertical intra-industry trade also applies to precision machinery.

The vertical intra-industry or interprocess trade has been developing rapidly since the mid-1980s. While the absolute value of Asian affiliates' procurement of electrical and electronic components from their parent firms increased by a multiple of 2.5 from 1986 to 1992, Asian affiliates' sales (or production) of finished electrical and electronic products increased even more rapidly by a multiple of 4.5.

At the same time, sales of finished electric and electronic products to local markets of host countries in Asia increased most rapidly, by a factor of 5, together with the increasing procurement of components from the local markets and sales of components to Japanese parent firms.

For total manufacturing, intrafirm trade between Asian affiliates and Japanese parent firms dominates international trade between Asian affiliates and Japan. The share of intrafirm trade was particularly high for general, electrical, transport, and precision machinery for exports and imports at 80–90 percent and above. Thus, when Asian affiliates export to and import from Japan these machinery products, they do so predominantly with their parent firms. The prevalence of intrafirm trade is attributable to the well-established distribution networks of Japanese firms that can take good care of after-sales services, and also to the required stable supply of a large number of components for specific final products, reflecting the internalization advantages of FDI compared with arm's-length transactions.

From 1986 to 1992, the share of intrafirm exports and imports between Japan and Asian affiliates increased from 76.5 percent to 84.2 percent for exports and from 66.6 percent to 78.0 percent for imports of all manufactured products. The share of intrafirm trade for machinery products also advanced during the same period, suggesting that international production networks of Japanese firms have been rapidly developing in Pacific Asia in view of the increasing importance of planning and coordination of research, development, quality control, production, and distribution.

The revolution of information and communication technology has opened up new possibilities for coordinating transactions both within and between MNCs, and networks are emerging as a new organizational form that is intermediate between the hierarchy of the traditional firm and the arm's-length relationship of the market. Networking is also creating new types of international links in such sectors as autos and electronics. Intracorporate regional production networks are emerging most clearly in east Asia through Japan's FDI and overseas production. In these networks, a subsidiary in a specific location produces a component in the value chain for the firm as a whole. This form of intracorporate integration is very different from intercorporate, interindustry integration based on traditional international trade and investment.

In sum, this type of intrafirm trade, which is engaged in the vertical interprocess and horizontal intra-industry trade, has been supported by two interacting factors: one is higher living standards and greater technological capabilities in Asian host countries and the other is more pervasive buildup of international production networks through Asian affiliates by Japanese firms.

The form of technology transfer to Asian host countries varies, depending on the types and goals of Japan's FDI. In the case of import-substitution FDI in the early development stage of Southeast Asian countries, the whole line of standard low- and medium-technology products was transferred to host countries, together with technology and management know-how relating to equipment procurement, production management, and maintenance. The standard low-end products require a relatively limited number of parts and components. Furthermore, most such parts and components are not specific, but standardized. Therefore, Japanese subsidiaries increasingly procured those parts and components from local industries, through which technology was also transferred.

In the case of overseas production targeted at export expansion in overseas third and Japanese markets of low- to medium-end products such as radio cassettes, stereos, and window air conditioners, however, most of the required parts and components have been procured either from Japan or from Asian affiliates of Japanese firms. This procurement pattern reflects the inability of local industries in host countries to meet quality standards of exportable products for advanced countries' markets, including Japan.

For Japan, the continued appreciation of the yen and its still dynamic evolution of comparative advantage are the driving forces for such development of international production networks. While these developments substitute for both exports of finished products from Japan and their domestic production in Japan, equally important they encourage more exports of highly sophisticated, high value-added specific intermediate goods, parts, components, and capital goods from Japan, thus contributing to further upgrading of its domestic industrial and international trade structure.

Postscript and Update. As projected and anticipated in this chapter when it was first written, Japanese outward FDI and overseas production in Asian developing countries continued to expand even more rapidly in 1994–1995 because of the further appreciation of the yen and the associated upgrading of Japanese manufacturing industries. What

69

was notable in this respect during this period is that Japanese automobiles and more sophisticated home electronics and appliances such as large-screen color TVs, car stereophonic audios, and separate-type air-conditioners have started to lose comparative advantage even under the current exchange rate of about ¥105/U.S. dollar. These industries had been the stars of efficient Japanese manufacturing in the 1980s. Furthermore, the current exchange rate is close to the equilibrium exchange rate for the average of Japanese manufacturing industries in 1995 by our estimate. Net exports of these two industries have been rapidly declining in the past few years because of both declining exports and increasing imports. What is more relevant for Japan's trade with Asian developing countries is that these assembly industries have held a vast number of parts and components suppliers and that many of them have also lost comparative advantage. Several important results, therefore, have emerged:

• First, both Japan's total exports and imports of parts and components expanded rapidly. In particular, the value of these exports to and imports from Asia increased more or less in parallel by 65–80 percent in two years of 1994 and 1995.

• Second, the share of imports of consumer durables in their domestic demand (shipments) more than doubled from 6.3 percent to 13.2 percent in only three years from 1992 to 1995, compared with a relatively gradual increase from 1.8 percent to 5.6 percent during the period 1985–1991.

• Third, in 1995 China became the second largest origin of Japanese imports of home electronics and appliances, next to Malaysia, but surpassing South Korea, Thailand, and Singapore. Chinese exports, however, still concentrated on less sophisticated products such as tape recorders, hi-fi speaker systems, and small-screen color TVs.

Global Role of Pacific Asia in a Post–Uruguay Round and Post–Asian Miracle Era

Given the analysis in the first part of this chapter on such developments as the newly developing international division of labor in Asia and the deepening economic integration through FDI, this section of the chapter discusses how we should establish more constructive U.S.–Pacific Asian economic relationships in the near future. This issue cannot be effectively discussed without analyzing the recent U.S.-Japan bilateral economic relations. Therefore, this section first analyzes the two interrelated perceptions about Japan: doubts about Japanese absorptive capacity to import from Asia and the rest of the world and the perception behind the Framework Talks that Japan is an outlier. The discussion then turns to what we should do collectively in the context of APEC for establishing a more constructive U.S.–Pacific Asian economic relationship as well as for strengthening multilateralism.

Doubts about Japan's Absorptive Capacity to Import. While the U.S. economy has to expand net exports to rectify its external deficit, one of the critical questions has been whether and how Japan can play a leading role in absorbing increasing Asian and world exports. There are some doubts about Japan's absorptive capacity to import for the following two reasons. First, Japan's distinctive domestic resource endowments such as poor natural resources and rapid accumulation of physical and human capital have shaped its equally distinctive external trade structure of comparative advantage. On the one hand, Japan's imports are dominated by primary products, with small penetration of manufactured products, while on the other, its exports cover a wide range of manufactured products. Some claim that this trading pattern has prevented Japan from absorbing manufactured products exported from successively industrializing Asian countries. Second is Japan's distinctive business practices, characterized by long-term repetitive intrabusiness group transaction relationships. Such relationships occur among assemblers, component suppliers, distributors, bankers, and corporate stockholders. Some claim that such business practices further limit Japan's role as importer.

To see Japan's role of absorption, we should look, first, at its total export and import performance since 1985.

Since 1985, Japan's export share in its export world market has declined by 5–7 percent every year (except 1990), if measured in volume (table 3–5). That decline occurred since the volume of Japanese exports expanded only 20 percent in spite of the 80 percent expansion of Japanese export markets during the period of 1985–1994. Nevertheless, the nominal value of Japan's total exports increased by 100 percent during the same period, if measured in dollar value. This gap between the volume and the nominal dollar value of Japanese exports is attributable simply to the cumulative 60 percent rise in the dollar unit prices of exports of Japanese manufactured products under the cumulative appreciation of the yen of more than 100 percent against the U.S. dollar.

The performance of Japan's imports has been just the opposite. The volume of Japan's imports increased by 67 percent from 1985 to 1994 (see table 3–5), which is more than three times faster than that of exports. If measured in the nominal dollar value, Japan's imports increased by 79 percent, implying very limited rises in dollar unit prices of Japan's imports.

TABLE 3-5
Export and Import Performance of the United States and Japan, 1985–1994
(% change from previous year)

	1985	1986	1987	1988	1989	1990	1991	1992	1993	1994
				Export volumes[a]						
United States	1.6	4.2	10.0	19.3	11.8	7.3	7.5	6.6	2.0	4.7
Japan	5.0	−0.5	0.4	4.3	4.3	5.6	2.5	0.8	0.9	−0.7
				Export Performance[b]						
United States	−1.9	2.0	3.6	7.8	2.9	2.9	2.2	1.6	−0.8	−1.1
Japan	1.2	−1.4	−5.5	−5.1	−3.4	1.4	−3.4	−7.3	−5.7	−7.7
				Export Share in World Trade[c]						
United States	11.7	11.0	10.6	11.8	12.3	11.6	12.3	12.1	12.5	12.5
Japan	9.3	10.3	9.6	9.7	9.2	8.5	9.2	9.2	10.0	9.5
				Import Volumes[d]						
United States	5.9	8.6	4.2	4.0	4.4	2.4	0.5	10.4	10.3	7.7
Japan	0.6	9.7	9.0	16.7	7.9	6.0	2.8	−0.7	2.3	2.5

	Import Share of World Trade[e]									
United States	18.2	17.9	17.2	16.4	16.2	15.0	14.5	14.8	16.4	16.7
Japan	6.3	5.6	5.7	6.2	6.3	6.3	6.2	5.8	6.1	6.0
Exchange Rates										
Yen per dollar	238.6	168.5	144.6	128.2	138.0	144.8	134.5	126.7	111.2	104.3[f]
Effective Exchange Rates[g]										
U.S. dollars	144.0	121.2	104.6	99.6	103.5	100.5	100.0	97.3	98.3	98.5
Yen	69.9	91.1	97.2	106.6	102.5	95.1	100.0	106.1	126.0	134.7

a. Customs basis, percentage.
b. Difference in expansion between export volume and export markets.
c. Values for total goods, percentage.
d. Customs basis, percentage.
e. Import share of world trade percentage of values for total goods.
f. May 10, 1994.
g. Effective exchange rates (1991 = 100).
SOURCE: OECD, *Economic Outlook*, December 1993 and June 1994.

Thus, the volume of Japan's net exports (exports minus imports) has declined considerably since 1985, while losing 36 percent of the world market share through 1993. In sharp contrast, however, the nominal value of net exports, that is, the nominal trade account surplus, has increased from U.S. $56 billion in 1985 to 142 billion in 1993, mainly because of the terms-of-trade change in favor of Japan under the substantial appreciation of the yen.

In conclusion, contrary to the doubt about Japan's absorptive capacity to import, its net imports (imports minus exports) measured in volume that is the indicator of the net import absorption has considerably expanded since 1985, simply because the volume of Japanese imports increased more than three times faster than that of its exports. Furthermore, Japan has constantly lost its export market share in the world since 1985, contrary to the claim that Japanese possession of a wide range of globally competitive manufacturing industries should make possible the continued expansion of Japanese export share in the world market. These unfounded doubts and claims are due to the confusion between the absorptive capacity to import that should be measured in volume and the expansion of Japanese external surplus measured in nominal value.

The regional distribution of exports and imports and the trade balance of Japan, all measured in dollar value, have to be considered in the context of this general picture of the volume of its exports and imports.

The destination of Japan's exports has changed considerably since 1985. The U.S. share of total Japanese exports declined by about nine percentage points from 38.5 percent to 29.2 percent during the period 1986–1993, whereas the Southeast Asian share increased by more than twelve percentage points, from 20 percent to 32.5 percent. Compared with this substantial shift in the destination of Japan's exports, the increased share going to the European Community (EC) and the decreased share going to the Middle East and former socialist countries are less dramatic, though still significant (see table 3–6).

In contrast, changes in the regional distribution of the origin of Japan's imports have been less substantial, except for a larger decline in the Middle East share and the relatively large increase in the share of former socialist countries, particularly China, and the EC. The U.S. and the Southeast Asian share increased by two to three percentage points.

The Perception of Japan as an Outlier and Failure of a Result-oriented Trade Policy. To construct a more constructive economic relationship between the United States and Japan, the perception that Japan is an outlier or out-nation should be abandoned for two reasons.

TABLE 3–6: REGIONAL DISTRIBUTION OF EXPORTS, IMPORTS, AND TRADE BALANCE OF JAPAN, 1980–1993
(billions of U.S. dollars)

	1980	1985	1986	1990	1993
Trade account, total[a]	−10.7	46.1	82.7	52.1	120.2
United States	6.9	39.5	51.4	37.9	50.2
EC	8.8	11.1	16.7	18.5	26.3
Southeast Asia	−0.8	3.0	12.3	28.1	56.8
Middle East	−30.1	−17.8	−8.6	−21.5	−14.0
Ex-socialist	2.5	7.7	5.8	−7.1	−4.9
Percentage Distribution					
Exports, total[b]	100(129.8)	100(175.6)	100(209.2)	100(286.9)	100(360.9)
United States	24.1	37.2	38.5	31.5	29.2
EC	12.8	11.4	14.7	18.7	15.6
Southeast Asia	23.8	18.9	20.0	28.8	32.5
Middle East	11.1	6.9	4.7	3.4	3.7
Ex-socialist	7.1	9.2	6.7	3.4	5.7
Imports, total[b]	100(140.5)	100(129.5)	100(126.4)	100(234.7)	100(240.7)
United States	17.4	19.9	23.0	22.3	23.0
EC	7.4	6.9	11.1	14.9	12.5
Southeast Asia	22.6	23.4	23.3	23.3	25.2
Middle East	31.7	23.1	14.6	13.3	11.3
Ex-socialist	4.7	6.5	6.5	7.2	10.5

a. Custom-clearance basis
b. Billions of U.S. dollars in parenthesis.
SOURCE: Ministry of Finance, Japan, *Trade Statistics on a Custom Clearance Basis*, various issues.

First, there have been no clear-cut demonstrations in economic analysis that Japan's markets are "uniquely" closed. The possibility is high that Japan may be as closed or open as other advanced countries, particularly with regard to manufactured imports.

Second, that perception has strongly strengthened the notion that a radically different trade policy is needed for Japan, since the GATT cannot deal with the Japanese "problem." Such "solutions" as voluntary import expansion (VIE) and numeral targets—that is, managed trade—have gained currency. These approaches have also encouraged the use of the national trade policies to achieve the selfish interests of particular corporations.

The various origins of such perceptions should be better articulated and analyzed. The origins are threefold: (1) the persistently large external surplus of Japan; (2) the small penetration of manufactured imports and foreign direct investment into Japan; and (3) *keiretsu* and regulations.

Relations between the external surplus and exports of unemployment. The assertion that the external surplus of Japan is exporting unemployment abroad is wrong. Even the U.S. economy with a large external deficit can still export and import unemployment through business cycles. Movements of net exports (exports minus imports) in volume tend to be countercyclical, but such movements should not be labeled exporting unemployment or importing employment. Only when the exchange rate is deliberately manipulated by the authorities so as to expand net exports through the depreciation of a currency, that kind of policy should be labeled exporting unemployment.

Moreover, the locomotive effect of Japan's stimulus on U.S. employment should not be overemphasized. Laura Tyson once said that the reduction of Japan's surplus by $50 billion would increase U.S. jobs by 100,000–300,000 (*Wall Street Journal*, March 1, 1994). This number is equivalent to only a one-month increase in U.S. employment. It is quantitatively too small to discuss as a top priority by high-ranking officials.

In addition, in the 1990s, there have been virtually no specific industrial complaints or damages to American businesses caused by the reexpansion of Japan's surplus in the 1990s. This situation stands in sharp contrast to the phenomenon in the first half of the 1980s when Japan's net exports *in volume* considerably expanded. In the 1990s, however, the expansion of Japan's net exports *in value* has been attributable to more favorable terms of trade and quality effects, not the volume effects, as indicated by trade statistics on a custom-clearance basis (table 3–7). No wonder that there have been few concrete com-

TABLE 3–7
JAPAN'S TRADE BALANCE IN VOLUME AND PRICE,
ANNUAL AVERAGE, 1980–1994
(percent)

	1980–85	1985–90	1990–93	1994
Exports				
Dollar value	6.2	10.3	7.9	9.6
Volume	7.0	2.8	0.8	2.0
Price	− 0.7	7.3	7.1	7.5
Imports				
Dollar value	− 1.6	12.6	0.8	14.0
Volume	1.9	9.6	2.6	13.6
Price	− 3.4	2.8	− 1.7	0.3

NOTE: Custom-clearance basis: percentage change compared with year earlier.
SOURCE: Ministry of Finance, Japan, *Trade Statistics on Custom Clearance Basis*, various issues.

plaints from the American business community about the reexpansion of Japan's surplus in the 1990s.

Japan's low penetration of manufactured imports and foreign direct investment. The ratio of manufactured imports to GDP is an inadequate indicator of the "closedness" of the Japanese market, for at least two reasons. First, such a ratio for the United States was only 2.1 percent in 1960 and 3.5 percent in 1970, as compared with about 3 percent for Japan in the 1980s.

Second, the same ratio in real terms for Japan rose nearly three percentage points over the past two decades, whereas the same ratio in nominal terms has remained more or less unchanged. This is because manufactured import prices declined in relation to the GDP deflator owing to the continued yen appreciation, offsetting the rise in the ratio in real terms. What matters to world demand should be the ratio in real terms (figure 3–1).

On the low presence of multinational companies in Japan, we should, first of all, understand the fundamental determinants of FDI. We need to gauge carefully whether the extra costs that any FDI inevitably incurs in host countries compared with home countries because of different business practices, legal frameworks, language, and the like, are exceptionally high in Japan as a host country, or whether ownership advantages such as superior technology and management know-how held by MNCs of source countries are strong enough to overcome such extra costs.

FIGURE 3–1
RATIO OF VALUE OF MANUFACTURED IMPORTS TO
GROSS NATIONAL PRODUCT, 1975–1992

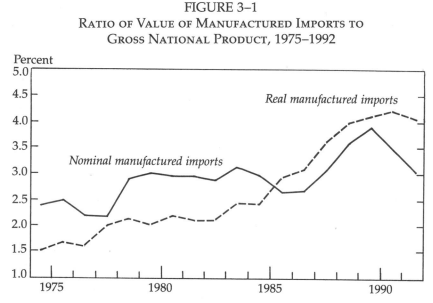

NOTE: Value of manufactured imports is based on a custom-clearance basis; yen denominated.

HISTORICAL TREND OF RATIO OF MANUFACTURED IMPORT PRICE
INDEXES TO GNP DEFLATOR, 1975–1992

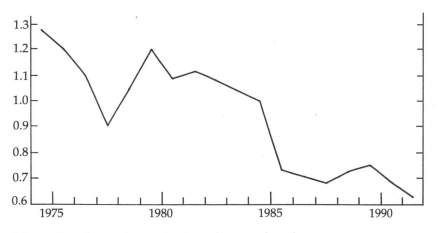

NOTE: Manufactured import price indexes are based on yen.
SOURCE: Japan Tariff Association, "The Summary Report on Trade of Japan," Economic Planning Agency, annual report on national account.

The links between FDI and trade can work in either direction of causality. For instance, the Vernon-type of product cycle theory suggests that trade precedes FDI. FDI may, in turn, induce greater trade than determined by conventional trade equations suggested by a trade theory in which relative strength of home and foreign demand and relative prices including exchange rate changes account for movements of exports and imports. Depending on the fundamental determinants (or theoretical yardstick) of FDI, the low penetration of MNCs in Japan may or may not be judged "too low."

Keiretsu *and price disparity between home and abroad.* On the question of *keiretsu,* the basic issue is whether it is collusive or exclusionary. Vertical *keiretsu* such as long-term repetitive transaction relationships between assemblers and component suppliers (that is, production *keiretsu*) cannot be more "exclusionary" than the in-house captive production system of major components by assemblers in the United States. Another vertical *keiretsu* such as distribution *keiretsu* cannot be collusive so long as manufacturers as suppliers of final products operate in competitive markets.

In this context, the issue of whether Japan's price disparity between home and abroad (that is, Japanese prices are higher at home than abroad) indicates a closed domestic market has become a central problem for debates.

In the due course of the SII (Structural Impediments Initiative), two official surveys on retail prices in Japan and the United States were conducted jointly by the MITI and the U.S. Department of Commerce (1989 and 1991). The surveys compare domestic and international prices of manufactured products *by country of origin* for both Japanese and foreign goods. "Surprisingly," manufactured products of Japanese origin showed little price disparity between Japanese and U.S. markets (as shown in table 3–8). That fact should not be confused by another that imported products in Japan were priced much higher at home than abroad. The difference arises because most of such higher-priced imported goods of foreign origins were food and brand-name products such as cosmetics and golf equipment. The question whether the vertical *keiretsu* is exclusionary should concern manufactured products of Japanese origin rather than imported food and brand-name products of foreign origin. These imported products have little to do with vertical *keiretsu* in such areas as automobiles and electrical machinery.

The Fair Trade Commission can officially challenge a horizontal financial *keiretsu* characterized by intercorporate cross-shareholdings within a business group and a main-bank system, if cross-shareholdings result in violations of the Anti-Monopoly Act. While

79

TABLE 3–8

COMPARISON OF U.S. AND JAPANESE PRICES FOR SELECTED GOODS
BY COUNTRY OF MANUFACTURE, 1991

Country of Manufacture	Number of Products Surveyed	Japanese Prices as % of U.S. Prices	Number of Products Priced Higher in Japan
Japan	40	98.6	12
United States	34	170.3	31
Other	20	165.9	19
Mixed	17	130.7	13
Total	112	137.1	75

SOURCE: C. Fred Bergsten and Marcus Noland, "Reconcilable Differences?—United States-Japan Economic Conflict," Institute for International Economics, June 1993.

members' activities can be coordinated within each business group, there must be an institutional basis for intergroup collusion (not intragroup collusion), if six or seven corporate groups in Japan want to work together to prevent entry and maintain high prices in a particular industry. In Japan, however, each business group comprises many kinds of industries. As a result, in each industry the competition is intense among different business groups unless the horizontal integration across business groups takes place with regard to a particular industry. Cross-shareholdings that are observed within a business group have prevented hostile takeovers by foreign companies or by companies belonging to other business groups.

The notion of impediments to market access has led the United States to a result-oriented rather than a rule-oriented trade policy and to unilateralism rather than bilateralism, let alone multilateralism. The perception of Japan as an outlier has come to the fore in this context. Efforts to resolve problems arising from the broad differences between the two economic systems should not be reduced to narrowly based trade-related arguments such as voluntary import expansion and numerical targets. Such an approach would serve only to worsen the confrontation between the two nations. The key question is neither whether capitalist systems differ from each other nor how to harmonize them, but how collusive and exclusionary business practices should be eliminated from any capitalist system through both domestic and international mechanisms, including the World Trade Organization.

Collective Action of the Pacific Asian Region. To discuss what Pacific Asia should do collectively in the near future, we should take into consideration a fundamental change in the international economy in the 1980s and 1990s: the "relative" decline of U.S. economic and technological hegemony as an inevitable result of successful catch-up of other advanced countries, including Japan. Because of this relative decline, the United States is no longer willing to act as the sole guardian of the multilateral system (Ostry 1994). In American eyes, the countries now catching up look like free riders on the multilateral system at the expense of the United States. The notion of the lack of a "level playing field" or unfairness has thus taken root, fostering protectionist sentiment in the United States.

Since the mid-1980s, the United States has developed a multitrack trade policy: (1) regionalism (such as NAFTA); (2) unilateralism (such as Super 301 of the 1988 Trade Act); and (3) multilateralism (such as the Uruguay Round). How this multitrack policy will evolve in the future is uncertain. It is, however, clear what Japan and Asia should do to direct U.S. policy toward rule-based multilateralism.

On the current international scene, however, a strange drama has been played, particularly between the United States and Pacific Asia: while Pacific Asia, led by Japan, should be in the best position to pedal the bicycle of a freer world trade and investment system and to enjoy the resultant benefits because of its dynamic economic development, it is the United States that has actually pushed Pacific Asian countries toward liberalization and deregulation, although it is often blamed for its drift to protectionism due to its eroding relative hegemony.

Japan and Asia should direct the U.S. multitrack policy toward rule-based multilateralism, for the following reasons:

• First, since Pacific Asia is likely to increase its share of world trade, this region will gain more from freer trade and investment than any other. Pacific Asia should not institutionalize the natural economic integration advancing through market forces of trade and investment as a formal preferential trading bloc. Although the intraregional ratio has increased in Pacific Asia (including China) from 36.5 percent to 45.0 percent between 1985 and 1992, the area is still highly dependent on extraregional trade: its trade with North America, the EC, and the rest of the world accounted for 22.9 percent, 14.3 percent, and 17.8 percent of its total external trade, respectively, in 1992. In fact, the extraregional export ratio of Pacific Asia (57.7 percent) is higher than that of North America (56.7 percent) and the EC (38.6 percent). Therefore, Pacific Asia needs MFN (most-favored-nation) based on a multilateral system. Any formal institutionalized trading bloc is bound to discriminate against nonmember countries, which is not in the interest of Pacific Asia.

• Second, an unprecedented number of countries have joined or seek to join the GATT, and many developing countries have initiated, on their own accord, market-oriented domestic and international liberalization and deregulation. Pacific Asia in a post–Asian miracle era, whose miracle was nurtured by outward-looking export promotion policy, should pursue rules-based multilateralism to support the developing countries.

• Third, in reality, liberalization requires some kind of political enforcement mechanism. Intraregional liberalization through regional political leadership and negotiations can be initiated for this purpose. While working toward regional liberalization on its own initiative, however, Pacific Asia should implement any regional trade liberalization on an MFN basis, by extending preferential treatment of intraregional liberalization to nonmember countries. This extension should not be conditioned by reciprocal liberalization; that is the thrust of the so-called open regionalism. Such regionally concerted liberalization in Pacific Asia should help prevent U.S. trade policy from drifting toward protectionism.

Pacific Asia should not be trapped in a prisoner's dilemma in a sense that a country will not want to engage in trade liberalization unless its trading partners agree to liberalize simultaneously, resulting in no action of liberalization that should benefit every country. Instead, Pacific Asia should pursue a prisoner's delight in a sense that a country can benefit from trade liberalization even if its trading partners do not reciprocate by liberalization, so that each country should liberalize for its own self-interest. This act of enlightened self-interest will add an extra boost to the world economy as well as to gain its own benefits from unilateral and regional liberalization through increased market exposure and greater efficiency. According to recent World Bank estimates, a 50 percent reduction in protection levels in East Asia would raise global income by more than $100 billion (or 0.4 percent of world income) above the baseline level for the year 2000. That number is about half the gains envisaged under the recently completed Uruguay Round (World Bank 1994). By benefiting the rest of the world, such concerted action in Pacific Asia would prevent the EC and North America from drifting into protectionism and inward orientation, incipient in their regional arrangements.

The Role of Pacific Asia in APEC. A big question remains whether Pacific Asia can really achieve this task. The East Asian miracle is characterized by a sound role of government intervention for economic development. Because of the success of such intervention, however, it has generally been difficult for the Asian governments to take the initiative in dismantling their own intervention because of vested interests. Needed deregulation and liberalization have tended to be delayed, justifying external pressures. This is the greatest dilemma facing Pacific Asia in a post-Asian miracle era.

Against this background, in the planning for the APEC leaders' meeting in Osaka in November 1995, the author recommended that Japan, as the host country, make the following two proposals:

- *Incremental, step-by-step liberalization.* The progress toward such liberalization will depend on the development stage of a member country.
- *Formation of a Non–NAFTA Pacific Caucus within APEC.* The purpose of this group would be to exert strong pressure against any drift of the EU or NAFTA toward protectionism.

The basic reason for the proposal of the incremental, step-by-step liberalization is the diversity of APEC member-countries, not only in language, religion, culture, and political system but also in the development stage of their economies. Income "disparity" is extremely wide, ranging from per capita annual income of more than $25,000 in the United States and Japan to only $500 in Indonesia and Vietnam. In contrast, the income difference between the top and the bottom is about five to one in the case of the EU. Economic systems are also different among APEC member-countries, covering both matured capitalist systems on the one hand and young, former socialist market economies in transition such as China and Vietnam on the other. Because of these economic and political diversities, it would be unrealistic to introduce a unified liberalization program to all APEC member-countries.

The incremental liberalization proposal can apply not only to the timing, speed, and degree of liberalization of the goods market but also to the sequential order of liberalization among the different areas of goods, finance, and services. In the case of Japan, for instance, it incrementally liberalized trade barriers in the goods market (excluding agriculture) only in the 1960s and throughout the mid-1970s, followed by the initiation of financial liberalization only in the early 1980s and of telecommunications and information services in the late 1980s.

While several ASEAN countries are reluctant to accept a unified approach for liberalization or to accept an APEC-wide free trade area, the United States is perceived to push young, developing countries too forcefully toward unrealistic liberalization not only for the goods market but also for financial and service areas. In addition, APEC

83

member-countries recognize that APEC is not a place for negotiations but a place for regional cooperation and development of consensus. For this reason, facilitation and cooperation have been emphasized over liberalization. By *facilitation* is meant, for example, simplified and unified custom-clearance procedures, harmonized standards and certification, and established principles and transparent laws for inward FDI. *Cooperation for development* includes advanced countries' assistance for human capital development, the nurturing of small and medium-scale enterprises, and technology transfer to developing APEC countries. The policy measures for such facilitation and development cooperation are decided on a basis of consensus. These are nonbinding targets efforts for member countries.

An important question now is how to advance the proposed incremental liberalization. Each member-country could formulate its basic outline for liberalization for the next five to ten years. Again in the case of Japan, it announced a basic outline for liberalization of tariffs and import quotas in the early 1960s. Resistance by industries with vested interests was often strong enough to block liberalization efforts of the Japanese government alone. In such circumstances, while turning the nation's own plan of liberalization into an international promise of liberalization and an established fact, the government was able to force private enterprises to prepare for the forthcoming liberalization, whereby Japan could achieve stronger international competitiveness of hitherto protected industries as well as better allocation of resources.

APEC member-countries can take similar action. First of all, each member country should produce its outline for liberalization, which each can design to fit its stage of economic development for the next five to ten years. At the APEC level, those outlines should be reviewed for content and implementation so that each member's outline becomes a regional promise. This review procedure should strengthen peer pressure and enhance the commitment to the implementation of the plan. In that way, a balance can be struck between the consensus-based traditional approach and the regional political pressure for liberalization in a way that would be more timely and binding than if left to individual countries.

This review procedure should also consider the extent to which so-called open regionalism can be effectively applied. While *regionalism* in this particular phrase means regional efforts for liberalization of APEC countries as well as regional efforts for facilitation and development cooperation, *open* means unconditional extension of liberalization by individual member countries to nonmember countries on an MFN basis. The extent to which such openness should apply can be discussed during the review processes.

84

The second proposal, formation of the Non-NAFTA Pacific Caucus (NNPC) within APEC, is aimed at exerting strong pressure against any drift of the EU and NAFTA toward protectionist and discriminatory actions. The justification for the formation of such an organization is straightforward; there should be a strong regional group that can counter inward-looking regionalism and protectionist movements by the EU and NAFTA. So far in Pacific Asia, no individual country, including Japan, has been strong enough to protest and exert effective pressure against discriminatory actions by the EU and NAFTA. No one should see the proposed NNPC as a custom union or free trade area; such an organization would be inconsistent with the very concept of open regionalism as well as with the spirit of the GATT or the WTO. The NNPC should work vigorously against, for example, abuses of antidumping or voluntary import expansion, and should direct bilateral and regional trade problems and disputes toward their solution and resolution on a multilateral basis by the WTO.

In passing, it should be noted that the proposed NNPC captures the thrust of the EAEG (East Asian Economic Group) or EAEC (East Asian Economic Caucus) put forward over the past several years by Malaysian Prime Minister Mahathir. The thrust is to form a strong Asian group so as to prevent the EU and NAFTA from taking discriminatory actions against nonmember countries, in particular the dynamic export-oriented Asian countries. Unfortunately, the concept of EAEG or EAEC has been extremely vague and hence the justification has been weak. The proposed NNPC, however, can be justified on two grounds, particularly when compared with EAEG or EAEC. First is the need for a regional group in Asia to act as a counterweight in disputes with Europe and the United States. Second, the criterion for the selection of members should depend on the purpose of such a group, but not on race. The aim of EAEG or EAEC is to forestall a drift of the EU and NAFTA toward protectionist actions and exclusionary measures that have often targeted Asian products. Thus, the qualification for membership should be non-NAFTA and non-EU. If both the purpose and the selection criteria of membership are thus justified, the proposed NNPC can be a more rational regional instrument for capturing the thrust of Prime Minister Mahathir's basic idea.

The proposed NNPC can also discuss how liberalization should proceed, either by an American "big-bang" approach or in an Asian gradual one. The presence of Australia in the NNPC as a non-NAFTA member country should, without the one-sided, coercive political pressure of the United States, enhance the opportunity to balance the two approaches for liberalization.

With these two proposals, Japan should be in a position to coordi-

nate the debate over timetables, outlines of liberalization, and exceptions by country or industry in a more harmonized way among all
APEC countries. Japan should also achieve a better balance among liberalization, facilitation, and cooperation, through securing market access for all countries in return for guarantees of ODA (official
development aid) and technology transfer.

Last, but not least, the important task for the United States and
Japan is as follows. The post–cold war era has clearly demonstrated
the increasing need for joint actions by the United States and Japan on
global issues such as environmental problems, including CO_2 emission
in China and former socialist countries, population control in lesser-
developed countries, cooperative science and technology development,
more constructive use of ODA, cooperation on AIDS, and drug control.
Our exercise of coleadership should be designed to develop the
world's stock of these public goods.

Postscript and Update. The key task for the APEC meeting in Osaka
in November 1995 was to draw an action agenda to implement the
Bogor Declaration of a year earlier, which had set the goal for trade
liberalization by 2010 for advanced countries and by 2020 for developing countries. The key concept for the adopted action agenda in Osaka
was Concerted Unilateral Actions, an idea along the line of the proposal made in this chapter.

In contrast, however, my second proposal for the formation of the
Non-NAFTA Pacific Caucus within APEC, aimed at exerting strong
pressure against any drift of the EU and NAFTA toward protectionist
and discriminatory actions, was not adopted. Instead, ASEAN (at present, seven member-countries including Vietnam and Brunei) now
plans to assist the economic development of Cambodia, Laos, and Myanmar (which would become ASEAN members in a few years), with
the help of Japan, South Korea, and China (southern provinces). In fact,
these thirteen countries for the first time held an East Asian Ministerial
Meeting at Kuala-Lumpur (Malaysia) in June 1996. The possibility is
high that a series of such meetings in the future would not only assist
in economic development of the three potential member countries of
ASEAN but also contribute to fighting against any drift of EU and
NAFTA toward protectionistic movements, as proposed through the
formation of the Pacific Caucus in this chapter.

References

Dunning, John H. "The Eclectic Paradigm of International Production:
A Restatement and Some Possible Extensions." *Journal of International Business Studies* 19, no. 1 (1988), pp. 1–31.

Ostry, Sylvia, and Richard R. Nelson. *Techno-Nationalism and Techno-Globalism*. Brookings Institution, Washington, D.C., 1994.

U.S. Department of Commerce. *The Joint DOC (Department of Commerce) / MITI (Ministry of International Trade and Industry) Price Survey: Methodology and Results*. Washington, D.C.: U.S. Department of Commerce, December 1989.

U.S. Department of Commerce. "Results of the 1991 DOC / MITI Price Survey." *U.S. Department of Commerce News*. May 1991.

Vernon, Raymond. "International Investment and International Trade in the Product Cycle." *Quarterly Journal of Economics* 80 (May 1966), pp. 190–207.

World Bank. *East Asia's Trade and Investment—Regional and Global Gains from Liberalization*. 1994.

4

U.S.-China Trade to the Year 2000

Guocang Huan

President William Clinton's decision to extend China's most-favored-nation (MFN) trade status on June 1, 1994, was a turning point in the development of U.S.-China relations, including trade ties between the two countries. The decision, an important step toward depoliticizing U.S.-China economic relations, created a new era of further expansion of trade between the two nations. Following the decision, the two governments started intensive negotiations over the protection of intellectual property right (IPR) and China's application for membership in the General Agreement on Tariffs and Trade (GATT). After tough negotiations, the two governments reached an agreement on the protection of IPR on February 26 (just a few hours before the U.S. deadline to impose sanctions against China), as reported in the *Asian Wall Street Journal*, February 27, 1995. Despite wide gaps between the two countries on various trade issues, on March 12, 1995, U.S. Trade Representative Mickey Kantor announced that Washington was willing to support Beijing's bid to join the World Trade Organization (WTO) as a funding member, according to the *New York Times*, March 13, 1995.

Meanwhile, the American business community has rapidly expanded operations in China. More than 150 of the *Fortune 500* companies have already approached the vast Chinese market directly; almost all major U.S. banks and securities houses have developed their own business dealing in China; many American legal and accounting firms also have been competing aggressively against their counterparts, notably from Japan, Hong Kong, and Europe. The United States is now China's second largest trading partner after Hong Kong and third largest investor after Hong Kong and Taiwan. In 1993, U.S. direct investment of U.S.$2.1 billion followed Hong Kong's U.S.$17.3 billion, and Taiwan's U.S.$3.2 billion. Japan's direct investment ranked fourth, reaching U.S.$1.3 billion. U.S.-China exports and imports have grown and will continue to do so.

Nevertheless, political and economic factors still constrain trade between the United States and China. The two governments differ broadly over human rights, nuclear proliferation, and, lately, the Taiwan issue. The two countries have been cooperating in various areas including the stabilization and de-nuclearization of the Korean peninsula, the maintenance of peace in Cambodia, the security in the Asian-Pacific region, and other political and security matters that require the participation of the United Nations (China is a permanent member of the Security Council and holds veto power). Nonetheless, the differences and conflicts between the two countries have often blocked expansions of their bilateral trade.

China's economic competitiveness with the U.S. market has surged, thanks to its economic reform and "open door" policy, which were begun in 1978 and have attracted a substantial foreign investment and strengthened China's export capacity. More important, Chinese companies and foreign-funded companies in China have become less and less dependent on Hong Kong as an intermediary in approaching the U.S. market and are successfully increasing direct sales to U.S. end users. Before 1993, more than 40 percent of China's total exports designed for the U.S. market went through Hong Kong. In 1993, the percentage dropped to 24 percent (Huan 1994a, 2). At the same time, U.S. sales (especially of industrial equipment and technology products) to China have increased significantly. American banking institutions have expanded their operations in China and Hong Kong. Between 1992 and the middle of 1994, most major American investment banks rapidly expanded their China-oriented operation at the expectation of making quick money. Nevertheless, the rise in U.S. interest rates and complications of conducting business deals in China have disappointed many American investment houses, which tend to expand quickly and then cut quickly.

Beginning in the second half of 1994, however, most American houses have reduced their China-oriented operation substantially. Nevertheless, those changes have had only limited impact on those U.S.-based multinational manufacturers. The U.S. trade deficit with China continued to widen substantially; in 1995, it reached U.S.$36.8 billion. Washington's negotiations with Beijing over China's WTO membership have made some progress. Such membership would require China to open its domestic market and liberalize its trade and foreign exchange practices as well as its financial markets. At the same time, the Chinese government has become increasingly concerned about the impact of WTO membership on its domestic industries and the survival of the state sector, in which 40 percent of the enterprises posted losses during 1994. In 1994, although China had a trade surplus of U.S.$5.3 billion, foreign-funded companies suffered a deficit of U.S.$18 billion, according to the Ministry of Foreign Trade and Cooperation of the People's Republic of China. China's balance of external trade is likely to be threatened by the heightening competition in both its domestic and overseas markets. In the United States, the deteriorating trade balance reflects its declining international competitiveness, especially with most Asian countries, while the policy debates over free trade and protectionism continue in Congress.

A few issues are relevant here. What are the basic trends in U.S.-China trade relations? What key factors are driving these trends? How can the business communities and governments in both countries further develop these trade ties? What basic policy issues face the U.S. government? How should Washington promote U.S. trade and other business interests in China, a rapidly growing and liberalizing market? To answer these questions, this chapter reviews the development of U.S.-China trade during the past decade, analyzes key factors that have driven this process, and discusses trends in the coming decade. Moreover, the chapter reviews China's policy toward regional trade blocs and its implications for U.S.-China bilateral trade. Finally, we provide some policy recommendations to the U.S. government on how to expand U.S. ties with China and promote U.S. business interests.

Historical Background of U.S.-China Trade

During the past two decades, U.S.-China trade has changed dramatically. In 1979, the United States and China normalized diplomatic relations. Over the next ten years, trade between the two countries expanded rapidly. In 1981, bilateral trade counted for U.S.$6.3 billion; U.S. imports from China were U.S.$1.9 billion, while its sales to China were U.S.$3.6 billion, generating a surplus of U.S.$1.7 billion. The United States accounted for 9.8 percent of China's total imports and 5.6 percent of its total exports, according to the U.S. Department of Commerce.

The main items initially sold by the United States to China were industrial machinery, telecommunication and computer equipment, grain, and chemical products. U.S. imports from China were primarily labor-intensive products such as textiles, toys, and machine tools, and primary goods, including mining products. At that time, American corporations had little knowledge about how to do business in China. To approach the Chinese market, they had to rely heavily on middlemen in other countries, primarily Hong Kong, or on overseas Chinese living in the United States. Nor was there any U.S. direct investment in

China, which would have enhanced trade ties between the two countries. Similarly, Chinese foreign trade companies did not have much direct access to the U.S. market. Most of these firms did not even have representative offices in the United States but had to depend on their branches in Hong Kong and overseas Chinese to conduct their business in the United States. Until the mid-1980s, most of China's imports and exports were handled by the Ministry of Foreign Trade, under which there were some ten specialized foreign trade companies. Most Chinese industrial companies did not have direct access to the international market.

During the following few years, commercial relations between the two countries developed rapidly. By 1988, total U.S. exports to China reached U.S.$5.1 billion, up 41.7 percent from 1981, while its imports from China jumped four and a half times from the 1981 level to U.S.$8.5 billion, resulting in a trade deficit of U.S.$3.4 billion. The United States became China's third leading trading partner after Hong Kong and Japan. A major part of Hong Kong's trade with China is reexports (accounting for more than 80 percent of Hong Kong's total exports) to China and other parts of the world, including the United States. At the same time, the structure of U.S.-China trade changed. American manufacturers significantly increased their sales of industrial (transportation, electronic, and electric) equipment and other industrial products, but China's imports of grain and other food products from the United States declined proportionally. At the same time, U.S. imports from China shifted more to labor-intensive manufactured goods such as shoes, toys and textiles.

An important development in bilateral commercial relations occurred as U.S. manufacturers began to commit direct investment in China. These investment projects were aimed mainly at China's cheap labor and low tax and tariff rates, especially in the coastal special economic zones (SEZs). Most of them were joint ventures (JVs) and were export-oriented. During these years, three major factors prevented U.S. and other foreign corporations that had JVs to increase their domestic sales in China significantly:

1. China's domestic purchasing power was still low, and Chinese managers and consumers were not familiar with foreign products.

2. Chinese policy was to encourage foreign investors and JVs to increase their exports but not to expand domestic sales. In 1984, the Chinese government issued a regulation that required foreign investors to sell 70 percent of their products to overseas markets; only 30 percent of their products could be sold in the domestic market. There were, however, exemptions to this regulation: JVs in SEZs and those whose products were considered import-substitution and high tech were al-

lowed to have a higher percentage of Chinese domestic sales. Never-theless, those consumer goods sold in the domestic market by JVs were taxed by Chinese customs according to comparable tariff rates.

3. Under the foreign exchange regime at that time, it was difficult for foreign investors to convert profits made in China into hard currencies through the Bank of China, the only bank that then handled currency conversion. There was no foreign exchange market. All conversion ap-plications, which were strictly related to permit for domestic sales, had to be approved by the State Administration of Foreign Exchange Con-trol. Those JV operations, however, enhanced American companies' understanding of the Chinese markets and broadened their contacts.

The year 1989 witnessed a huge setback of the expansion of U.S.-China commercial relations. Following the Tiananmen tragedy, the U.S. government decided to suspend high-level exchanges between the two nations and imposed sanctions against China, especially regarding technology transfers. Under pressure from Congress, trade unions, human rights organizations, and other special interest groups, the Bush administration linked the approval of extension of China's MFN trade status with its human rights practices. As the sale of high-tech equipment to China became increasingly restricted, many American companies decided to restrain their business expansion in China, and a few pulled out from the Chinese market. As a result, the expansion of U.S.-China commercial ties slowed significantly.

Nevertheless, bilateral trade continued to develop until 1990, when China suffered a policy-driven recession that reduced its import demand from the United States. In 1989, bilateral trade between the two countries rose to U.S.$17.8 billion, from U.S.$13.6 billion in 1988, with U.S. exports of U.S.$5.8 billion and imports of U.S.$12 billion. Con-sequently, the U.S. trade deficits widened to U.S.$6.2 billion, from U.S.$3.4 billion the year before. In particular, U.S. sales of high-tech industrial equipment to China dropped. In the following year, the growth of U.S. exports to China declined 20.8 percent at U.S.$4.8 bil-lion, while its imports from China soared 26.7 percent to U.S.$15.2 bil-lion. At the same time, the growth of U.S. investment in China dropped substantially. The tense political relations between the two countries appeared to have a strong impact on their commercial ties.

The situation began to change in 1992, when the Chinese govern-ment decided to make great efforts to boost its economic growth and reform. Following Deng Xiaoping's trip to China's southern coast in the beginning of the year, China's reform and growth suddenly blos-somed. As capital inflow accelerated, demand for imported capital and consumer goods jumped. At the same time, Chinese exports to major member-nations of the Organization for Economic Cooperation and

Development (OECD) picked up strongly. Despite the deep U.S. recession, U.S. imports from China actually soared, partially because of China's competitiveness in labor-intensive industries and partially because Hong Kong, Taiwan, and South Korea accelerated their direct investment in China, which strengthened the country's export capacity. Moreover, the recession increased U.S. consumer demands for cheap goods imported from overseas, especially from Asia. China's dynamic developments attracted many American companies, which expanded their presence and were able to increase their sales in China. Thus, although the U.S. government, especially Congress, continued politicization of commercial relations between the two countries by intensifying the annual debate over MFN status, the expansion of trade and investment between the two countries accelerated.

By the end of 1992, U.S.-China bilateral trade surged 65.5 percent above earlier 1992 levels, to U.S.$33.1 billion. U.S. exports to China rose 54.2 percent, to U.S.$7.4 billion, while imports from China soared 69.1 percent to U.S.$25.7 billion, leaving a U.S. deficit of U.S.$18.3 billion, according to the U.S. Department of Commerce. The United States remained China's third largest trade partner after Hong Kong and Japan. More important, the structure of U.S.-China trade continued to change: China became increasingly competitive in the American labor-intensive goods market, while its sales of machinery products to the United States increased sharply. Meanwhile, U.S. companies remarkably increased their exports of high-tech and capital-intensive products, such as aircraft, computers, automobiles, and other industrial equipment. Simultaneously, U.S. exports of consumer goods and services to China began to soar, reflecting in part structural changes in the Chinese economy, strong growth in the purchasing power, and major shifts in consumer preference, as well as the rapid progress in the integration of the Chinese economy into the world market.

U.S. direct investment in China also surged. In 1992, this investment climbed up to U.S.$519 million, third behind Hong Kong and Taiwan. Unlike most Hong Kong investors, however, American investors were attracted to China not only by low tax rates and cheap labor, but also by China's domestic market potential, which was supported by its strong growth. U.S. investment in China tended to large operations, focusing not only on the Chinese coast but also on inner provinces and producing a wide range of consumer and capital goods. The market orientation in this area began to shift from exports to China's domestic market for several reasons. China's domestic consumer demand (especially for foreign products either imported from overseas or manufactured by JVs in China) strengthened; the Chinese government began to loosen its restrictions on foreign investors' domestic sales and to encourage direct foreign investment by providing tax incentives and legal protection; and China's newly formed foreign exchange market became increasingly active, although the supply of foreign exchange was in heavy demand and the government's control over the market remained relatively tight.

The uptrend in U.S. direct investment supported its exports to China, as American companies had to bring in equipment, technology, parts, components, and, sometimes, raw materials, which were mostly exempt from import tariffs, to facilitate their manufacturing operations in China. In most cases, American companies were able to choose the best Chinese companies with which to work and often used their existing market distribution network, which sharply increased market capability of the U.S. firms in the domestic market. Moreover, teaming up with solid Chinese companies made it easier for American companies to deal with Chinese regulatory agencies and other government authorities in charge of the management of the domestic market and matters of foreign exchange. JV operations can also provide renminbi (RMB), the Chinese currency, which can be used to facilitate domestic sales.

With respect to bilateral relations between Washington and Beijing, little progress was made before the summer of 1994, when President Clinton decided to remove the link between trade ties with China and human rights issues and granted China the MFN trade status without attaching any political conditions. The turning point was September 1993, when the State Department submitted a policy recommendation to the White House suggesting a shift in China policy to "engagement" from confrontation. The Clinton administration took a few months, however, to readjust its policy. In response partially to active lobbying efforts by American defense industries, Washington also significantly loosened the restrictions against transfer of defense-related technology and the sale of weapons to China. Political tension between the two governments began to decline, and the two countries resumed military exchange programs. In the international community, Washington and Beijing have extended their cooperation at the United Nations on nuclear nonproliferation as well as on the stability of the Korean peninsula. The general atmosphere improved.

In 1993, commercial ties between the United States and China expanded rapidly. The total amount of bilateral trade rose 21.5 percent, year to year, reaching U.S.$40.2 billion. U.S. imports from China grew 22.6 percent, year to year, to U.S.$31.5 billion, while exports to China rose 17.6 percent, reaching U.S.$8.7 billion and resulting in a trade deficit of U.S.$22.8 billion, according to the U.S. Department of Commerce. Total U.S. investment reached more than U.S.$3.5 billion in 1994. Yet, U.S. investment projects tend to be long-term, large, and oriented to the domestic market. American banks and investment houses have become more active in the Chinese market and compete successfully against most British and Japanese firms. In 1993, the Chinese government allowed twenty-two large Chinese state-owned companies to raise equity abroad. American firms primarily coordinated this effort. This is partially because the large size of most of these deals required additional (to Hong Kong) listing through the format of American deposit rights (ADR) or global deposit rights (GDR) in either New York or London. Over the past two years, Chinese banks and other institutions have increased their bond issues in the overseas markets. Most of these deals were managed by U.S. investment houses. In the insurance industry, AIG was the first foreign company to be allowed to enter the Chinese market.

U.S. exports to China have continued to change structurally. China's export of manufactured goods to the United States has continued to rise, while U.S. sales of industrial equipment and consumer goods have accelerated. At the same time, the growth of U.S. grain exports to China has slowed and reflects China's successful efforts in boosting its agricultural production, as well as a major shift in Chinese consumer preference: residents now consume less grains and more foods such as fruit, vegetables, and meat. In both 1992 and 1993, the United States was China's second trading partner, after Hong Kong. More important, in terms of China's export, the U.S. market is far larger than the Japanese market, China's third largest market.

Dynamics of U.S.-China Trade

Several factors explain the development of Sino-American trade relations. The major factor is China's domestic changes. Since 1978, the Chinese economy has grown 9.5 percent, and its foreign trade has expanded an average of 18 percent per year (*Statistics Year Book of China* 1994, 20–28). More important, China has been integrated rapidly into the world market, and the institutional gap between the Chinese economy and market economies overseas has narrowed sharply. As a result, the interdependence between the Chinese economy and the world market has risen quickly, while China's international competitiveness in the labor intensive goods market has increased significantly. Moreover, rapid economic growth and implementation of the open-door policy have substantially changed China's demand as well as the domestic environment for foreign investment.

The key domestic factors that promoted China's exports are its economic reforms, including the government's industrial strategy, to develop labor-intensive, small-scale, and export-oriented manufactur-

95

ing industries. China's efforts to liberalize foreign trade and the administration of foreign exchange, as well as new policies to attract foreign direct investment, have also been important. Between 1978 and 1992, China's light industry grew an average of 15.6 percent per year while heavy industry expanded 13.7 percent. Most light industry was labor-intensive and export-oriented. In addition, the government made great efforts to promote rural industry, especially along the Chinese coast. These enterprises are usually small or medium-sized and easily able to change their products in response to overseas demand. By 1992, rural industry produced more than one-third of total industrial output and sold nearly 35 percent of total exports. In 1978, China's average labor costs were only about 7 percent those of Hong Kong. In 1993, its average labor costs in manufacturing industry were about 10 percent those of Hong Kong and 9 percent those of Taiwan, respectively. Cheaper labor was a major factor supporting China's expansion of export-oriented manufacturing industry and its overseas sales, especially to major OECD nations.

In addition, the Chinese government made strong efforts to decentralize its central planning system by granting local authorities great autonomy and recourse to promote local economic growth, especially on the Chinese coast. At the same time, it set up four special economic zones and later expanded the practice to the entire Chinese coastal area to attract direct foreign investment and promote exports. From 1979 to 1988, the Chinese government required foreign investors to balance their own trade and to export 70 percent of products manufactured in China; only 30 percent of their products could be sold in the domestic market. Those companies that were considered high tech or produced goods deemed "import-substitute" could be exempted from these rules. The government, moreover, reduced its administrative control over state-owned companies and supported the expansion of collectives and privately owned operations. The government also encouraged the development of export-processing industries by providing tax and other policy incentives to foreign contractors, mainly from Hong Kong. These policies have improved the efficiency of Chinese industry and strengthened its export capability.

From 1978 to 1992, China's single largest export item was textiles and apparel products, which accounted for 15 percent—nearly 30 percent of China's total direct sales to the United States. Other major export products were footwear, electronics, machinery, and machine tool products. Nevertheless, the jump in exports of these products has taken place only since 1988, when China's machine-building industrial production and foreign direct investment in those industries intensified.

⅄· The development of Sino-U.S. trade relations has been strongly affected by a second factor, the trade ties of other Asian countries with both China and the United States. Since the end of the 1970s, the labor and land costs of Asia's tigers have continued to leap and resulted in a decline in their competitiveness in labor-intensive industries; between 1984 and 1994, the average labor costs rose 10 percent, 12 percent, and 13.5 percent per year in Hong Kong, Taiwan, and Korea. In both Taiwan and South Korea, moreover, the democratization process has encouraged the development of the labor movement, pushing higher production costs. At the same time, the strong economic growth of these countries has resulted in accelerated domestic spending, which further weakened their competitiveness abroad, especially in labor-intensive industries. Asian tigers thus began to upgrade their industrial structure from labor-intensive to semitechnological and capital-intensive. Hong Kong, of course, began to upgrade its industrial structure much earlier by relocating its labor-intensive manufacturing operations to China. By the end of the 1970s, Hong Kong manufacturers started to subcontract to Chinese companies to produce textiles and other labor-intensive goods for the OECD nations.

During this process, the tigers have invested heavily in infrastructure projects, R&D, service sectors, and technology and capital-intensive industries. Their overseas activity during this period can be divided into three phases: first, subcontracting of manufacturing and export orders to those countries whose production costs were much lower than their own but whose cultural and political environment were favorable; second, the relocation of their own labor-intensive industries into the above-mentioned countries, primarily for export-processing operations; and third, to accelerate their overseas investment simultaneously targeting the host countries' domestic markets. Hong Kong started this transformation by the end of the 1970s, by developing export-processing operations in China. Since then, Hong Kong has remained China's top trade partner as well as investor. Investment from Hong Kong has brought China not only capital resources but technology, management, and an overseas distribution network, which together have boosted China's exports, especially to the United States. Both Taiwan and South Korea, however, began to upgrade their industrial structure during the mid-1980s. Despite their efforts to explore markets in Southeast Asia, they regard China as a huge source of cheap labor, which can be used to enhance their exports to OECD nations. Over the past few years, their direct investment in China has accelerated. More important, unlike in earlier years when Taiwanese and South Korean investment was mainly in small and medium-sized labor-intensive firms, more large and semi-capital and technology-intensive manufacturers have transferred their production

97

facilities to China. Between 1990 and 1994, thanks to relaxation of tension between the two sides of the Taiwan Strait, almost all major Taiwan corporations set up operations in China.

The results of this transformation have been remarkable. During the first few years, both China and the tigers were able to increase their sales to OECD nations, especially to the United States, as China obtained new market access and strengthened its overseas competitiveness, while the tigers' export gains derived from China's cheap labor and low rate of taxation. The tigers most value on their exports, however, added outside of China. This situation began to change in the beginning of the 1990s, when direct foreign investment, much from the tigers, spiraled in China. Increasingly, multinational manufacturers, including those from the tigers, relocated their production facilities to China and Southeast Asia and exported their completed products directly from the host countries. Meanwhile, helped by foreign investors and its own reform process, China's export capability has also been enhanced.

Since 1986, China has had a trade surplus again in dealings with the United States. Between 1986 and 1994, China experienced trade deficits against the United States every year for a total of U.S.$106.7 billion, according to the U.S. Department of Commerce. Nonetheless, China generated a trade surplus of *U.S.$485.7* billion against Hong Kong. Meanwhile, Hong Kong's total trade surplus against the U.S. reached U.S.$22.1 billion, according to Trade Statistics Dissemination Section and Census and Statistics Department, Hong Kong government. Hong Kong accounted for more than 40 percent of China's total exports during these years, reflecting China's high degree of dependence on Hong Kong for channeling its goods to major OECD markets, especially the U.S. market. Most Chinese manufacturers did not know the international market well, nor did they have direct access to markets overseas, as the Ministry of Foreign Trade, through various foreign trade companies, controlled most of China's imports and exports. This situation was particularly true for the labor-intensive products market, which is highly unstable and more dependent on the reliability of an overseas distribution network.

Nevertheless, this situation began to change in 1993, when China was able to reduce sharply the percentage of its sales to Hong Kong of its total exports in 1992 from 44.1 percent to 24.0 percent. During the first half of 1994, Hong Kong's share of China's total exports stood at 26.8 percent. The sharp reduction was attributable to two major factors. First, Chinese companies themselves became more competitive in the international market as the Chinese government granted them greater access to foreign exchange and the right to sell their products directly to foreign markets. Moreover, Chinese managers have developed their own distribution network in OECD countries and have become less dependent on Hong Kong intermediaries. Second, foreign investors have rapidly expanded their operations in China. Unlike Chinese companies, most enjoy their own distribution network and do not have to rely on Hong Kong to channel their products to OECD markets. In particular, China's direct and indirect (through Hong Kong) sales to the United States have skyrocketed and reflect the fact that China, along with other members of the Association of Southeast Asian Nations (ASEAN), has taken over the American labor-intensive goods markets from the tigers. More important, China's own manufacturing capacity and management skills have developed.

At the same time, Japan and the tigers have significantly increased their intraregional trade within Asia and reduced their dependence on U.S. and European markets. With the exception of South Korea, whose export growth to the United States has been fueled by its successful efforts to upgrade its automotive, electronic, and chemical industries, export growth of other Asian tigers (especially Taiwan and Hong Kong) has slowed. Yet, Taiwan's export of electronic, electric, chemical, and textile products to the United States has continued to grow strongly, reflecting the progress made in restructuring its industries as well as its trade. Similarly, Hong Kong's exports and reexports to the United States have undergone some major structural changes: sales of labor-intensive products have slowed, while exports of services and technology-oriented goods have continued to grow strongly.

Third, the development of Sino-American trade has been influenced by U.S. domestic economic growth, structural changes in the U.S. economy, and the trade and political relationship between the two countries. The U.S. restructuring process has major implications for U.S.-China trade ties. It has raised the U.S. demand for labor-intensive goods imported from overseas, including from China. Because of China's rising competitiveness in labor-intensive industries and because the Asia tigers have accelerated their efforts to transfer their labor-intensive production facilities to China, the growth of its exports of labor-intensive products to the United States has been particularly strong. Between 1978 and 1990, China's exports of manufactured goods to the United States grew 20 percent per year. Since 1991, it has further grown 20 percent per year. Manufactured goods now account for more than 80 percent of China's total exports to the United States, compared with 60 percent in 1980. Fourth, trade relations reflect the growth of China's imports from the United States.

China's imports of other American products, however, have been strongly affected by bilateral relations, both political and economic, between the two countries. After the Tiananmen tragedy in June 1989,

99

for example, the U.S. government tightened its restrictions against technology transfer to China, and the U.S. Congress's annual debate on the extension of China's MFN trade status was politicized. These events strongly affected the bilateral trade ties, as it became much more difficult for American companies to sell high-tech–oriented products to China.

In 1990, China's imports from the United States actually dropped 16.2 percent, compared with 1989. At the same time, each year between 1992 and 1994, the Chinese government made large orders of U.S. products before early June, when the U.S. Congress and administration had to finalize their decision on the extension of China's MFN trade status. More recently, in the fall of 1994, the Chinese government sent two major trade delegations to visit the United States; these signed many purchasing agreements with major American corporations in an attempt to influence Washington's policy toward China's application for GATT membership. These efforts have had a major impact on China's imports of transportation and telecommunication equipment from the United States.

The machinery industry is perhaps one of the best examples to demonstrate the competitiveness of U.S. companies in China. In 1993, China's imports of industrial machinery constituted approximately 20 percent of its total imports, of which the U.S. share was about 12 percent. Other major suppliers include Hong Kong (a major partner in reexports from OECD countries and Taiwan), Germany, and Japan. Nevertheless, Japan and the European Economic Community have been taking the lead in selling China key industrial machinery, because the technology that they provide to the Chinese is more suitable, because their governments have provided credit to support their sales in China, and because these countries are more flexible in the transfer of technology to the Chinese. Indeed, before 1986, Japan was China's leading supplier of industrial machinery. Since then, however, the EEC has taken the lead and provides more than one-third of industrial equipment sold to China. The major shift occurred partly because European, especially German, companies are more willing than their Japanese counterparts to transfer technology to China along with their industrial equipment.

Meanwhile, U.S. machinery exports to China have increased over the past sixteen years, but the U.S. share of the total market remained more or less the same until 1993, when U.S. direct investment in China climbed and the U.S. government further loosened restrictions on technology transfers to China. The U.S. Import and Export Bank of the U.S. Treasury Department, however, remained conservative in extending credit to U.S. companies for their sales to China. At the same time, many European governments and the Japanese government have continued to provide governmental loans to the Chinese government; some of the loans are often used to purchase industrial equipment manufactured in the country concerned. These governments have also extended cheap credit to support exports by manufacturers from their countries to China. Moreover, many Japanese governmental agencies, including the Bank of Japan, the Ministry of International Trade and Industry, and the Ministry of Finance, have sponsored many detailed research projects on China's economic, political, and legal developments and have supplied these data to Japanese corporations.

Nevertheless, the budgetary shortage has constrained the American embassy in Beijing and consulates in other Chinese cities and Hong Kong from conducting a broad and detailed survey on the Chinese economy. In addition, the data from their quite limited surveys are considered secret and, for the most part, are not made available to American companies. Without strong government support, many American companies have remained at a disadvantage in the Chinese market vis-à-vis their European and Japanese competitors.

Another interesting case is Hong Kong, whose share of the Chinese imported machinery market (especially those for manufacturing production) has risen quickly since 1987; this increase reflects the rise of Hong Kong's and Taiwan's direct investment in China as well as the more active approach of some multinational companies (mainly from OECD nations) to the Chinese market through Hong Kong. Also, the corporate income-tax rate in Hong Kong is only 17 percent. It is much easier for Hong Kong branches or subsidiaries to sell high-technology–related products to China. Before 1991, the Taiwanese government did not allow Taiwanese companies to carry out direct investment in China; and there is still no direct shipping between the two sides of the Taiwan Strait. As a result, Taiwanese manufacturers have to rely on Hong Kong to transfer their sales to China. Similarly, until 1994, there was neither direct shipping nor trade between China and South Korea. Korean companies had no choice but to sell their products to China through Hong Kong.

China's Policy toward Regional Economic Organizations

Historically, China has never initiated any proposals on forming regional trade or economic organizations in the Asia-Pacific region. Only recently China has become active in approaching various regional and international trade and other economic organizations such as GATT/WTO and the Asian-Pacific Economic Council (APEC) and conditionally supporting proposals from other Asian nations to form new regional trade and economic organizations.

A few factors explain China's policies. First, China was not a major trading power until recently. Before 1978, China was extremely isolated from the work market at large, and its political relations with most market economies were tense. Moreover, China had adapted a strategy of "self-reliance" based on a central-planning economic system. Under this strategy, China did not import products that it could manufacture domestically even at higher prices than overseas, and the government invested huge resources to build up its own comprehensive industrial system at heavy costs and with poor efficiency. The aim was to reduce China's imports as much as possible. Before 1978, foreign trade made up only about 5 percent of its gross national product. Much of its trade went through Hong Kong but was not directly conducted with major OECD nations. Foreign trade at that time was not on the top of the government's foreign policy and economic policy agenda. Political motivation (to break its isolation in the international community) rather than economic benefits often determines the government's approach in its economic relations with countries in the region.

Over the past sixteen years, however, all those factors have changed dramatically. China is no longer isolated in the international community; rather it has been rapidly integrated into the work market at large. Currently, foreign trade contributes about 40 percent of the country's total GNP. Economic interdependence between China and other parts of the world has significantly increased. More fundamentally, China no longer follows the strategy of self-reliance but actively promotes export processing and imports of technology and industrial equipment. To expand its foreign economic ties, to develop its trade relations with other nations, and to attract foreign investment have become key components of its foreign economic policy. Instead of using economic tools to reach political, security, or even ideological objectives, the Chinese government has shifted its policy priority to creating a relatively peaceful international environment and obtaining the maximum possible resources from overseas for its economic growth. For the first time since 1949, when the Chinese Communist Party took power, the government in Beijing has implemented a strategy to integrate the Chinese economy into the world economy at large. This goal significantly increased China's dependence on overseas capital resource, technology, management know-how, and markets. In particular, interactions between China and countries around the Asian-Pacific region have heightened. More than 85 percent of China's total trade is conducted with the region, and nearly 90 percent of foreign investment in China comes from the region.

Second, during the 1960s and most of the 1970s, the expansion of trade ties between China and most countries in the Asian-Pacific region was constrained by political relations. During those years, there was no direct trade between China and many Asian countries. China's political relations with most ASEAN nations, South Korea, and Japan were tense. Hong Kong functioned as the intermediary between China's and overseas markets. There were tough restrictions against selling technology-oriented products to the former Communist bloc, including China. At the same time, China was much more dependent on the former Soviet bloc. During the 1950s, the former Soviet Union and East European nations helped China build its entire structure of modern industries; this process resulted in the latter's high dependence on Soviet-made technology and industrial equipment. Moreover, during those years, trade between those countries did not require hard currency. Such a high degree of economic dependence on the former Soviet bloc, most of whose members had almost no influence in the Asian-Pacific region at that time, constrained China's ability to deal with Asian countries in the region. Meanwhile, before President Richard Nixon's trip to Beijing in 1971, China, which was actively supporting various radical groups fighting against their own governments in the region, was Washington's priority containment target in the Asian-Pacific region. Such a political and economic environment made it difficult, if not impossible, for China to play on active role in regional economic affairs.

Now the cold war is over. China has improved its political ties with most countries in the region and plays an active and constructive role in reducing regional tensions and building stability, especially in the Korean peninsula and Indochina. Ever since 1972, when Sino-Japanese relations normalized, China's economic and political relations with Japan have developed smoothly. Japan was the first OECD nation to lift sanctions against China after the Tiananmen tragedy. Over the past decade, the Japanese government has provided China a large amount of concessional government loans. Political tensions between the two sides of the Taiwan Strait have also fallen substantially, and business relations between them have expanded rapidly, although Beijing and Taipei have not worked out a realistic formula to settle their political disputes.

Despite territorial disputes between China and ASEAN states and Vietnam over the South China Sea, neither side seems to be motivated to escalate those disputes up to military confrontations. China's relations with the United States have gone through a number of difficult stages, especially since the Tiananmen tragedy in June 1989. In September 1993, however, the Clinton administration decided to shift its China policy and to repair its ties with China. In June 1994, the administration delinked China's MFN status with the country's human rights conditions, and over the past two years, the two countries have resumed military exchange programs. These fundamental changes have made it possible for China to downplay its security and political concerns in its foreign economic relations and to make more efforts and resources to make its economic relations depend on countries in the region.

Third, before the end of the 1970s, China's volatile domestic politics and economy as well as its weak international competitiveness prohibited it from actively participating in international competition. During those years, China's economic growth was frequently interrupted by its own domestic political campaigns, power struggles within the leadership, and the government's mismanagement of development strategy. Moreover, gaps in the economic systems between China and market economies were wide and constrained interactions between them. Chinese managers simply did not know much about changes and trends in the international market. Nor did the country's system enable them to respond quickly to overseas demand. Consequently, China's export capability was weak, and it had only limited foreign exchange for imports. The trade regime in the Asian-Pacific region can and did operate without China's active participation.

But China's economic system and structure have changed dramatically since the beginning of the 1980s. During most of this period, political tensions have generally been low, and the government has demonstrated strong ability of maintaining social stability. While the government has made great progress in liberalizing its economic system and building up new institutions, the country's economic growth has been strong. More important, its dependence on overseas markets, capital, and technology has soared, and China has become more active in the international marketplace. The Chinese economy has been rapidly integrated into the world economy at large, especially the Asian-Pacific market. In Asia, China now is the second leading exporter after Japan, and it is the first destination of international direct investment.

Moreover, China's trade ties with other countries in the region have expanded rapidly, partly because of China's own domestic needs and its strengthened export capability and partly because Japan and the tigers have accelerated their direct investment, which requires them to bring in industrial equipment, parts, and components into China. More recently, supported by its strong economic growth, China's domestic demand for imported consumer and capital goods has risen strongly and its own investment in the region, mainly in Hong Kong, has also picked up. China is the major investor in Hong Kong, for example, with a total estimated capital investment of U.S.$25 billion. Consequently, China is playing an increasingly active and important role in the region's economic affairs.

Fourth, the region's trade structure has changed dramatically over the past ten years. Before the end of the 1970s, trade with the United States and European countries dominated most Asian countries' imports and exports. The Asian countries were less developed, and their domestic demand was constrained. Most of them adapted an export promotion strategy by selling their labor-intensive manufactured goods to American and European markets. With the exception of Japanese investment in the tigers, the flow of capital and goods among Asian countries was limited. Thus, individual Asian countries' dependence on U.S. and European markets was high. Meanwhile, those underdeveloped Asian countries, such as ASEAN nations, did not appear to have strong export capability. China, conversely, did not have substantial trade ties with most Asian countries (except Japan), although through Hong Kong it imported limited industrial equipment, crude oil, and grain from some OECD nations and exported primary goods. Nor was there any direct investment from other Asian nations to China. Thus, China did not share many common interests with other Asian countries in dealing with non-Asian countries, notably the United States and European countries.

Since the end of the 1970s, however, many fundamental changes in the structure of Asian external trade have affected their dealings with China. Trade between Japan and the tigers has expanded rapidly, and Japan's trade surplus against the tigers has widened rapidly; the tigers' dependence on Japanese technology and capital resources deepened. While Japan and the tigers have successfully increased their exports to the United States and Europe, the structure of their direct sales to those countries has changed significantly: with a few exceptions, growth of their exports of labor-intensive goods has slowed, while sales of technology and capital-intensive products to the United States and Europe have soared; this change reflects mainly those countries' efforts to upgrade their industries and trade. Trade between Japan and the tigers on the one side and other Asian countries on the other has expanded rapidly. More important, China and most ASEAN nations have become increasingly competitive in labor-intensive industries and developed a strong capability of exporting those products to OECD nations as well as to the tigers, in part because Japan and the tigers have relocated many labor-intensive manufacturing facilities to China and ASEAN nations.

As a result, China now shares many economic interests with other Asian countries, although they may also compete against one another for capital resources and markets. China and most ASEAN countries, for example, would like to increase their sales to OECD nations and may act collectively to cope with the rise in international protectionism in the developed world as well as pressure from regional and subre-

105

gional trade blocs in other parts of the world. Direct investment from Japan and the tigers has played a major role in promoting China's exports to the United States and Europe. If OECD nations impose protectionist measure or sanctions against China, investors from Japan and the tigers that conduct export-oriented manufacturing operations in China may be hurt.

Nevertheless, China's policy toward regional trade organizations has been cautious. While actively participating in the Asian-Pacific Economic Council, China has made strong efforts to join the GATT/WTO. Yet the nation has been reluctant to support Malaysia's proposal to form a regional trade organization excluding countries in North America and Europe, especially the United States. Nor has China shown any interest to initiate or sponsor any other regional trade clubs in Asia.

For China, active membership in APEC—which is not a trade bloc but rather an international forum through which leaders of member countries can exchange their views on various international and regional economic issues—can enhance its international status and support its efforts to increase its portfolio in the international community, especially when China's relations with language deteriorated. Moreover, since Taipei is also a member of APEC, Beijing wants to make sure that APEC will not become an international organization in which Taipei can get the upper hand in its competition against Beijing for influence in the international community.

Beijing, nonetheless, realizes that a regional or subregional trade bloc excluding the United States will not serve its interest. Nor will such a bloc be realistic. China is too vulnerable to possible U.S. retaliation. In recent years, the U.S. market has been about 25 percent of China's total exports, and the dependence is likely to rise in the coming years, as Taiwan, Hong Kong, and Japan accelerate their export-oriented direct investment in China. Moreover, most other nations (Japan and the tigers) in the region are unlikely to join Malaysia's efforts, as they, too, are highly dependent on the American market. A major trade war will damage all countries involved. Unless forced, China is unlikely to take any initiatives to propose an exclusive regional trade organization in the Asia-Pacific region.

Prospects for U.S.-China Trade

The further expansion of economic relations between the two countries will be determined by the following major factors: China's economic growth, as well as its export capacity and its demand for imported goods; the likelihood that China will join the WTO by the middle of 1995; political relations between the two countries; competition from other countries for both U.S. and Chinese markets; and U.S. growth and structural changes in its economy as well as its trade policies.

By all estimates, China should be able to continue its rapid economic growth, although this process may become volatile during the next two or three years as the country's political succession approaches. The government's macroeconomic management may weaken because of mounting inflationary pressure and unemployment and a lack of effective monetary, fiscal, and other policy instruments. Both internal and external demand are likely to surge in the coming years. Rising domestic demand will be fueled by the need for capital investment as well as structural changes in Chinese consumer behavior.

The distribution of wealth between the state and society, the share of fiscal revenue between the central government and local authorities, and the rise of the service sector are also important factors. China's savings rate is likely to remain at the level of about 35 percent, as the Asian traditional culture will continue to encourage individuals to save while the government (at both central and local levels) should be able to continue its high saving and investment policies because of its influence on the business community.

Externally, China's competitiveness (relatively lower production costs and higher productivity vis-à-vis many Asian and South American developing countries) will continue to ensure strong demand for its labor-intensive products, mainly from OECD nations and the tigers. Moreover, the surge in direct foreign investment in China should strengthen its export capacity, as these investments further improve China's management skills, market connections, technology, and capital resources. At the same time, these countries will continue to upgrade their own industries by relating their labor-intensive industries overseas and opening up their domestic labor-intensive products markets.

On the supply side, China's high domestic savings will ensure a continuation of high growth in fixed capital outlays. More important, intensified capital investment in infrastructure projects in recent years, which is partially financed and managed by foreign investors, should improve significantly the country's industrial productivity and support further growth. Foreign direct investment should continue to soar, as China's domestic market for both capital and consumer goods will continue to boom, especially after China joins the WTO. Chinese managers' and consumers' preferences, moreover, will most likely lean toward foreign-made products. Yet, to set up manufacturing facilities in China will enhance the ability of multinational corporations to increase their competitiveness in China's domestic market. If China joins the WTO in the middle of 1995, its domestic market will open further, and the liberalization of its trade, financial, legal, and foreign exchange systems will accelerate. The existing institutional disadvantage between itself and market economies overseas will narrow and more direct foreign investment will be attracted.

China's economic reform, the most important institutional support for rapid economic growth, is most likely to continue. The decentralization drive will continue, as it is needed to speed up the reform and economic growth, while the central government, for both political and economic reasons, is unlikely to be able to recentralize its power. In recent years, both in China and overseas, the argument for recentralizing fiscal and political power has been based on the definition of state capacity. Scholars often confuse the state's macroeconomic management ability with its fiscal power by assuming that the more fiscal revenue the central government receives (especially vis-à-vis both local authorities and the private or nonstate sector), the more its macroeconomics management ability will strengthen.

They have missed the following points:

- The decentralization process is one of most important dimensions of the Chinese reform and economic takeoff over the past sixteen years.
- The Chinese central government's record of investment efficiency has been poor; more central government revenue means lower efficiency for the whole economy.
- China is in a transitional period from a central planning system to a market-oriented economy.
- What is needed is not recentralization, which cannot be done anyway, but rather a set of macroeconomic management mechanisms, such as a more effective central bank, legal structure, and taxation system (which is partially operated by local authorities). To build these new mechanisms does not mean necessarily that the central government should increase significantly its share of total state revenue, but the government should rather accelerate its reform process and place these new mechanisms in the new market structure. This new structure should enhance the central government's macroeconomic management without damaging local authorities' incentive and their ability to manage local reform and growth.

In the coming years, the government is likely to develop financial markets further; if well-structured and managed, these markets will increase the efficiency of capital and improve its macroeconomic management. The government will continue to reform. The central bank is expected to strengthen its role in managing the economy by developing open-market operations and the bond market and by granting commercial banks greater autonomy in governing their own credit policies. China's nonstate sector (including collectives, private ownership, and foreign-funded companies), which produced more than 50 percent of total industrial output in 1994, will continue to grow much faster than the state sector. Meanwhile, the government has had little alternative but to speed its efforts to privatize the state sector. In fact, China has already made some progress in establishing social welfare and retirement systems. If China were to join the WTO in 1995, its foreign trade and foreign exchange administration would be liberalized further.

To be sure, China's economic growth will face certain major challenges. First, the country's infrastructure facilities are still unable to address the needs of strong economic growth. Currently, China's railway system can meet only 65 percent of the need; air transportation and telecommunications systems are underdeveloped; only a few provinces have highways; and China's power generation capacity can meet only 75 percent of the nation's requirements. China's efficiency in power use is far behind that of OECD nations. To solve these bottlenecks, government will have to implement more flexible policies governing foreign investment in these areas, improve efficiency, and direct more domestic capital resources to infrastructure projects.

Second, stability and consistency in macroeconomics management will have to be improved. To do so, the government will have to strengthen coordination and balance between its reform strategies and its various macroeconomic policies. Moreover, China will have to reform the banking system and financial markets and create new instruments for the central bank to manage its monetary policies. Similarly, the legal and taxation systems need further improvement. The central government should be able to stabilize growth as well as its own policies.

Third, the government will have to reform and privatize the state sector, more than 40 percent of which currently loses money, as the sector has been challenged by both the nonstate sector and foreign investors. If China joins the WTO, these challenges will become more severe, especially for capital- and technology-intensive industries in the domestic market, although some labor-intensive industries will benefit from the membership.

Nevertheless, a rapid privatization program, which requires effective financial, legal, and social welfare systems, will significantly slow growth and raise unemployment and underemployment, which may jeopardize the country's political stability. Moreover, WTO membership will require China to open its domestic market much more widely to foreign products both imported to China and manufactured in China by foreign investors, which usually team up with the best Chinese companies. Thus, a large number of rural industrial companies, which have grown fast and have created most of the jobs during the past sixteen years, will soon lose their competitiveness in the domestic market.

Fourth, the high population growth rate will remain a major challenge. Currently, China's total population is about 1.2 billion, and its natural birth rate (after deducting the natural death rate) is about 1.2 percent, which means about 14 million new lives each year. More important, strong agricultural growth and changes in rural lifestyle have released a large surplus of labor; half of these workers (estimated at 80 million) have already moved to urban areas, especially in the coastal regions, to seek either long-term or seasonal jobs. Meanwhile, the pressure of underemployment on nonprofitable state-owned companies will continue. Currently, the official unemployment rate is just 2.8 percent. But the number of underemployed workers in the state sector is estimated at 15–20 million. If the government accelerates its privatization program and foreign competition intensifies because of its expected WTO membership, the pressure of unemployment and underemployment will further mount.

Fifth, how to balance external accounts will remain a major challenge. In 1993, China had a trade deficit of U.S.$12.2 billion. But the trade deficits generated by foreign-funded companies jumped to U.S.$16.5 billion. During the first three quarters of 1994, thanks to a 10 percent depreciation of the RMB against the dollar and a more than 20 percent drop against the deutsche mark and Japanese yen, China experienced a turnaround in its trade balance, generating a small surplus of U.S.$1.2 billion. Nevertheless, foreign-funded companies had a deficit of U.S.$10.6 billion. In both 1993 and 1994, foreign-funded companies imported about 40 percent of China's total imports and exported nearly 30 percent of its total exports.

Foreign-funded companies have become a major source of the trade imbalance because of their need to import capital goods (machinery, parts, and components) for their manufacturing operations in China and the rising demand by Chinese consumers and managers for foreign-made consumer and capital goods manufactured both overseas and in China. Nevertheless, this phenomenon differs from the experience of Japan, South Korea, and Taiwan during earlier years, when capital inflow along with imported capital goods soon strengthened the manufacturing capacity of those economies to target overseas markets. Over the past three years, large foreign-funded companies in China have been focusing increasingly on China's domestic market, while their import of capital goods, most exempt from import tariffs, has soared. If China were to join the WTO in 1995, its domestic market

110

would open wider, and the competitiveness of foreign investors in China would intensify. As a result, their imports would continue to rise.

These five major challenges may weaken the Chinese government's macroeconomic management in the short term, but this problem should be rectified in the medium and long term if the government adopts appropriate, well balanced, and effective policies. For American companies, this prognosis for the Chinese economy promises a huge potential market, as China's rapid economic growth will require more financial resources, technology, and capital goods imported from overseas. More important, if the Chinese reform continues and if China joins the WTO, the institutional gap between China and Western market economies will further narrow, and the Chinese economy will be further integrated into the world economy at large. These trends will significantly improve China's investment environment and provide U.S. manufacturers greater access to the Chinese market if the U.S. government can provide effective policy support and U.S. companies can devise effective marketing and investment strategies. At the same time, China's exports of labor-intensive goods and some technology- and capital-intensive goods, which respond to the progress of capital inflow and technology transfer to China, will rise strongly.

It is in the interests of both sides for China to join the international trade organization. Beijing without WTO membership would face an intensified trade war with the United States. Such a development would injure China's economic ties with key OECD nations, especially the United States, and damage in particular exports from its labor-intensive industries. China's ability to raise capital from overseas to finance its modernization drive would be severely impaired. Politically, if Taipei were to join the WTO before Beijing, China's "one-China" position would be compromised. Notwithstanding these consequences, if Beijing were to join the WTO by making further major concessions (especially as a "developed" country), many of its industries would be hurt severely and its economic growth would be damaged. The high stakes involved here will heighten internal policy debates.

Should, however, China be unable to join the WTO, U.S. interests would also be hurt. An intensified trade war between the two countries would seriously damage American business interest in China. The situation would place U.S. corporations at the severe disadvantage in the Chinese market vis-à-vis their European and Japanese competition, as European and Japanese governments took advantage of U.S.-China tensions and the Chinese government retaliated against U.S. policy by turning to its competitors. A trade war between China and the United States would have the effect of reducing the U.S. trade deficit with

111

China. It would protect the U.S. labor-intensive goods market from cheap Chinese products, an increasingly large portion of which are manufactured by foreign-funded (including American-funded) companies in China. A trade war, however, would be unlikely to recreate U.S. labor-intensive production or to preclude the entry of cheap products from other countries. Moreover, launching a trade war with China would not help U.S. companies obtain greater access to the Chinese market but rather undercut their competitiveness in the market relative to other countries. Such a policy, therefore, would not improve the U.S. trade balance. While this policy would satisfy certain sectors in the United States, such as trade unions in labor-intensive industries, manufacturers, especially those producing high-tech industrial equipment, would be hurt. By the same token, American consumers would wind up paying high prices for products made domestically. Whether the relationship between Beijing and Taipei will be destabilized if China is rejected by the WTO remains to be seen.

If, however, Washington allowed China to join the WTO without making further concessions, the United States would also weaken its commercial ties with China. If China failed to meet the necessary criteria, it would be difficult for the United States to narrow the gap in its trade balance with China and to obtain greater access to the Chinese market needed by U.S. industry. It would also be more difficult to induce the Chinese government to conform to international practices in intellectual property protection and to open its domestic market, including the financial and service markets, to foreign investment and goods.

There is, however, a middle ground whereby both nations can solve their dispute over China's application for WTO membership. While the Chinese side will insist on joining the trade organization as a developing nation, the nation is likely to make further concessions concerning protection of intellectual property rights. China will also concede greater access to its domestic manufactured goods market and accept the reduction of disparities in the treatment of Chinese and foreign companies in China. Reduction of tariff and nontariff trade barriers will also be conceded by China.

For the United States, the key issue is not whether China is treated as a developing nation, but rather how to work out numbers with China that will reflect China's reality as well as the realistic concessions that China can make in order to join the WTO.

Political relations between China and the United States have gone through a long and difficult transition since the Tiananmen tragedy in June 1989. While Beijing has made some concessions on issues concerning human rights and the nonproliferation of nuclear technology and other weapons of mass destruction, China has been supportive of many U.S. international demands, especially through the mechanism of the United Nations, in which China enjoys a veto power at the Security Council. These actions include the invasion of Haiti, intervention in the former Yugoslavia, and the war and later sanctions against Iraq. On the Korean peninsula, Beijing has cooperated with Washington on the nuclear issue, the reduction of tension between the North and South, and the post–Kim Il-Sung transition.

Meanwhile, the Clinton administration has gradually tuned down its ideological criticisms of China. More important, the government has begun to separate political and ideological issues, including matters of human rights, from its economic policies toward China. The two armies have renewed their exchange programs, which were suspended shortly after June 1989. Although the atmosphere still needs much improvement, at the working levels officials from both countries can cooperate and have worked together to solve their disputes. What is needed are more frequent and direct communications between top leaders of the two countries and a more realistic approach in dealing with each other.

Competition for the Chinese market is likely to intensify in coming years. Many OECD nations and Asian tigers continue to be attracted by China's rapid economic growth. The surge in China's demand for advanced capital and consumer goods, its increasingly liberalized economic system and trade administration, and rapidly rising purchasing power will all contribute to the growing, magnetic appeal of the Chinese market. As China's political and economic relations with most OECD nations have been improving—and will continue to do so—OECD member governments can be expected to increase policy support for their national companies, support that will include low-interest government credits to back company sales and company loans to China.

Multinational companies from other OECD nations will compete effectively against U.S. firms by urging their own governments to improve relations with Beijing and by expanding their operations, especially direct investment projects. These companies will increasingly focus on the Chinese domestic market and transfer technology to their Chinese partners. Similarly, companies from other Asian countries are likely to make comparable efforts to expand investment and sales in China.

These trends will put pressure on American companies to increase their market share and undertake direct investment projects in China. The situation will also affect U.S.-China trade. The more direct investment and governmental loans undertaken by a given country, the easier it will be for that country to increase its exports to China. Such

113

efforts will broaden both knowledge and the distribution network that companies will develop in China and render their products more competitive in that market. This is true particularly because the Chinese government has always used trade, especially imports, as an instrument to manage its relations with other countries.

Conclusions

China's economic growth in the coming decade will remain strong, although the process of modernization may experience short-term volatility during the next two or three years because of the coming political succession. Both domestic and external demand will remain strong, while the upswing in internal and external supplies will support continued growth. Moreover, China's reform and open-door policy are unlikely to be reversed, because the country's economic, political, social, and cultural structures have already changed profoundly. Rather, the post–Deng Xiaoping leadership, regardless of its identity, has little choice but to reform further open-door policies if this leadership is to meet the demands of the majority of the population and narrow the institutional gap between China and overseas market economies.

On the external front, while China has been integrated increasingly into the world economy at large, the interdependence between the Chinese economy and market economies overseas has deepened. Competition for the Chinese market and for the international labor-intensive goods markets will intensify. China's demand for financial resources, technology, and industrial equipment will soar, and its competitiveness will rise.

Meanwhile, the United States will continue its efforts to upgrade its industrial structure and make further attempts to increase its exports and reduce its trade deficit. At least in the near future, U.S. demand for cheap capital and consumer goods imported from Asia, including China, will continue to soar. By the same token, U.S. dependence on the overseas market, including that of China, will rise markedly.

Fundamentally, U.S. long-term strategy toward China should be based on the principle of free trade, not protectionism. This strategy should look forward to open further the Chinese market, narrow the institutional gap between China and Western market economies, and integrate the Chinese economy into the world economy at large. Such a strategy will require Washington to encourage Beijing in its economic reform and open-door policy and to follow the basic principles of GATT (or WTO). The United States itself must not turn in the direction of nationalism and isolation. An open China resting on market mechanisms will promote economic growth, stability, and democracy and will raise its demand for overseas capital, technology, industrial equipment, and consumer goods. It will thereby provide great trade and investment opportunities for the American business community.

U.S. strategy should include the following key components:

1. support for Beijing's reform and open-door policy
2. encouragement to China for the opening of its domestic market, internationalizing of its foreign trade and foreign exchange administration, as well as its financial system, and the further removal of tariff and nontariff trade barriers
3. provision of more effective policy support for American corporate operations in China and promotion of U.S.-China trade and other economic relations
4. assistance to nongovernmental institutions in training a new generation of Chinese policy makers and technocrats and improvement of Chinese understanding of international economic, business, and legal practice, as well as Washington's decision-making process

This long-term strategy will have to be coordinated with short-term policy objectives and approaches in dealing with China. It is in the interest of the United States to have China join the WTO, obey principles of intellectual property protection, further liberalize its various markets as well as its foreign exchange administration, and improve its legal system. These goals should be achieved through bilateral and multilateral negotiations. Nevertheless, both sides should demonstrate sufficient flexibility and avoid needless trade wars. It is in the interest of the United States to coordinate its policies toward China with the policies of other nations, including those of many developing and Asian nations. Without such coordination, Washington's efforts will not be effective but will rather impair its own fundamental interests and weaken its competitiveness against other countries in the Chinese market.

Washington's economic policies toward China should continue to be separate from its political and security concerns. Solid U.S.-China economic relations will support Washington's long-term political objectives in China: democracy, internal stability, regional stability, and peace. To make a new linkage between economic instruments and narrowly defined political objectives will reduce the administration's decision-making power and leave little flexibility to the management of China policy. U.S. decision making would then be hostage to various special interest groups. Without economic progress in China and its integration within the world market, the United States is unlikely to reach many of its fundamental political objectives. What should be linked, however, is U.S. long-term economic strategy toward China

115

and its regional and global political and security objectives, including free trade, stability, democratization, and peace.

Washington needs to redefine its policies of support for the American business community in China. The Import-Export Bank and the Agency for International Development should become more active in support of American corporation sales and investment in China. The demand for policy support from trade unions and labor-intensive manufacturers should be well balanced with those of other manufacturers that are capable of increasing their sales in China with appropriate and effective U.S. policy support, and that of the financial industry. Other government agencies should also be more proactive in helping U.S. corporate operations in China.

These policies should promote U.S. economic and business interests in China, open the Chinese market wider for American corporations, strengthen U.S. competitiveness, and support the expansion of bilateral trade ties between the two countries. This will benefit as well China's growth, reform, and open-door policy. In the long run, these policies will promote regional and global prosperity, peace, and stability.

References

Almanac of China's Foreign Economic Relations and Trade, 1994/5. Bejing, China: 1994.

Hong Kong Year Book. 1994.

Huan, Guocang. "China Tackles Its External Trade Gap." Economic Research Note (New York: J. P. Morgan, October 7, 1994a): 2.

———. "China's Urban Unemployment Problem." Emerging Market Economic Research. J. P. Morgan & Co., 1994.

Statistical Year Book of China. Bejing, China: 1994.

5
Korean–U.S. Economic Relations under the New Global Order

Il SaKong and Taeho Bark

As the twentieth century enters its last few years, a new world order is emerging. At least four factors have contributed to the rapid demise of the old order and the creation of a new one: the end of the cold war; the relative decline of the economic strength of the United States; advancements in information-related technologies; and the conclusion of the Uruguay Round of multilateral trade negotiations, with the subsequent launching of the World Trade Organization (WTO).

An Economic Context

With the end of the cold war, countries around the world have been pursuing "economics first" policies, as economic interests have become more important relative to security concerns in their domestic and international policy agendas. International relations are now largely determined by economic interests, and competition in international markets is intensifying to an unprecedented degree.

With the relative decline in the economic might of the United States, particularly with respect to Germany and Japan, and the demise of the Communist bloc, a multipolar world has been emerging. This environment necessitates a collective leadership, one that can provide the necessary public goods for the world economic system—that is, free trade and a stable financial environment. Consequently, the burden sharing for providing public goods becomes a serious issue under collective leadership; frequent disputes and friction are bound to arise. At the same time, there is a danger of repressive, inward-looking regionalist and protectionist movements.

Under the old order, the United States assumed a large part of the cost and responsibility for providing the public goods. These include the creation of such multilateral institutions as the International Monetary Fund (IMF), the World Bank, and the General Agreement on Tariffs and Trade (GATT). The United States also implemented the Marshall plan and the Dodge plan, to help reconstruct war-torn economies and to make multilateral institutions viable. In addition, it opened its own economy to the rest of the world. Not only was the United States capable of providing these public goods; it also had strong incentives to do so.

Before World War II, the United States, although the dominant industrial power, did not exercise the necessary leadership for the world. In fact, the United States maintained an isolationist attitude; and as a result, the world suffered, the United States being no exception. Soon, of course, the country realized its interest in preserving the well-being of all nations, both for economic and security concerns. In particular, the United States needed the overseas markets for its industrial products. The Truman Doctrine further bolstered the U.S. desire to have the free world prosper economically. Thus, the United States began to exercise strong economic leadership, and it maintained this role after the war.

Today, however, the United States is finding it increasingly burdensome to maintain that role by itself. The relative decline in its economic strength has made the nation less capable of playing that role, and the end of the cold war weakened the political incentive for bearing the burden.

The rapid advancement in the information technologies has accelerated and will continue to drive the trend of globalization. Consequently, competition in the global markets will become increasingly intense. Firms and strategic alliances are being restructured across national borders to stay competitive.

The conclusion of the Uruguay Round and the formation of the WTO will strengthen the multilateral trade system. With a wider scope and strengthened institutional setup, the WTO system will further promote intensified trade competition in the global marketplace. But the Uruguay Round agreement did not achieve trade liberalization in goods and services to the extent that major participants called for. Many of the more contentious issues remain unresolved, and newly emerging trade-related issues such as environment, competition, and investment policies are not covered by the agreement. Much effort will be necessary to ensure that the World Trade Organization (WTO) effectively responds to the new challenges.

Confronted by these changes in the world economic environment, policy makers in each nation are trying to redirect their economic policies. Obviously, the United States and Korea are no exceptions. In adapting to the changing global economic environment and the stiffer competition, the Korean government decided to take various measures to enhance the nation's economic competitiveness. In doing so, Korea has set about deregulating and liberalizing its economy. Since taking office in February 1993, President Kim Young Sam has committed his administration to carrying out a series of economic reforms. Nonessential government controls and regulations have been amended or abolished, and further liberalization in the trading of goods and services is being pursued. In addition, Korea's trade-related laws and practices are also being reformed, to bring them into conformity with the existing multilateral rules.

At the same time, to take full advantage of the globalization trend and strategic alliances, the Korean government made special efforts to facilitate the globalization of the Korean economy. Incoming foreign direct investment and strategic alliances have been especially encouraged. The Korean government has declared its desire to make Korea "the best place in the world to do business."

The priority of the Clinton administration is also clearly shifted toward economics, especially trade. At the outset of the administration, the White House established the National Economic Council, signifying the Clinton administration's emphasis on economic matters. The administration has repeatedly expressed its assurance that trade is central to U.S. foreign policy.

The trade policy of the United States has evolved dramatically from the end of World War II to the present.[1] Between the end of World War II and the 1960s, the United States relied primarily on multilateral channels to achieve its trade-policy goals. The multilateral route was the most effective for the United States during this period because, as the dominant economic power of the Western world, the country could achieve its objectives in a multilateral framework. Since there was little competition for American firms either in domestic or in foreign markets, the best interest of the nation was served by maintaining as liberal a domestic market as possible, and by pushing for lower trade barriers in other countries through multilateral means. Furthermore, by pressing for trade liberalization through multilateral channels instead of opting to use more aggressive unilateral or bilateral means, the United States avoided frictions that could have alienated its allies in the ideological struggle against the spread of communism.

Thus, it was not until the 1980s that the United States began to change its posture on trade policy. In the early 1980s, however, as it

---

1. For the most recent overview of the evolution of the U.S. trade policy, see Baldwin (1995).

was suffering from the twin deficit problems of government budget and international trade, the United States resorted frequently to approaches other than multilateral ones in pressuring its trading partners. For example, the United States began to use unilateral and bilateral trade measures more aggressively, such as antidumping and countervailing duty laws and the now well-known section 301, super 301, and special 301 trade laws.[2]

The current U.S. trade policy focuses not only on protecting domestic industries from "unfair" foreign competition, but also on strengthening the domestic economy through expanding exports, through pressing to deregulate foreign markets, and through liberalizing the foreign investment environment for U.S. firms.[3] In particular, the United States has targeted several economies, including Korea's, as big, emerging markets, and it is developing specific export-expansion strategies for each of these markets.[4] This strategy is called the big emerging markets (BEMs) policy, and it is viewed as one of the key components of the Clinton administration's commercial and trade policy.[5]

Obviously, the Korean government's liberalization policies and its emphasis on the globalizing Korean economy would provide various new opportunities for U.S. businesses. At the same time, the changes in the trade policy direction of the United States outlined above have direct implications for Korea on all the unilateral, bilateral, regional, and multilateral levels of its trade relationship with Korea.

This chapter will examine Korean-U.S. relations, as follows. First, we briefly review the evolution of Korean-U.S. economic relations. Second, we assess the recent status of Korean-U.S. trade relations. Third, we analyze the recent trend of Korea's foreign trade and investments, and changes in the pattern of trade and investments. Fourth, we briefly

---

2. Under super 301, the U.S. trade representative is required to identify trade priorities, including priority countries and practices, to be investigated under section 301 of the 1974 trade act. Special 301 sets up a more aggressive mechanism for enforcing intellectual property rights protection.

Along with these trade measures, in the second half of the 1980s, the United States tried to resolve its huge trade deficits through exchange-rate realignments with Japan, Germany, and some newly industrializing Asian countries.

3. Trade policy has been given a much higher priority in the U.S. public policy agenda, as the external sector in the U.S. economy grew from 6.7 percent in 1960 to 17.5 percent in 1994.

4. The Chinese Economic Area (including China, Hong Kong, and Taiwan), India, the Association of South East Asian Nations (ASEAN), Korea, Vietnam, Mexico, Brazil, Argentina, South Africa, Poland, and Turkey are economies identified by the United States as big emerging markets.

5. For detailed contents of the BEMS policy, see *Business America* (1994).

present Korea's view on the Asia-Pacific Economic Cooperation (APEC). Fifth, we look at recent industrial alliances between U.S. and Korean firms. Finally, we suggest policy recommendations for the future of the Korean-U.S. economic cooperation.

Evolution of the Korean-U.S. Economic Relationship

The modern Korean-U.S. relationship can be traced back to the end of World War II, in 1945. The relationship started primarily as one of security, and economics between the two countries were essentially on a recipient-donor basis until the early 1960s.

When Korea adopted an outward-looking development strategy in the early 1960s, however, the United States became not only its most critical source of private capital and technology but also the single most important market for Korean exports of manufactured goods. Such an economic relationship remained throughout the 1970s, and Korea enjoyed an outstanding industrial development.[6]

There were no major trade disputes between the two nations during this period. The smooth bilateral trade relationship can be explained by two important factors. First, Korea's exports amounted only to a small portion of the total U.S. imports. Moreover, the bilateral trade balance had favored the United States throughout most of the 1970s. Second, because of Korea's limited market size, the U.S. private sector did not have much interest in the Korean market. In fact, the United States had in general very limited interest in foreign markets.

In the 1980s, however, a fundamental shift took place in that relationship. The shift resulted from the dramatic changes in the economic conditions of both countries. First, Korea's rapid economic growth over the previous two decades had transformed it into one of the newly industrialized economies (NIEs), which began to export more industrial products to the United States. Furthermore, Korea started to record a trade surplus with the United States, reaching a peak of $9.6 billion in 1987. Second, the U.S. economy started to experience serious difficulties, namely the growing deficits in external trade and in the federal budget, while the dependence of the U.S. economy on international trade had simultaneously increased, reaching the level of Germany's and Japan's.[7] With its sudden rise in income level, Korea was emerging as a promising market for American goods and services. U.S. firms began to show an interest in the Korean market. At the same time, U.S. firms began to regard imports from Korea as a threat.

---

6. See SaKong (1993) for a comprehensive overview of Korea's economic development experience.

7. See note 3.

The first U.S. reaction was a defensive one, utilizing quotas, countervailing duties, and antidumping actions to protect its domestic producers.[8] The United States paid special attention to protecting those industries that were losing competitiveness, such as the textiles, shoes, color television, and steel industries.[9] By the mid-1980s, however, the U.S. strategy turned more aggressive, as the U.S. government shifted its policy direction from restricting imports toward more actively promoting exports. Accordingly, the United States began to demand that Korea open its market, using aggressive unilateral and bilateral measures. Threatening to resort to retaliatory actions under section 301 of the 1974 Trade Act, it began to exert pressure on Korea to open up its domestic market for American goods and services.

Trade tensions between Korea and the United States reached their peak in 1988 and 1989, when the United States introduced the 1988 Omnibus Trade Act with the super 301 provisions. U.S. pressure was concentrated in areas where U.S. industries were deemed competitive, including agriculture, telecommunications, and financial services. With Korea's rapidly rising current account surpluses, the United States also put pressure on the Korean currency to appreciate.[10] The U.S. demand was further extended to the protection of intellectual property rights. An agreement was reached between the Korean and U.S. governments in 1989.

In short, the Korean-U.S. economic relationship turned around in the mid-1980s, from being an aid recipient-donor relationship to being an equal partnership in trade. With its reduced economic affordability and the end of the cold war, the United States started to insist on the principle of reciprocity in dealing with its trading partners. As the Korean market share in the U.S. increased and the bilateral trade balance turned unfavorable for the United States, Korea became an important target for market opening, with the threat of retaliatory measures.

Recent Korean-U.S. Trade Relations

Korea and the United States have not experienced major, visible trade conflicts in recent years. A number of continuing trade issues, however, have yet to be resolved. These include the automobile-market opening, financial-market deregulation, shelf-life regulation on meat products, sanitary measures for imported food and agricultural prod-

---

8. For a recent overview of the evolution of Korean-U.S. trade relations, see Young (1995).

9. See Bark (1991).

10. See Williamson (1989).

ucts, the import approval system of telecommunications equipment, the testing of medical devices, and the intellectual property rights protection of trademarks and computer software.

Recently, the United States went to the WTO dispute settlement process with the cases of shelf-life regulation practices and sanitary measures for imported food and agricultural products in Korea.[11] The United States has also threatened to retaliate against Korea's practices in the testing of medical devices and the approval of the telecommunications equipments.

These individual trade issues are not so great as to threaten trade relations between Korea and the United States. The ever expanding list of specific trade issues, however, could jeopardize the seemingly smooth Korean-U.S. trade relations.

Since Korea's trade balance, as well as bilateral balance vis-à-vis the United States, became negative, Korea has not been a major target of the aggressive U.S. unilateral or bilateral trade measures in recent years.[12] Various U.S. complaints about Korean market accessibility, however, have become louder than ever before. U.S. Trade Representative Mickey Kantor, in commenting on U.S. trade issues at the U.S. Senate, recently mentioned that Korea was "one of the toughest markets in the world."[13]

In his recent assessment of U.S.-Korean trade relations, Daniel Tarullo said, "If one were to look at the individual components of our bilateral economic dialogue . . . the frustrating financial discussions and endless debates over non-tariff barriers—it would be easy to be pessimistic about the U.S.-Korean bilateral economic relationship." Tarullo went on to say that "our future economic relationship depends to a great extent upon the Korean government's ability to sustain and implement its liberalization policies."[14] In fact, these views are not exceptional in the United States today. Paradoxically, the same views were expressed when the Korean government set the goal of making

---

11. The case of the shelf-life regulation practices has been resolved by reaching an agreement between the two governments in July. The Korean government will completely lift up the regulation starting from July 1, 1996. With this new regime, manufacturers are responsible for designating the shelf lives of their own products. The case of the Korean sanitary and phytosanitary system, which is still pending, is expected to be resolved without major confrontation.

12. In contrast, the United States continued to record much larger trade deficits with other major Asian trading partners, such as Japan and Taiwan. In addition, China has become a major trade surplus country with the United States in the 1990s.

13. See Kantor (1995).

14. See Tarullo (1995).

"Korea the best place in the world to do business."

Are Americans exaggerating the reality or blaming others for their own problems? Or does the Korean government lack credibility, for not living up to the official rhetorical level?

Tarullo himself provides the correct perspective for answering these questions when he says, "I am uncertain whether President Kim's commitment to globalization will be reflected in thousands of lower-level bureaucratic decisions that affect foreign businessmen in Korea. Another problem is what appears to us to be a lack of support for internationalization among the Korean public. It is not clear that Koreans see President Kim's globalization concept as something more than increasing Korea's exports."[15]

It is true that there is still a widespread public ambivalence toward economic liberalization and market opening in Korea today. Of course, this ambivalence must be cleared up with a stronger leadership commitment to liberalization and market opening. In fact, the Korean government's globalization policy should include programs for changing people's ways of thinking. Needless to say, liberalization and market opening are not only inevitable but desirable for the Korean economy, no matter how painful they are in the short run.

Korea has done for its economy in one generation what today's industrialized countries did in two or three. Consequently, people's attitudes simply do not keep up with the pace of economic development.

Old habits and old virtues die hard, no matter how outdated they may be. For example, the current generation still so vividly remembers those chronic balance-of-payment–deficit days that it is difficult for the generation not to consider trade surplus per se as always desirable. Therefore, market openings and liberalization that might reduce surpluses (or increase deficits) are viewed as undesirable. It is important for the Korean government to help the general public, including lower-level bureaucrats, change their way of thinking in this regard.

At the same time, it is also important for the United States to realize that unilateral or bilateral measures can be counterproductive to those reform-minded governments of trading partners. For instance, in the case of super 301, any U.S. firm can file a complaint with the U.S. Trade Representative (USTR) concerning a foreign country's alleged unfair trade laws or practices, and the USTR can take action according to its findings to coerce the foreign government to remove such alleged trade barriers, whether visible or invisible. This sort of unilateral, particularistic approach becomes counterproductive because it instigates

---

15. Ibid.

the general public's hostile reaction to necessary reforms for the countries involved.

There are always domestic adversaries of market opening and liberalization in any country. As such unilateral or bilateral trade pressures from outside become politicized, those domestic adversaries inevitably gain strong ground for delaying or jeopardizing any unilaterally initiated liberalization programs. It is much easier for this camp to appeal to the general public that trade liberalization is for the benefit of other nations, such as the United States.[16]

Consequently, both trading partners will end up suffering. It is therefore important to depoliticize bilateral trade issues by taking them to multilateral dispute settlement procedures, that is, the WTO dispute settlement procedures, for mutual gains.

Recent Trends in Korea's Foreign Trade and Investment

Korea's trading volume has been steadily increasing in recent years, despite the sluggish economic condition prevailing in the industrialized economies. In 1994, Korea's total exports increased to $96.0 billion, which accounted for about 2.3 percent of total world exports for that year. Korea's total imports reached the $102.3 billion level (table 5–1).

Korea's rising international trade coincides with its increasing direct investment abroad. As shown in table 5–1, Korea's overseas direct investment maintained a level slightly higher than $200 million in 1988; this has been on the rebound in the 1990s, however, reaching more than $2.3 billion in 1994. In contrast to the rapid expansion of Korea's overseas direct investment, foreign direct investment in Korea has been staggering since its peak in 1991. But with the introduction of the comprehensive, five-year Foreign Investment Market Opening plan announced in June 1993, the incoming foreign direct investment too started to increase.[17]

As seen in table 5–2, Korean exports to developed economies are steadily decreasing. The United States, however, is still the largest export market for Korea, although Korea's export volume to the United States has continued to decline following its peak in 1988. A similar

---

16. See SaKong (1993).

17. In 1994, foreign direct investment in Korea reached $1.3 billion. This increase in foreign capital inflows was driven partly by the increase in plant and equipment investment associated with Korea's economic recovery. The increase is also attributed to the improved investment environment in Korea, including the simplified investment procedure, and the better protection of intellectual property rights.

TABLE 5–1
KOREA'S FOREIGN TRADE AND INVESTMENT, 1988–1994
(billions of U.S. dollars)

	1988	1989	1990	1991	1992	1993	1994
Exports	60.7	60.5	65.0	71.9	76.6	82.2	96.0
	(2.21)	(2.04)	(1.92)	(2.06)	(2.05)	(2.21)	(2.29)
Imports	51.8	60.2	69.9	81.5	81.8	83.8	102.3
	(1.83)	(1.96)	(2.00)	(2.26)	(2.13)	(2.23)	(2.37)
Overseas direct investment	0.224	0.570	0.959	1.125	1.255	1.317	2.347
Foreign direct investment	1.284	1.090	0.803	1.396	0.894	1.044	1.317

NOTE: Numbers in parentheses are percentage shares of Korean exports and imports in the world exports and imports markets, respectively.
SOURCES: International Monetary Fund, *Direction of Trade Statistics Yearbook* (Washington, D.C.: IMF, 1995); Ministry of Finance and Economy, *Trends in Foreign Investment* (Seoul: MFE, 1995); Bank of Korea, *Overseas Investment Statistics Yearbook* (Seoul: BOK, 1995).

TABLE 5–2
KOREA'S EXPORTS TO SELECTED INDUSTRIALIZED AND
DEVELOPING REGIONS, 1988–1994
(billions of U.S. dollars)

	1988	1989	1990	1991	1992	1993	1994
Industrialized regions	45.7	44.8	45.4	44.8	42.9	42.5	48.1
United States	21.5	20.2	19.4	18.6	18.1	18.1	20.6
Japan	12.0	13.2	12.6	12.4	11.6	11.6	13.5
Europe	9.6	8.4	10.5	11.1	10.4	10.2	11.2
Developing regions	13.9	14.3	16.8	25.9	33.1	35.6	42.6
Asia	8.7	9.6	11.4	16.2	21.4	26.2	30.9
Latin America	1.5	1.6	2.0	2.2	4.9	3.8	5.1
Europe	0.2	0.2	0.5	1.8	1.1	1.6	1.6
Africa	0.8	0.9	1.0	2.5	2.2	1.2	1.9
Middle East	2.5	1.9	1.9	3.2	3.5	2.9	3.1

SOURCE: International Monetary Fund, *Direction of Trade Statistics Yearbook* (Washington, D.C.: IMF, 1995).

TABLE 5–3

KOREA'S IMPORTS FROM SELECTED INDUSTRIALIZED AND
DEVELOPING REGIONS, 1988–1994

(U.S.$ billion)

	1988	1989	1990	1991	1992	1993	1994
Industrialized regions	38.8	44.3	49.7	57.0	54.2	55.3	68.3
United States	12.7	15.4	16.9	18.9	18.2	18.0	21.6
Japan	15.8	17.2	18.6	21.1	19.5	20.0	25.4
Europe	7.0	7.6	9.7	11.5	11.3	11.8	14.9
Developing regions	10.1	12.2	15.4	23.7	26.4	25.7	29.5
Asia	5.5	6.6	7.8	13.0	13.9	14.0	16.3
Latin America	1.5	1.5	1.8	2.3	2.5	1.8	2.7

SOURCE: International Monetary Fund, *Direction of Trade Statistics Yearbook* (Washington, D.C.: IMF, 1995).

pattern is found in Korea's exports to Japan and Europe. Korean products exported to these two industrialized regions have either declined or have stayed at a steady level in recent years.

Korea's exports to developing economies tell quite a different story, though. Exports from Korea to other developing economies are on the rise, reaching more than $40 billion in 1994, close to the value of exports absorbed by developed economies in the same year. In particular, the Asian market has emerged as receiving the largest proportion of goods and services produced in Korea.

Table 5–3 shows the recent trend in Korea's imports of foreign goods and services. The sales performance of the U.S. and Japanese firms in the Korean market still dominates that of other countries. Their market shares have declined significantly in recent years, however, reflecting the fact that Korea has recently diversified its sources of imported goods to a wider region of the world. In particular, the level of imported goods in Korea from the Asian market in 1994 has more than tripled since 1988. Currently, imports from Asia significantly exceed those from Europe.

The distribution of the shares of Korea's exports and imports to various regions of the world is found in table 5–4. In 1994, 50.1 percent of Korea's total exports were sent to developed economies, whereas 66.8 percent of Korea's total imports came from developed economies. These figures represent a dramatic decline from those recorded six years ago, when both exceeded 70 percent. These shares for the Asian developing economies have recently improved quite dramatically. In 1994, for instance, Korea sent 32.2 percent of its total exports to the

TABLE 5–4

REGIONAL DISTRIBUTION OF KOREA'S EXPORTS AND IMPORTS, 1988–1994
(percent)

	1988	1989	1990	1991	1992	1993	1994
Exports							
Industrialized regions	75.3	74.0	69.8	62.3	56.0	51.7	50.1
Developing regions	22.9	23.6	25.8	36.0	43.2	43.3	44.4
Asia	14.3	15.9	17.5	22.5	28.7	31.9	32.2
Imports							
Industrialized regions	74.9	73.6	71.1	69.9	66.6	66.0	66.8
Developing regions	19.5	20.3	22.0	29.1	32.9	30.7	28.8
Asia	10.6	11.0	11.2	16.0	17.1	16.7	15.9

SOURCE: International Monetary Fund, *Direction of Trade Statistics Yearbook* (Washington, D.C.: IMF, 1995).

Asian developing economies, a phenomenal increase from 14.3 percent in 1988.

The recent surge in Korea's exports to the Asian developing countries is attributed, among others, to the rapid economic growth of China and ASEAN. An increase in exports to Hong Kong and Taiwan is also a factor behind the expanded Korean exports to the Asian developing economies.[18] The rise in Korea's direct investment in the Asian developing economies is yet another factor in Korea's export growth in this region.

The increasing dependence on developing economies is not a phenomenon unique to Korea. Other economies are also expanding their markets in developing economies. The Korean dependence on developing economies, however, appears to be much stronger than other countries', as indicated by the regional concentration ratio, computed by dividing the ratio of Korean exports to a particular region by the ratio of world exports to the same region (table 5–5).

The concentration ratio for exports to developed economies declined continuously, from 1.04 in 1988 to 0.74 in 1994. In direct contrast, the concentration ratio for exports to developing economies in 1994 is almost double the ratio in 1988. As seen in table 5–5, though, the concentration ratio of Korean imports from both developing and devel-

18. In 1994, Korea exported 11.9 percent of its goods to ASEAN, which is the highest among the Asian developing economies. China absorbed 6.5 percent of the exported goods from Korea, while Hong Kong and Taiwan together absorbed 11.2 percent of Korean exports.

TABLE 5–5
REGIONAL CONCENTRATION RATIO OF KOREA'S EXPORTS AND IMPORTS,
1988–1994

	1988	1989	1990	1991	1992	1993	1994
Exports							
Industrialized regions	1.04	1.03	0.96	0.86	0.78	0.75	0.74
Developing regions	0.82	0.84	0.93	1.28	1.49	1.40	1.38
Asia	1.09	1.17	1.31	1.52	1.78	1.84	1.77
Latin America	0.64	0.69	0.81	0.81	1.77	1.12	1.20
Imports							
Industrialized regions	1.02	1.01	0.97	0.97	0.95	1.02	0.96
Developing regions	0.71	0.74	0.83	1.04	1.10	0.96	0.82
Asia	0.83	0.82	0.83	1.06	1.10	0.95	0.82
Latin America	0.87	0.78	0.78	0.75	0.75	0.47	0.50

SOURCE: International Monetary Fund, *Direction of Trade Statistics Yearbook* (Washington, D.C.: IMF, 1995).

oped economies is quite stable in the 1990s.

Changes are also observed in Korea's overseas direct investment. Korea's overseas direct investment in the 1990s is characterized by an increasing tendency to concentrate in the Asian region. Traditionally, the final destination of Korea's overseas direct investment has been North America. In the 1990s, however, the focus of the attention has shifted to the Asian region (see table 5–6), where the costs of production are low and the governments are offering favorable investment environments for foreign investors. Since 1991, more capital started to flow into Asia than to North America, with China being the largest recipient of Korean foreign investment.

Unlike foreign direct investment abroad, foreign direct investment in Korea shows virtually no change in pattern (see table 5–7). The developed countries are still the major suppliers of foreign capital in Korea. Although the European Union (EU) has increased its investments in Korea recently, the United States and Japan are still the largest investing countries in Korea. In particular, Japan has emerged as the leading supplier of foreign capital in Korea in 1994, exceeding the United States, which had invested the largest amount of capital in Korea throughout the early 1990s.

As previously indicated, Korea's trade with developing economies, particularly with the Asian developing economies, has significantly increased, while Korea's dependence on the U.S. market has

129

TABLE 5–6
KOREA'S DIRECT INVESTMENT OUTFLOW, 1988–1994
(U.S.$ million)

	1988	1989	1990	1991	1992	1993	1994
North America	99.3	282.9	436.0	463.3	391.6	386.1	573.3
United States	92.9	153.8	352.9	395.2	346.9	379.6	530.8
Latin America	14.2	55.4	35.7	41.5	36.0	44.4	49.1
Asia	45.3	129.6	300.5	431.3	555.7	546.2	1092.0
Japan	6.5	10.2	11.2	14.9	63.6	57.9	58.0
ASEAN	29.0	86.9	235.5	325.9	248.4	138.1	165.4
China	—	6.3	16.0	42.5	140.6	271.7	640.8
Europe	19.3	19.6	95.2	92.4	144.1	189.6	455.8
Middle East	41.2	31.6	40.3	58.6	75.3	85.7	38.3
Africa	1.5	8.4	26.5	18.0	29.0	30.7	115.8
Oceania	3.0	41.9	26.2	20.2	23.4	34.7	22.4
Total	223.8	569.6	959.3	1125.4	1255.0	1317.4	2346.6

SOURCE: Bank of Korea, *Overseas Investment Statistics Yearbook* (Seoul: BOK, 1995).

TABLE 5–7
KOREA'S DIRECT INVESTMENT INFLOW, APPROVAL BASIS, 1988–1994
(U.S.$ million)

	1988	1989	1990	1991	1992	1993	1994
North America	289.0	320.7	335.4	311.8	433.7	343.8	323.4
United States	284.4	319.4	317.5	296.3	379.2	340.7	310.9
Asia	712.7	525.3	257.3	248.5	170.3	391.6	569.1
Japan	697.3	466.0	235.9	226.2	155.2	286.0	428.4
ASEAN	0.6	15.1	14.2	10.6	1.6	9.1	25.5
China	—	2.8	0.1	0.7	1.1	6.7	6.2
Europe	242.9	216.9	207.0	824.4	282.2	307.4	406.7
Middle East	3.6	1.3	0.0	3.3	4.3	0.1	10.7
Total	1283.8	1090.3	802.6	1396.0	894.5	1044.3	1316.5

SOURCE: Ministry of Finance and Economy, *Foreign Direct Investment Securities* (Seoul: MFE, May 1995).

declined. The index that indicates the relative dependence of Korean exports on the U.S. market is computed by dividing the market share of Korean exports in the United States by the Korean export share in the world and is shown in the last column of table 5–8. The index

TABLE 5–8
KOREA'S EXPORTS TO THE UNITED STATES, 1988–1994
(billions of U.S. dollars)

	U.S. Imports from Korea (A)	U.S. Total Imports (B)	Korea's Total Exports (C)	World's Total Exports (D)	Korean Exports' Market Share in the U.S. (E = A/B)	Korean Exports' Market Share in the World (F = C/D)	E/F
1988	21.2	459.8	60.7	2743.7	0.046	0.022	2.08
1989	20.5	493.3	60.5	2963.1	0.042	0.020	2.04
1990	19.3	517.0	65.0	3383.2	0.037	0.019	1.94
1991	17.7	509.3	71.9	3484.6	0.035	0.021	1.68
1992	17.3	552.6	76.6	3728.8	0.031	0.021	1.52
1993	14.9	600.0	82.2	3713.3	0.025	0.022	1.12
1994	20.4	689.3	96.0	4184.6	0.030	0.023	1.19

SOURCE: International Monetary Fund, *Direction of Trade Statistics Yearbook* (Washington, D.C.: IMF, 1995).

shows a decline from 2.08 in 1988 to 1.19 in 1994. A similar trend is found with respect to its imports from the United States, although not as striking as in the case of Korean exports to the United States. As shown in table 5–9, the U.S. share of Korea's imports has declined modestly but continuously. Following a peak in 1989, the U.S. share in Korea's imports declined to 21 percent in 1994.

The rapid growth of the developing economies, coupled with the economic slowdown of the industrialized countries, has led to the deepening of trade and investment relations between Korea and other developing countries. In particular, encouraged by the geographical proximity, Korea has been expanding its relations with the other Asian developing economies. An enhanced trade and investment relationship with the Asian developing economies has been followed by the declining dependence of Korea's external sector on the U.S. economy. The continuous rapid growth of the Asian developing economies will induce Korea to expand its trade relations further with these countries, reducing its relative dependence on the U.S. market.

In short, Korea is becoming less dependent on the United States as a market for its exports. As the globalization trend accelerates, Korea will continue to diversify its export markets—that is, newly emerging markets of Asia, Eastern Europe, and Latin America. Despite the recent decline in the level of trade volume between the two countries, however, the United States is still one of Korea's major export markets, as

TABLE 5–9
U.S. Exports to Korea, 1988–1994
(billions of U.S. dollars)

	Korea's Imports from the U.S. (A)	Korea's Total Imports (B)	U.S. Total Exports (C)	World's Total Exports (D)	U.S. Exports' Market Share in Korea (E = A/B)	U.S. Exports' Market Share in the World (F = C/D)	E/F
1988	12.7	51.8	319.4	2743.7	0.25	0.12	2.11
1989	15.4	60.2	363.8	2963.1	0.26	0.12	2.08
1990	16.9	69.9	393.1	3383.2	0.24	0.12	2.08
1991	18.9	81.5	421.7	3484.6	0.23	0.12	1.92
1992	18.2	81.8	447.4	3728.8	0.22	0.12	1.85
1993	18.0	83.8	465.4	3713.8	0.21	0.13	1.71
1994	21.6	102.3	512.4	4184.6	0.21	0.12	1.72

SOURCE: International Monetary Fund, *Direction of Trade Statistics Yearbook* (Washington, D.C.: IMF, 1995).

well as one of its most important sources of capital and technology.[19] Nonetheless, it is also true that as Korea diversifies its export and import markets, the U.S. leverage in trade negotiations will decline.

Korea's View of APEC

During the first APEC economic leaders' meeting in Seattle, the leaders of the Asia-Pacific area presented a vision for APEC. At the Bogor meeting, a concrete time table was formulated for the completion of free trade in the Asia-Pacific region. In Osaka, the leaders agreed to a framework for implementation of trade and investment liberalization. This year's Philippines meeting will adopt individual "comparable" action plans.

Although the Osaka meeting clearly enhanced the credibility of APEC, many still are reluctant to recognize the meeting's significance. Many trade economists believe that the "flexibility" clause in the action plan hampered the Bogor Commitment, arguing that it will be used as a shield behind which Asian countries will protect themselves from the United States and other bilateral pressures to open their markets. In addition, the U.S. role was not as prominent as it should have been, nor did it take the lead either in making a significant down pay-

19. In 1994, Korea's exports to the United States regained their growth momentum, with a healthy 13.3 percent increase over 1993.

ment or in promoting an ambitious trade agenda. The Clinton administration apparently decided to postpone all new trade initiatives until after the 1996 election.

As for its role in Osaka, Korea also left something to be desired. The Korean government was quite concerned about the possibility of having to accelerate the liberalization of its market for agricultural products beyond its capacity. Thus, it insisted on the inclusion of the "flexibility" principle in the action agenda. By so doing, however, the Korean government gave APEC member-economies the impression that it was less than fully committed to achieving free trade and investment in the Asia-Pacific region.

Even with all the diverging assessments, the Osaka action agenda contained general principles that provided some specific guidance and outlines for future trade liberalization in the Asia-Pacific region. Although APEC emphasizes the importance of voluntary participation among its members, the principles would act as the fundamental agreement to all future agreements of APEC. Therefore, it would be unwise to interpret members' disagreements over the liberalization process as a sign of difficulty in achieving substantial progress in trade liberalization. The difficulties that arose during the Osaka meeting were, in fact, a reflection of the member-economies' true intentions of achieving trade liberalization. The future of this scheme of the general principles will entail serious discussions of detailed liberalization processes and member-economies' evaluations of each other's actions. Furthermore, APEC members will need to formulate sectoral action plans and address most-favored-nation (MFN) principle issues with non-APEC members.

Korea was one of the cofounders of APEC and hosted the third APEC ministerial meeting in Seoul in 1991. President Kim Young Sam was one of the early supporters of President Clinton's proposed leaders' meeting in Seattle, and Korea served as the first chair of the APEC Committee on Trade and Investment. Considering that Korea has been one of the greatest beneficiaries of the multilateral trading system during the post–World War II era, it has a great stake and great responsibility in strengthening and deepening global and regional cooperation through APEC.

Despite various policy agendas to liberalize and deregulate the domestic market, there has always been a concern among Korea's trading partners that "the reforms will not be fully implemented as originally proposed." President Kim's recent globalization initiative is creating awareness regarding the importance of market opening and providing a favorable trade and investment environment as a key element in Korea's long-term economic success. The overall trade and investment climate, however, is slow to gain acceptance by its trading partners.

Therefore, Korea should, first of all, offer a plausible but envisionary liberalization package. It is of crucial importance for Korea's long-term interests to lead, and not lag behind, neighboring Asian developing countries in eliminating barriers to trade and investment. Should these efforts succeed, the liberal trade forces in APEC will be strengthened, which will, in turn, translate into further increase in trade and investment in the Asia-Pacific region.

Second, Korea could contribute to deepening economic cooperation within APEC by serving as a mediator between developed economies and developing economies. Despite the substantial progress in recent years, the pace and agenda of trade and investment liberalization of APEC economies are divergent, mostly because of the member-economies' differing stages of economic development. Korea, in cooperation with other like-minded member-economies, might be able to serve as a pacesetter or consensus builder on future APEC agendas.

Third, Korea could intensify efforts to bridge developed and developing economies, especially in the area of technology transfer. It would be highly sensible for firms in developed economies to make greater use of Korea's strength in manufacturing technology while Korea assists late-developing economies in manufacturing less sophisticated products.

There is no doubt that the linkages the United States has forged with the economies of the Asia-Pacific are crucial to the future economic prosperity of the United States. Thus, the potential of APEC for serving American as well as regional interests is also considerable. Through APEC, the United States has pursued some concrete results and gained progress in such areas as promoting trade and investment liberalization, spurring greater economic involvement in the world's most dynamic region—which acts as a counterweight against possible European protectionism—and preventing the creation of an East Asian economic bloc dominated by Japan.

In order to achieve these goals, it is desirable for the United States, among others, to establish a strong and pragmatic leadership in APEC, with a long-term strategy toward a greater sense of global responsibilities. In this light, it would be counterproductive if the trade liberalization agenda of the United States is perceived as being designed mainly to extract new trade concessions or to attack internal practices of some economies. Rather, the U.S. initiative and agenda in APEC must look to consensus building for successful discussion on regional cooperation based on the understanding that member-economies have divergent views on the pace and priorities with which APEC should move forward.

Strategic Industrial Alliances

The changing pattern of Korea's international economic relationship demands a reevaluation of the Korea-U.S. relationship. It is difficult to see rapid quantitative trade expansion between the two countries in the future. But there is also ample room for qualitative improvement in the bilateral trade relationship, such as increasing intraindustrial trade between the two countries.[20] More efforts are also needed to enhance industrial cooperation between the two countries, particularly in the area of high-tech industries. By combining U.S. technology with Korea's manufacturing capability, both countries could greatly strengthen their respective competitive positions in this era of global competition.

Strategic industrial alliances are not popularly utilized, even among Korean firms. In 1994 and 1995, however, substantial progress was made in the strategic industrial alliances between the United States and Korean firms, thanks to a number of measures. First of all, Korea has made a greater effort to protect intellectual property rights and improved the environment for foreign direct investment through deregulations and new incentives. More industrial cooperations between the two countries are now being initiated by private sectors rather than by the governments.[21] The imperatives of globalization and intensified competition have led Korean firms to look beyond Korea's borders for access to technology. Korean firms view strategic industrial alliance with U.S. firms as a means to enhance their own technical capabilities and to reduce Korea's significant technological dependence on the Japanese.

---

20. According to the Ministry of Trade, Industry, and Energy, the importance of intraindustrial trade in Korea-U.S. trade relations has greatly increased. The proportion of intraindustrial trade of the total bilateral trade, in value terms, increased from 18 percent in 1983 to 52 percent in 1993.

21. Since the early 1990s, it has been an important policy of the Korean government to engage the United States in various programs of industrial cooperation with Korean firms. In January 1994, the Korean government even set up the Korea-U.S. Industrial Technology Cooperation Foundation to assist industrial cooperation between the two countries effectively. In contrast, from the beginning, the U.S. government has not been positive on the idea of engaging itself in promoting industrial alliances. With the asymmetric attitudes of the two governments, government-led programs of industrial cooperation between Korea and the United States were not successfully implemented.

TABLE 5–10
KOREA'S TECHNOLOGICAL ACHIEVEMENTS, 1994

Area	Status	Remarks
Automobiles	Fifth largest in the world	Samsung entry critical factor
Semiconductors	Dominates DRAM market	Massive new investments, movement into nonmemory
Information technology	Moves in LCD technology	Entry into multimedia
Telecommunications	Satellite & fiber optics	Building own info-highway
Nuclear energy	Top three of world nuclear power developers	Could become exporter to SE Asia
Aerospace	Defense-tied capabilities	Collaborative effort for midsize Asia plane

SOURCE: *Business Week*, July 31, 1995.

Korea has emerged as one of the most rapidly growing countries with manufacturing strength, and it could be the U.S. strategic partner. As shown in table 5–10, Korea has enhanced its technological capabilities in several high-tech areas. Korea is also an attractive emerging market,[22] and the possible future unification of the peninsula increases Korea's market potential for American firms. Given its geographic location in East Asia, Korea can also be useful to U.S. businesses operating in Asia as a platform from which they can enter the markets of Japan, China, ASEAN, and Vietnam.

In November 1993, the Ministry of Trade, Industry, and Energy and the Department of Commerce agreed to establish a private sector–led industry advisory group consisting of subgroups in nine high-tech industry sectors: (1) semiconductors, (2) computers, (3) machine tools, (4) aerospace, (5) telecommunications equipment, (6) medical equipment, (7) environmental facilities, (8) automobiles, and (9) electric power equipment. Representatives from these supervisory bodies meet together for the efficient coordination of the process of industrial alli-

22. As of 1993, Korea's GNP was about equal to that of all the ASEAN countries combined, although ASEAN boasts a total population seven times the size of Korea's.

TABLE 5–11
TECHNICAL COOPERATION BY MAJOR CHIP MANUFACTURERS, 1994

Company	Number of Cooperation	Major Partner
IBM	31	256MB DRAM (Siemens/Toshiba)
AT&T	24	0.25 micron circuit widths (NEC)
HP	17	0.35 micron circuit widths (AMD)
Siemens	17	256MB DRAM (IBM/Toshiba)
Motorola	15	Microprocessors (IBM)
Toshiba	13	256MB DRAM (IBM/Siemens)
Matsushita	13	ICS (National Semiconductor)
Texas Instruments	12	Acer (Taiwan)/Portugal plant (Samsung)
Samsung	10	256MB DRAM (NEC) & RISC (ARM)

SOURCE: *Korea Economic Weekly*, April 3, 1995.

ances between business firms from the two nations.[23]

Among the high-tech industry sectors, the semiconductor industry has perhaps made the greatest progress in establishing strategic alliances between the two nations. In this industry, while U.S. firms have primarily been systems builders, Korean companies have focused on components manufacturing. This type of complementarity offers some potential for expanded cooperation. The case of Anam is particularly illustrative in this regard. Anam, through its cumulative experience in packaging technology for semiconductor production, has worked with a number of U.S. firms and been able to move into lead frame manufacturing and photomask production.[24] Another recent example of a successful alliance involves the decision by Hewlett Packard to build a high-end work station in Korea in cooperation with Samsung, which ranked ninth in the world in key technology alliances in semiconductors (see table 5–11). By forging ahead together, they have effectively penetrated the global minicomputer and printer markets.

Despite the fact that there are many other examples of recent industrial and technical cooperation between these two countries, as we can see in table 5–12, the present state of "strategic industrial alliance"

23. Similar types of industrial cooperation between the two countries can be found in electronics, telecommunications, and aerospace industries.

24. See J. Kim (1994).

137

TABLE 5–12
RECENT COOPERATION BETWEEN U.S. AND KOREAN FIRMS

Korean Firm	U.S. Firm	Type and Area
Samsung	IGT	Acquisition (codevelop hi-fi speakers)
Samsung	AST	Acquisition (computers/multimedia)
Samsung	Motorola	Alliance (codevelop PDA)
Samsung	Sanctuary	Alliance (codevelop CD-ROM)
Hyundai	AT&T-GIS	Acquisition (nonmemory chip tech)
LG	Microsoft	Alliance (codevelop PDA)
LG	Zenith	Acquisition (advanced image tech-HDTV)
Anam	Group Geotek	Alliance (information/telecom tech)

SOURCE: *Korea Economic Weekly*, July 21, 1995.

has yet to develop further. Additional efforts must be made by both nations in this regard. The Korean government must continue its policy of making the Korean business environment comparable to those of OECD nations.[25] The U.S. firms, however, must not forget that some of the big corporations in Korea are exploring new technological sources other than the United States, such as Russia and Japan.

Expanded U.S.-Korean industrial and technological cooperation will offer substantial benefits for both countries, as well as for the firms in each country. A new basis for long-term cooperation between Korea and the United States must be established. In this era of global competition, it is most appropriate to foster a mutually beneficial "strategic industrial alliance" between Korean and American firms.

---

25. The Korean government has given particular attention to reform and deregulation. Although there has been much progress in this regard, evaluations by the business community, both domestic and international, still do not appear to be satisfactory. According to a 1994 survey by the Korea Institute for Industrial Economics and Trade (KIET), Korea's ranking was particularly low with respect to the role of the government. A similarly sobering conclusion was reached in the *1995 World Competitiveness Report* issued by the IMD in Switzerland. In terms of the role of the government, Korea had steadily held the position of twenty-fourth among the forty-nine countries surveyed.

Toward Forward-looking Cooperative Korean-U.S. Economic Relations

Perhaps no two other nations, geographically so far apart, historically so unrelated, and culturally so different, have maintained such a close relationship throughout the post–World War II era as have Korea and the United States.

Aside from the security relationship, the United States provided public aid, then private capital and technology, and most important, the markets for Korean exports in the past. The Korean economy succeeded with them, or rather the United States succeeded in its own policies. In this regard, Korea and the United States should respect each other and should continue to maintain a mutually beneficial cooperative partnership in the future.

From the Korean perspective, the United States will have to continue to be the most important market for its exports and, even more important, its source for advanced technologies. Today, Korea is about to join the ranks of the industrially developed nations.[26] To join those ranks successfully, Korea needs more advanced technologies to produce high value-added products and sophisticated management know-how, which are usually bundled with equity participation in the form of foreign direct investments (FDIs) or joint ventures. Strategic industrial alliances of various sorts are other avenues for acquiring them.

It is in Korea's interest to facilitate foreign direct investments, joint ventures, and strategic industrial alliances by making "Korea the best place in the world to do business." Once that is done, it is not difficult to expect that U.S. firms would become the most important partners for their Korean counterparts, considering their past close relationship.

It is important for Koreans to realize that countries all over the world are competing to attract global firms that possess much needed capital and technology. Korea simply cannot afford to be left out of this global trend. It is therefore critical to make Korea indeed the best place in the world to do business, not only for Korean firms, but also for foreign firms. In light of this, both domestic and international deregulation and liberalization policies should be accelerated.

In this regard, it is again worth reminding potential foreign business partners of the following: according to a recent survey, while 67.7 percent of those Koreans surveyed approve of outgoing foreign direct

---

26. Korea officially applied for membership in the Organization for Economic Cooperation and Development (OECD) in March 1995, with the expectation that it would become a member before the end of 1996.

investment, only 36.1 percent approve of incoming foreign direct investment. The discrepancy must reflect Korea's historical background. Korea was under Japanese colonial rule until only a few decades ago. Consequently, Koreans in general are still concerned about foreign domination of their industries, or new imperialism. In fact, that is why most laws, rules, and regulations regarding FDIs and joint ventures were made difficult and complicated. Moreover, in implementing these laws and regulations, the bureaucrats interpret them in a manner that often makes it even more difficult for foreign firms to do business in Korea.[27]

Nevertheless, U.S. firms have to do their part in adapting to such local environments. They should be more sensitive toward the needs of the host country and its cultural and emotional factors. They should also ask themselves the following questions: How much training and R&D activities are done in Korea? When such activities are carried out, how much effort is being made to inform the Korean people of such activities? How many Koreans occupy top management positions? Whenever there are problems of doing business in Korea, is there a tendency to rush to write or file complaints to the U.S. government officials and politicians, instead of making an effort to solve the problems by appealing to the relevant agencies in Korea?

It is important for both partners to make a special effort to establish a closer cooperative base for mutual gain, particularly in this age of globalization.

The inconsistency in the approach of the U.S. government to trade issues can dampen Korea-U.S. cooperative efforts. This inconsistency arises from the two-track U.S. approach—that is, U.S. reliance on unilateral and bilateral as well as multilateral means in pressuring its trading partners for their market opening.[28]

---

27. In fact, Korea is exceptional among developing nations in that it relied little on foreign direct investment or joint ventures in the course of its earlier development. In addition to the historical reason, there was an obvious economic reason as well. With the fixed exchange rate regime under a chronic inflationary situation, borrowing was a preferable alternative for Korean firms to choose. As a result, Korean firms relied heavily on borrowed capital. At the same time, they obtained their needed technology primarily through licensing agreements and purchasing patents. For a detailed discussion, see SaKong (1993).

28. Bhagwati (1995) criticized that the U.S. trade policy of obsession with further expansion and creation of free-trade areas, instead of concentration on multilateralism at the WTO, is a mistake. Bayard and Elliot (1994) also recommended the U.S. government abandon the unilateral policy measure of super 301 provisions for attacking import barriers in other countries.

The recent U.S.-Japanese auto and auto-parts deal settled outside the WTO framework is a good case in point. The U.S. decision to stay out of the recent WTO agreement on banking and financial services is another example. The insistence on the part of the United States, still the most international trading partner, to leave unilateral or bilateral avenues open significantly reduces other trading partners' multilateralism and multilateral institutions—namely, the World Trade Organization.

As for Korea, a continued liberalization and market opening in the coming years is inevitable, not only to adapt to the rapidly changing global economic environment but also to enhance its economic competitiveness. Therefore, it is in Korea's interests to have a well-sequenced comprehensive liberalization program, preferably preannounced. The United States could help Korea and itself by dealing with bilateral trade and investment issues through a comprehensive package approach on a regular basis with Korea, instead of relying on counterproductive, particularistic, unilateral case-by-case approaches.

It is in the U.S. and Korean mutual interests to help strengthen the multilateral institutional framework and to rely diligently on multilateral dispute settlement procedures. In this connection, while Koreans have to get out of the "hermit kingdom mentality," the United States has to overcome "diminished giant syndrome." It is much more beneficial for a medium-sized country like Korea to help strengthen the multilateral institutions and abide by their rules and regulations than to take every trading partner on a one-on-one basis. Even with the reduced influence of the United States in determining the global economic order, still the United States is expected by the rest of the world to exert appropriate leadership. Consequently, any visibly diminished U.S. commitment to multilateralism is bound to weaken the very foundation of multilateralism. In this regard, the United States should join the WTO agreement on financial services as early as possible. By doing so, it would show the world that it is still strongly committed to strengthening the WTO.

At the same time, Korea and the United States should work together to counter the rising trend of discriminatory regionalism. It is worth reminding the United States that the new proposal of the Trans-Atlantic Free Trade Area (TAFTA), in addition to the extending of NAFTA, is viewed as a negative factor for multilaterialism by the rest of the world.

Both Korea and the United States should recognize the importance of the trans-Pacific economic linkage and commit themselves to maintaining the integrated unity of the Asia-Pacific region. Regional cooperation within APEC would reduce the obstacles to trans-Pacific trade and would allow both countries to reap the benefits of increased specialization between the two sides of the Pacific that are complementary to each other in terms of resource endowments and cost structures.

The two countries should promote the successful progress of APEC, focusing on three aspects: trade and investment liberalization, trade facilitation, and the economic development of the Asia-Pacific region.[29] To date, the United States has focused most of its attention on trade and investment liberalization.[30] Korea and the United States should cooperate closely to achieve more balanced progress, addressing all three aspects with equal concern.[31]

In this way, the United States can allay the fears of its East Asian neighbors, while Korea can further the momentum of economic cooperation in the Asia-Pacific region. Such cooperation could be effective in closing the existing gap between Western legalism and East Asian pragmatism, as an approach to trade liberalization. Additionally, the new trade issues of the environment, labor, and competition policies are another area for a closer cooperation between the two countries. Korea can play an intermediary role by reconciling the different positions of the developed and developing nations on these issues.

For a Northeast Asian subregional economic cooperation, Korea, Japan, and the United States could establish a subregional economic development bank, such as the Northeast Asian Development Bank.

To overcome the mutual suspicion and distrust still prevalent in this region, it is highly desirable for Japan, Korea, and China together to engage in forward-looking constructive activities for the region

---

29. There have been discussions on the idea of forming an FTA between Korea and the United States since 1989, when a USITC report identified Korea, as well as Taiwan, ASEAN, and the Pacific Rim region, as potential FTA partners with the United States. While Korea continues to evaluate the merits of forming an FTA with the United States or joining NAFTA, attention has shifted toward APEC as a means of strengthening Korea–U.S. economic relations and countering the trend toward regionalism. For the most recent discussion concerning the idea of Korea's forming an FTA with the United States or joining NAFTA, see Bark (1994), Dornbusch (1994), and K. Kim (1994).

30. Korea is determined to place the highest priority on implementing the free-trade goals of APEC as outlined in the Bogor Declaration agreed to at the APEC leaders' meeting in Indonesia. Conflicts may arise, however, between Korea and the United States concerning trade liberalization schedules. While the United States expects Korea to follow the fast-track liberalization scheme targeted for 2010, Korea's official position is to complete liberalization by 2020. For the U.S. perspective on the future progress of APEC, see Bergsten (1995).

31. For the Japanese perspective on a balanced package proposal, see Yamazawa (1995).

through the Northeast Asian Development Bank. It seems especially beneficial for Japan to establish a basis for mutual respect and trust in the region before it exerts the global leadership demanded by the international community. The United States, as a Pacific nation, should also actively participate in this endeavor.

This bank might play a critical role in helping to transform formally planned economies into market-oriented economies and in maintaining regional stability. The abundant natural and human resources available in this region—that is, in North Korea, Russia, and China—along with the modern technology and capital provided by Japan and the United States, as well as the most recent development experience and middle-level technological know-how of South Korea would provide an ideal complementary basis for the region's economic development and stability.

Korea also needs the United States to help establish and maintain its firm position in the international economic and political arena, so that Korea can play an important intermediary role within such regional or multilateral arenas as APEC and the WTO, reconciling differences in perspective between the developed and developing nations.

Korea is a pioneer nation in that it has succeeded in its economic development before many follower nations. Korea was considered a basket case not only by the international community but also by leading development economists, until Korea chose the right strategy of outward-looking development. The strategy was the most effective one in taking full advantage of the sound GATT-Bretton Woods system, established and supported by U.S. leadership.

Consequently, most follower nations and formerly planned economies are keenly interested in emulating Korea. Obviously, Korea should devote more of its energy and resources to sharing its experiences with those countries. At the same time, the international community, especially the United States, should support Korea in establishing its appropriate position, particularly in multilateral institutions, such as the WTO, IMF, World Bank, and OECD.

References

Balassa, Bela, and John Williamson. "Adjusting to Success: Balance of Payments in the East Asian NICs." *Policy Analyses in International Economics*, vol. 17 (1987).

Baldwin, Robert E. "U.S. Trade Policy under the WTO." University of Wisconsin-Madison, 1995.

Bark, Taeho. "Anti-Dumping Restrictions against Korean Exports: Major Focus on Consumer Electronic Products." KIEP Working

Paper 91-02, Korea Institute for International Economic Policy, 1991.

———. "Prospects for a U.S.-Korea Free Trade Agreement." Manuscript. Seoul: Korea Institute for International Economic Policy, 1994.

Bayard, Thomas O., and Kimberly Ann Elliot. *Reciprocity and Retaliation in U.S. Trade Policy.* Washington, D.C.: Institute for International Economics, 1994.

Bergsten, C. Fred. "APEC: The Bogor Declaration and the Path Ahead." Working paper. Washington, D.C.: Institute for International Economics, 1995.

Bhagwati, Jagdish. "U.S. Trade Policy: The Infatuation with Free Trade Areas." Conference paper. Washington, D.C.: American Enterprise Institute, 1995.

Business America. "The Big Emerging Market." March 1994.

Business Week, July 31, 1995.

Dornbusch, Rudiger. "The United States and Korea in the Asia-Pacific Region: An American Perspective." In *The Political Economy of Korea-United States Cooperation,* edited by C. Fred Bergsten and Il SaKong. Washington, D.C.: Institute for International Economics, 1994.

International Management Development Institute. *The World Competitiveness Report 1995,* September 1995.

Kantor, Mickey. Statement before the Senate Finance Committee. April 4, 1995.

Kim, Joo-Jin. "Korea-U.S. Alliances and Joint Research and Development in the Semiconductor Industry." *Korea Economic Weekly,* June 13, 1994.

Kim, Kihwan. "U.S.-Korean Bilateral Relations: A Korean Perspective." In *The Political Economy of Korea-United States Cooperation,* edited by C. Fred Bergsten and Il SaKong. Washington, D.C.: Institute for International Economics, 1994.

Korea Economic Weekly, April 3, 1995.

———, July 21, 1995.

SaKong, Il. *Korea in the World Economy,* Washington, D.C.: Institute for International Economics, 1993.

Tarullo, Daniel. "U.S.-Korea Economic Relations." Presented at the Korea-U.S. Twenty-First Century Council, Washington, D.C., February 9, 1995.

Williamson, John. "Exchange Rate Policy in Hong Kong, Korea, and Taiwan." Statement before the Subcommittee on International Trade, Committee on Finance, U.S. Senate, 1989.

Young, Soogil. "Korea-U.S. Economic Relations in the 1990s: Conflict or Cooperation?" Presented at the Korea-U.S. Twenty-First Century Council, February 9, 1995.

Yamazawa, Ippei. "Japanese Approaches toward APEC: Osaka Agenda." Tokyo: Hitotsubashi University, 1995.

6
Taiwan's New Growth Pattern of Shifting Dependency

Yu-Shan Wu

Like other developing countries, Taiwan uses its cheap labor and relies on international trade to achieve sustained high growth. Low wages, however, are always relative to labor productivity. The gap between the wage level and labor productivity represents the competitiveness of the exports from the country. The essence of trade-dependent growth is to raise productivity faster than wages so that the country's exports enjoy high competitiveness on the world market. The foreign exchange earned can then be used to import producer goods and to raise productivity further.

It can be argued that exchange rate manipulation or wage controls can serve the same purpose, that is, to keep exports competitive on the world market. Manipulating exchange rates, however, always brings about distortions in resource allocation and often induces inflation through more expensive imports. Wage levels hinge on the degree of economic development of the country, the structure of the labor market, and the policies of the government. It is easy to maintain low wages when the economy is still at a low level of development, when there is an abundant supply of labor, and when the government enforces its low-wage policy. Wage control is difficult, however, when the economy has been growing rapidly, when there is full employment, and when the government lacks the ability to suppress union activities and labor movements. Productivity growth, therefore, is the only long-term solution to the problem of sustaining economic growth in a trade-dependent economy.

Two elements in Taiwan's economic development, productivity growth and foreign trade, are crucial. Since the 1950s, two stages of import substitution and two stages of export expansion have occurred. During each stage of import substitution productivity rose. During each stage of export expansion, Taiwan cut into the world market through its mature production technology and relatively cheap labor.

Import substitution sheltered native industries so that they could later become the base for launching export expansion. A successful export expansion then raised the wage level, making further productivity growth imperative; but it also provided the means for upgrading the industrial structure through the accumulation of foreign exchange and the import of producer goods and technology. Through an alternate succession of import substitution and export expansion, Taiwan's economy has sustained a high growth rate over the past four decades.

The 1950s—The First Import Substitution

When Taiwan was retroceded to the Republic of China (ROC) following the end of World War II, economic ties with Japan were abruptly severed. Mainland China was for a while the major market for Taiwan's principal exports (rice and sugar), but that link was also terminated with the Communist takeover on the mainland in 1949. During the 1950s, the United States supplied more than 40 percent of Taiwan's imports, while Japan again became the major outlet for Taiwan's agricultural exports. Taiwan's trade deficit with the United States was then met by U.S. aid, which totaled $1.5 billion (unless otherwise stated, dollar amounts refer to U.S. dollars) from 1951 to 1965. The ROC government used the same aid to nurture food-processing and textile industries on the island. This was the first stage of import substitution. High tariffs, import controls, and a multiple exchange-rate scheme were instituted to protect nascent domestic industries. As a result, gross national product grew 56.1 percent between 1952 and 1958. The momentum, however, soon subsided with a saturated domestic market. Because deepening of import substitution was considered impossible considering Taiwan's small market size, the government then pushed for export expansion based on the very same industries that grew under primary import substitution. The United States, eager to terminate direct economic aid, also applied pressure to Taiwan to shift to export expansion.

The 1960s—The First Export Expansion

Between 1958 and 1961, a reform of foreign exchange and trade, a nineteen-point program of economic and financial reform, and a Statute for Encouragement of Investment took place. Through these measures, the incentive structure shifted away from favoring production for the domestic market toward encouragement of exports. The timing was optimal, as the 1960s were a golden decade of world trade. The Dillon Round and the Kennedy Round of General Agreement on Tariffs and

Trade (GATT) negotiations significantly lowered the tariffs of the industrialized countries. Taiwan took advantage of this unique opportunity and targeted the U.S. market. Taiwan's exports to the United States grew from $18.9 million in 1960 to $564.2 million in 1970, a thirtyfold expansion, compared with Taiwan's total export expansion of ninefold during the same period. In 1967, the United States for the first time surpassed Japan as Taiwan's largest export market. One year later, Taiwan registered the first-ever trade surplus with the United States (table 6–1). The U.S. market also took an increasingly larger share of Taiwan exports, from 11.5 percent in 1960 to 38.1 percent in 1970.

The 1960s were a decade of successful export expansion based on labor-intensive manufactures. During that time, textiles and apparel were the mainstay of Taiwan's exports to the United States, followed by footwear and wood products and then by electrical and electronic products (table 6–2). The textile industry was nourished by government subsidy and U.S. aid in the 1950s. The private entrepreneurs, brought up under the protectionist policies in the industry, now moved to the export sector to take advantage of the new incentives there. Textiles and apparel remained the dominant export industry until the 1970s. Here is an example of Taiwan's indigenous industrial strength, a successful case of the government's industrial policy (Wu 1994a, chap. 5). Footwear, wood, and other miscellaneous consumer manufactures, such as plywood, toys, sporting goods, traveling equipment, and the like, benefited from American wholesalers and importers who looked abroad for cheaper products to meet domestic competition.

Taiwan's small and medium enterprises met their demand for flexibility of production. The American buyers then placed orders, transferred unsophisticated technology, and practically guaranteed markets for local producers. This demand-driven phenomenon rose and fell in a short time, making Taiwan the leading producer for the U.S. market for a while and then shifting to other cheaper overseas manufacturing bases. These industries were never considered strategic by Taiwan's economic planners, and their growth should be attributed mainly to the importers' demand.

In the late 1960s, the most rapid industrial expansion occurred in electronics (table 6–2). This industry was the first in postwar Taiwan directly linked with foreign investment. Many American giants, such as Ford Motor, TWA, RCA, and Admiral, set up subsidiaries in Taiwan to produce for the U.S. market. The Export Processing Zones established by the government clearly facilitated the inflow of foreign capital at this critical juncture. In 1970, 49 percent of all the electronics firms registered in Taiwan were foreign owned, which accounted for 80 per-

147

TABLE 6–1
TAIWAN'S TRADE WITH THE UNITED STATES, 1947–1994
(millions of U.S. dollars)

Year	Taiwan's Export to United States	U.S. Share of Taiwan's Export (%)	Taiwan's Import from United States	U.S. Share in Taiwan's Import (%)	Taiwan's Trade Surplus with United States
1947		0	9	0	−9
1948	1	0	6	0	−5
1949	2	0	53	0	−51
1950	3	0	23	0	−20
1951	6	0	41	0	−35
1952	4	3.5	86	45.7	−82
1953	n.a.	4.2	n.a.	38.7	n.a.
1954	n.a.	5.4	n.a.	46.4	n.a.
1955	5	4.4	96	47.5	−91
1956	7	5.6	81	42.0	−74
1957	5	3.5	85	49.9	−80
1958	10	6.2	84	37.3	−74
1959	14	8.6	84	36.1	−70
1960	19	11.5	113	38.1	−94
1961	43	21.9	131	40.6	−88
1962	53	24.4	115	38.0	−62
1963	54	16.3	151	41.6	−97
1964	81	18.6	139	32.5	−58
1965	96	21.3	176	31.7	−80
1966	116	21.6	166	26.7	−50
1967	168	26.2	247	30.7	−79
1968	278	35.5	240	26.5	38
1969	399	38.0	292	24.1	107
1970	564	38.1	364	23.9	200
1971	859	41.7	408	22.1	451
1972	1,251	41.9	543	21.6	708
1973	1,677	37.4	953	25.2	724
1974	2,037	36.1	1,680	24.1	357
1975	1,823	34.3	1,652	27.8	171
1976	3,039	37.2	1,798	23.7	1,241
1977	3,636	38.8	1,964	23.1	1,672
1978	5,010	39.5	2,376	21.5	2,634
1979	5,652	35.1	3,381	22.9	2,271

TABLE 6–1 (continued)

Year	Taiwan's Export to United States	U.S. Share of Taiwan's Export (%)	Taiwan's Import from United States	U.S. Share in Taiwan's Import (%)	Taiwan's Trade Surplus with United States
1980	6,760	34.1	4,674	23.7	2,086
1981	8,163	36.1	4,766	22.5	3,397
1982	8,759	39.4	4,563	24.1	4,196
1983	11,334	45.1	4,646	22.9	6,688
1984	14,868	48.8	5,042	23.0	9,826
1985	14,773	48.1	4,746	23.6	10,027
1986	19,014	47.7	5,433	22.4	13,581
1987	23,685	44.1	7,648	21.8	16,037
1988	23,467	38.7	13,007	26.2	10,460
1989	24,036	36.2	12,003	23.0	12,033
1990	21,746	32.4	12,612	23.0	9,134
1991	22,321	29.3	14,114	22.5	8,207
1992	23,572	28.9	15,772	21.9	7,800
1993	23,478	27.6	16,722	21.7	6,756
1994	24,345	26.2	18,043	21.1	6,302

n.a. = not available.
SOURCE: Data for 1947–1990, Baldwin, Chen, and Nelson 1992, p. 4. Data for 1990–1993, *Taiwan chung-yao ching-chi pien-tung chih-piao* (Taipei: Chung-Hua Institution for Economic Research, April 1994), p. 11. Data for 1994, *Liang-an ching-chi t'ung-chi yueh-pao* (Taipei: Mainland Affairs Council, November 1995), pp. 56–57.

cent of all investment funds. Local firms were catching up only in the 1970s. Gradually, electronics developed into the most technologically advanced industry on the island, offering hope for continued growth of the economy when labor became much dearer. The successful development of textiles and apparel, consumer manufactures, and electronics in the 1960s brought about a booming export sector that fueled Taiwan's economic growth. As a result, before the first oil crisis Taiwan enjoyed stable prices and high growth without significant business cycles. At the same time, the island's economy was increasingly dominated by medium and small enterprises, proliferating in the export sector.

In the 1960s not only did Taiwan's exports boom and flow toward the U.S. market but also imports of industrial raw materials and capital goods from Japan increased. Just as the United States surpassed Japan

TABLE 6–2
TAIWAN'S PRINCIPAL EXPORTS TO THE UNITED STATES, 1955–1990
(% of total exports)

Year	Textiles and Apparel	Electrical and Electronic Products	Consumer Manufactures
1955	19.3	0	1.2
1956	11.4	0	1.2
1957	23.1	0	3.8
1958	23.5	0	13.4
1959	29.8	0	15.6
1960	31.4	0	11.5
1961	14.5	0	17.5
1962	32.4	0.2	21.8
1963	15.0	1.0	29.1
1964	20.6	1.5	30.5
1965	21.5	5.6	30.6
1966	18.3	12.2	32.2
1967	20.8	16.4	31.6
1968	22.0	21.0	31.3
1969	25.6	20.2	30.7
1970	28.9	20.1	28.5
1971	33.7	19.7	28.6
1972	24.6	26.7	31.7
1973	22.1	30.0	31.9
1974	22.5	28.7	28.9
1975	26.2	20.7	31.9
1980	18.8	20.3	37.4
1985	16.3	18.1	35.0
1990	12.2	18.1	22.4

SOURCE: Ministry of Finance, *Annual Statistics of Exports and Imports, the Republic of China, Taiwan District,* various issues; cited in Baldwin, Chen, and Nelson 1992, p. 13.

as Taiwan's leading export market in 1967, so Japan exceeded the United States and became the major import supplier for Taiwan in 1964. In 1971, Taiwan obtained 44.5 percent of its total imports from Japan, compared with 22.1 percent from the United States (Baldwin, Chen, and Nelson 1992, 31). The United States and Japan thus traded places from their previous positions in the 1950s.

Among Taiwan's three major imports—agricultural products, industrial raw materials, and capital goods—the United States remained the primary provider in the first category after the 1960s, thanks to the ROC government's procurement policies (the Bulk Commodity Import

Regulation, the "Buy American Missions," and the like) that favored American exporters. But Japanese providers managed to dominate the last two categories. This occurred because the new entrepreneurs in Taiwan were mainly native Taiwanese who had received a Japanese education during the colonial period and had a natural tendency to seek market know-how, technical assistance, and a supply of producer goods from Japanese firms. The U.S. importers, most of them wholesalers, did not favor products with U.S.-made components or parts. The Japanese trading firms, the *sogo shosha,* that handled procurements in Taiwan and sold on the U.S. market, however, preferred the use of Japanese capital goods and intermediate materials and by doing so encouraged local producers to import from Japan. The same phenomenon can be found in the procurement policy of Japanese subsidiaries in Taiwan that overwhelmingly imported components and parts from Japan. The American subsidiaries, though, showed no such preference for products made in the United States. Thus Taiwan gradually developed a trade pattern of high export dependence on the United States and high import dependence on Japan. In this scheme, Japan was the upstream provider, Taiwan the downstream producer, and the United States the end market.

The 1970s—The Second Import Substitution

Bottlenecks emerged in the early 1970s. The ROC was facing major economic and political difficulties. The first oil crisis brought about a worldwide recession and touched off protectionism in the West. Taipei was dislodged from the United Nations as Beijing took the China seat in 1971. Japan shifted its diplomatic recognition from the ROC to the People's Republic of China (PRC) in 1973. And finally in 1975 the old paramount leader Chiang Kai-shek died as the island experienced its first export decline since 1956. Chiang Ching-kuo, son of Chiang Kai-shek, took over political power and came up with a new economic package: ten major construction projects on the island were launched as the core of a second import substitution. The emphasis was on petrochemicals, steel, and ship building; the production of capital goods was the focus of the new industrialization drive.

This phase was Taiwan's deepening of its import substitution, though the industrial structure did not overwhelmingly tilt toward heavy industry, as in the case of South Korea. There was a division of labor between the public and the private sectors of the economy. The state enterprises and the corporations owned by the party in power, the Kuomintang (KMT), made massive investments in the protected heavy industries, while the small and medium private enterprises continued to dominate the export sector, which was governed by the same export-promoting policies installed in the 1960s. The state enterprises concentrated on the domestic market, while the private enterprises expanded on the international market. A link was established between the two, as the heavy industries became the upstream providers of capital goods for the downstream producers, as in the case between the petrochemical industries and textiles and apparel. This vertical integration contributed to the increasing competitiveness of Taiwan's industry. Although wages continued to rise throughout the 1970s and the price of oil surged toward the end of the decade, productivity gains were much greater, and a significant comparative advantage emerged.

During the 1970s, the United States, the major market for Taiwan's exports, made significant efforts to regulate bilateral trade between the two countries. In 1971, Washington and Taipei reached an agreement to control the flow of wool and man-made textile and apparel products. By establishing a large base of exports in the 1960s, Taiwan was actually guaranteed a sizable market share in the United States under such regulations. The Multi-Fiber Agreement of 1974 did not change this picture. Also to Taiwan's advantage was the U.S. Trade Act of 1974 that established the Generalized System of Preferences (GSP). Taiwan swiftly became one of the biggest beneficiaries. Thus, for example, a full 39 percent of Taiwan's total exports to the United States in 1979 was covered by GSP's preferential treatment. In that year, Taiwan reaped $160 million in tariff savings, which put the country at the top of all GSP beneficiaries (Baldwin, Chen, and Nelson 1992, 19). It is obvious that limited market regulation on the American side did not dampen Taiwan's export drive.

The second import substitution of the 1970s did not lessen Taiwan's import dependence on Japan. Although the public sector had a clear pro–United States bias in its investment policy, that bias simply meant that when exports to the United States were down, probably owing to a U.S. recession, the government would come up with a counter-cyclical policy and urge the public sector to increase imports from the United States. Hence the exports to the United States and the imports from it were conversely related, with the export series leading the import series by one year (Baldwin, Chen, and Nelson 1992, 34). When the exports to the United States were rising and the economy ran smoothly, imports were dominated by private firms that preferred Japanese products. The trade pattern established in the 1960s, export dependence on the United States and import dependence on Japan, was sustained throughout the 1970s.

The 1980s—The Second Export Expansion

Taiwan's exports continued to surge in the 1980s, taking full advantage of the productivity gains from the second import substitution of the previous decade and the island's relatively cheap labor. Here, one saw the second stage of export expansion. The derecognition of the ROC by the United States in 1979 and the second oil crisis of the same year did not dampen Taiwan's economic vitality, as foreign investment continued to pour in after the political shock and Taiwan's exports registered record growth.

Foreign trade became highly imbalanced, with Taiwan's enjoying unprecedented surpluses against its major trading partners, particularly the United States. In 1986, for example, Taiwan's total trade surplus was 21.1 percent of GNP, a phenomenon one can observe only in oil-producing countries during the oil crises (Liang and Hueh 1990, 35). In 1987, Taiwan's trade surplus vis-à-vis the United States reached an unprecedented $1.6 billion. Here foreign investors (from both the United States and Japan) played a significant role in using Taiwan as a major manufacturing base for exporting to the U.S. market (Wu and Ch'en 1988, 70). From 1984 to 1986, Taiwan's export dependence on the American market was 47.7 to 48.8 percent, compared with an average of 23.5 percent in the 1960s and 38 percent in the 1970s.[1] It is obvious that during the decade Taiwan had become increasingly dependent on the United States, even with the severance of official ties between the two countries. Taiwan became the second largest source of the U.S. trade deficit and, as a result, was targeted by Washington for currency appreciation, voluntary export restraint agreements, and all kinds of unfair trade practice investigations. In 1989, Taiwan lost its GSP privileges with the United States. Obviously, Taiwan's export expansion hit its limit.

The 1980s were primarily a decade of export expansion, with the state doing little to promote import substitution.[2] As in the past, trade-propelled high growth raised wages to a new high, making a third import substitution imperative for Taiwan's economic development in

---

1. The high concentration of Taiwan's exports in the U.S. market in the early 1980s had a lot to do with the appreciation of the U.S. dollar against other major currencies at that time. Because the NT dollar was pegged to the U.S. dollar, Taiwan's exports suffered from a heavy loss of competitiveness on international markets other than in the United States.

2. The only exception was the Science Based Industrial Park in Hsinchu founded in 1980 to promote the computer industry.

the late 1980s and early 1990s. This time, however, Taiwan faced an entirely different political environment. In the past, Taiwan had a strong "capitalist developmental state" (Johnson 1985). Both Chiang Kai-shek and Chiang Ching-kuo amassed indisputable power in their hands and entrusted economic bureaucrats, such as K. Y. Yin and K. T. Li, with managing the economy (Wu 1994a, chap. 5). The state was in a position to shift the direction of economic development for the country. The previous import substitutions and export expansions were all designed and promoted by the state. The 1980s, however, witnessed the surge of opposition political forces, factionalization of the ruling KMT, rise of prolabor and environmentalist movements, political liberalization and democratization, and, finally, the death of Chiang Ching-kuo in 1988. Production costs rose sharply, but labor productivity did not grow accordingly. What was missing was a major effort to upgrade Taiwan's industrial structure, as in the 1950s and 1970s. As a result, Taiwan's exports became increasingly less competitive on the international market.

Since the late 1980s, products made in Taiwan have captured a slimmer and slimmer share of the U.S. market. Taiwan's trade surplus with the United States also declined steadily. Part of this phenomenon has to do with the rising new Taiwan (NT) dollar, which appreciated against the U.S. dollar by 15.8 percent in 1987, 10.2 percent in 1988, and another 7.5 percent in 1989, under great pressure from Washington. Before this dramatic appreciation, the exchange rate was NT$37.84 to the dollar. In 1990–1994, the rate settled between NT$26.93 and NT$25.16 to the dollar. When the exchange rate stabilized in the early 1990s, however, Taiwan's trade surplus with the United States began to decline rapidly. It was down 10.1 percent in 1991, 5 percent in 1992, 12 percent in 1993, and another 8.3 percent in 1994. Clearly, something other than the exchange rate was at work to cause this phenomenon (table 6–3). The root of the problem was rising production costs and fleeing capital.

During the 1980s not only did Taiwan's export drive gradually lose momentum but also the island's imports from Japan rose sharply, as local manufacturers found themselves tied to Japanese providers and trading firms and suffered from the rising yen. At the same time, the United States made every effort to open Taiwan's domestic market to increase imports of American products. Intensive bilateral negotiations began in 1981. In 1985, Premier Yu Kuo-hwa commissioned an Economic Reform Committee, which produced a report calling for liberalization and internationalization. In this context, Taiwan gradually opened up its domestic market, a process accelerated with the ROC's bid for membership in the GATT (now the WTO). The biggest benefi-

TABLE 6–3
TAIWAN'S MARKET SHARE IN THE UNITED STATES, TRADE SURPLUS WITH
THE UNITED STATES, AND EXCHANGE RATE TO THE DOLLAR, 1986–1994
(percent)

Year	U.S. Market Share		Taiwan's Trade Surplus with U.S.		Exchange Rate	
	Exports	Growth rate (%)	Millions of $	Growth rate (%)	NT$ to U.S.$	Growth rate (%)
1986	5.37		13,581		37.84	
1987	6.12	13.97	16,037	18.1	31.85	−15.8
1988	5.67	−7.35	10,460	−34.8	28.59	−10.2
1989	5.20	−8.29	12,033	15.0	26.41	−7.5
1990	4.62	−11.15	9,134	−24.1	26.89	1.8
1991	4.75	2.81	8,207	−10.1	26.81	−0.3
1992	4.68	−1.47	7,800	−5.0	25.16	−6.2
1993	4.35	−7.05	6,864	−12.0	26.93	7
1994	4.04	−7.13	6,294	−8.3	26.24	−2.6

SOURCE: *Liang-an ching-chi t'ung-chi yueh-pao* (Taipei: Mainland Affairs Council, Nov. 1995), pp. 58, 64, 67; *Taiwan chung-yao ching-chi pien-tung chih-piao* (Taipei: Chung-Hua Institution for Economic Research, April 1994), p. 11.

ciary of Taiwan's opening-up policy was not U.S. firms, however, but Japanese companies with their intricate links to Taiwan's businesses.

The Cross-Strait Investment Surge

At the turn of the decade, Taiwan was unable to implement a large-scale import substitution. With production costs in general and wage levels in particular rising rapidly, Taiwan was hard pressed to find a solution for its trade-dependent economy. Just at this juncture, Taiwan was offered a unique opportunity to seek cheap labor overseas to maintain its export edge. With the political thaw across the Taiwan Strait, Taiwan's labor-intensive industries hurried to invest on the Chinese mainland to prolong their life spans. This strategy entails no gains in productivity, as Taiwan's investors were more interested in using the mainland's cheap labor than in investing in R&D. As long as the wage level on the mainland is low, however, Taiwan's trade-dependent economy will remain vigorous.

Mainland China was in its own stage of export expansion, based on production technologies that Taiwan mastered in the 1960s and 1970s. In 1988, after five consecutive years of trade deficits, Beijing made a critical decision to shift the focus of its open-door policy away from introducing Western technology toward earning badly needed foreign exchange through exporting labor-intensive products, a strategy based on its comparative advantage. Following Wang Jian's "grand international circulation" theory, Premier Zhao Ziyang decided to plunge China's east coast into the world market (Sah 1991, 101–2). The mainland economy thus embraced export expansion, very much like what had happened in the newly industrialized economies of East Asia several decades before.

This point is where Taiwan's investment fits in. Labor-intensive and oriented toward the international market, Taiwan's export industry is a perfect source of direct foreign investment for mainland China at this critical juncture. Following good economic logic, the PRC's State Council promulgated the Regulations Encouraging Taiwan Compatriots to Invest on the Mainland (the twenty-two articles), later followed by the Law on Protection of Investment by Taiwan Compatriots in 1994. Provinces then competed in offering privileges to Taiwan investors, including tax holidays, duty-free imports, land-use rights, permission to purchase bonds, and special areas exclusively for Taiwan investment (*Ta-lu t'ou-tzu chih-nan* 1991, 112–13). Besides these favorable policies, other "pull" factors include geographical proximity, cultural similarities, great market potentials, access to raw materials, GSP treatment that mainland exports enjoy on the U.S. market, and much lower production costs on the mainland. On the "push" side are a surging NT dollar, rising labor and land costs, pressure from the environmentalists against industrial pollution, and increasing competition from other Asian countries based on low wages. In some cases, Taiwan firms were asked by Western importers to establish manufacturing bases on the mainland (Li Tsung-che 1994, 78). In 1990, the ROC government finally legalized investment activities by Taiwan businessmen on the mainland in an effort to gain information on the outflow of capital from the island and to direct it better.

As a result, Taiwan's investment on the mainland grew by leaps and bounds. It started in 1987 with 80 investment projects and $100 million. Next year it grew to 430 projects and $600 million. The investment surge was not deterred by the Tiananmen incident at all, as witnessed by the fact that at the end of 1989 Taiwan investors had launched 1,000 projects involving $1 billion. This trend steamed ahead into the 1990s. In 1993, Taiwan's investment hit the $10 billion mark, making Taiwan the second largest foreign investor on the Chinese mainland, next only to Hong Kong and Macao.[3] According to a conser-

---

3. In 1993, the Ministry of Economics approved 9,329 projects involving $3.2 billion for investment on the mainland. These figures are widely considered below the actual numbers.

156

TABLE 6–4
OFFICIALLY APPROVED INDIRECT INVESTMENT ON THE
CHINESE MAINLAND, 1991–1994
(thousands of U.S. dollars)

Year	Cases	Amount
1991	237	174,158
1992	264	246,992
1993	9,329	3,168,411
1994	934	962,209
Total	10,764	4,551,770

SOURCE: Investment Commission, Ministry of Economic Affairs; cited in *Liang-an ching-chi t'ung-chi yueh-pao* (Taipei: Mainland Affairs Council, August 1994), p. 42; *yueh-pao* (Feb. 1995), p. 34.

vative official estimate (*Mainland Affairs Council* 1994), mainland China was the principal outlet for Taiwan's overseas investment in 1993. With $3.17 billion in 9,329 cases, Taiwan's mainland investment accounted for 66 percent of the total (table 6–4). This figure was six times as large as Taiwan's investment in the United States, which ranked second as a recipient of Taiwan's outflowing capital or eleven times as large as Taiwan's investment in Southeast Asia. Mainland investment continued to dominate Taiwan's overseas investment in 1994. At any time of the year, one can find roughly 20,000 Taiwan firms and 200,000 Taiwan businessmen and technicians on the Chinese mainland, many of whom have moved their families over to the mainland. Despite this activity, Taiwan's mainland investment is still characterized by its small scale and low technology content. Thus, for example, only 5.8 percent of the products manufactured by Taiwan-invested firms on the Chinese mainland are of higher quality than similar products made in Taiwan, compared with 8 percent in the case of Taiwan's investment in Southeast Asia and 72 percent in the case of the United States (Li Tsung-che 1994, 79).

The cross-strait investment has a decisive effect on Taiwan's industrial structure and export capacity. Thus, for example, more than 80 percent of Taiwan's shoemaking industry has been transplanted to the mainland. As a result, in 1991 shoes made in mainland China captured 45 percent of the U.S. market, a share enjoyed by products from Taiwan in 1986. Mainland investment also affected local capital markets, interest rates, and the effectiveness of the government's monetary policies. Thus, when the Central Bank was pursuing an expansionary policy by lowering interest rates, the economy responded slowly, for a large portion of the released capital flowed to the mainland and contributed little to capital formation in Taiwan.

Investment-driven Trade

The same hypergrowth characterizes the investment-driven trade across the Taiwan Strait, which grew from a low of $1.7 billion in 1987 to more than $17.8 billion in 1994 (table 6–5).[4] Cross-strait trade has become the main source of Taiwan's total trade surplus.[5] With Taiwan's trade surplus against the United States declining steadily, while its trade deficit with Japan is rising at a higher rate, cross-strait trade has become the main reason that Taiwan has avoided developing a trade deficit. The other side of the coin is that without the trade deficit mainland China accumulated with Taiwan in 1993 ($12.9 billion), the mainland would have had a trade surplus that year (it had a total deficit of $12.1 billion). In 1994, Taiwan's trade dependence on mainland China was 10.02 percent; its export dependence was 17.22 percent. According to some estimates, by 1996 mainland China will surpass the United States and become Taiwan's largest trading partner.

The cross-strait trade is highly unbalanced. If one takes a look at the trade balances between Taiwan and mainland China from 1987 to 1994, an unmistakable fact immediately stands out: Taiwan enjoys an increasingly larger trade surplus (figure 6–1). In 1987, when Beijing's economic incentives were not yet in full play, Taiwan exported $1.3 billion worth of goods to the mainland, while importing $289 million

---

4. The cross-strait trade is always underestimated for two reasons. First, researchers usually rely on the statistics provided by the Hong Kong government, but Hong Kong is by no means the only entrepot for cross-strait trade. Second, only reexport trade is calculated in the Hong Kong government's statistics, leaving out transshipment trade and triangular trade. It is estimated by Chien Tse-yuan that cross-strait trade reached $14.8 billion in 1992 (the Hong Kong government's official number is $7.4 billion) if transshipment and triangular trade of that year are included (Chien 1993; 76). The ROC government calculates the difference between Taiwan's export to Hong Kong (FOB) and Hong Kong's import from Taiwan (CIF) during the same period of time and adds that difference to the official figure released by Hong Kong's customs service. The result is $15.1 billion for 1993, and $17.9 billion for 1994. In the following discussion, I will use this last set of figures.

5. In 1993, out of the $7.9 billion trade surplus that Taiwan accumulated, $6.5 billion, or 82 percent of total surplus, was from cross-strait trade. If we use the ROC government's estimates that include transshipment trade, Taiwan's surplus against the mainland in 1993 was $12.9 billion, or 163 percent of Taiwan's total trade surplus.

TABLE 6–5

CROSS-STRAIT TRADE THROUGH HONG KONG, 1979–1994

(millions of U.S. dollars)

	Total Trade		Taiwan's Exports to Mainland		Taiwan's Imports from Mainland		Taiwan's Trade Dependence on
Year	Volume	Growth rate	Volume	Growth Rate	Volume	Growth rate	Mainland
1979	77.8		21.5		56.3		0.25
1980	311.2	300.18	235.0	994.41	76.2	35.39	0.79
1981	460.0	47.61	384.8	63.49	75.2	−1.35	1.05
1982	278.5	−39.37	194.5	−49.38	84.0	11.76	0.68
1983	291.3	4.60	201.4	3.55	89.9	6.94	0.64
1984	553.3	89.74	425.5	111.27	127.8	42.18	1.06
1985	1,102.7	99.30	986.8	131.92	115.9	−9.28	2.17
1986	955.6	−13.35	811.3	−17.78	144.2	24.43	1.49
1987	1,705.2	78.45	1,266.5	56.11	288.9	100.35	1.71
1988	2,720.9	59.57	2,242.2	77.04	478.7	65.67	2.47
1989	3,918.8	44.03	3,331.9	48.60	586.9	22.61	3.31
1990	5,160.0	31.67	4,394.6	31.89	765.4	30.41	4.23
1991	8,619.5	67.04	7,493.5	70.52	1,126.0	47.11	6.20
1992	11,666.6	35.35	10,547.6	40.76	1,119.0	−0.62	7.60
1993	15,096.7	29.40	13,993.1	32.67	1,103.6	−1.38	9.32
1994	17,881.2	18.44	16,022.5	14.5	1,858.7	68.42	10.02

SOURCE: *Liang-an ching-chi t'ung-chi yueh-pao* (Taipei: Mainland Affairs Council, August 1994), p. 31, 32; *yueh-pao* (Nov. 1995), pp. 24, 26.

worth of products from across the strait, giving the island a trade surplus of $978 million. In 1988, Taiwan's cross-strait exports jumped to $2.2 billion, imports rose to $479 million, and Taiwan's surplus reached $1.8 billion. This trend continued into the 1990s, when Taiwan amassed a surplus of $3.6 billion in 1990, $6.4 billion in 1991, $9.4 billion in 1992, $12.9 billion in 1993, and $14.2 billion in 1994. In the last year, Taiwan's exports constituted 90 percent of total trade across the Taiwan Strait.

Not only was there a steadily rising trade surplus in Taiwan's favor, but also the island's export dependence on the mainland market (as calculated by the mainland's share in Taiwan's total exports) increased over the years. In 1988, mainland China accounted for 3.70 percent of Taiwan's exports. That figure rose to 12.95 percent in 1992 and 16.47 percent in 1993 (figure 6–2). The same can be said of the mainland's import dependence on Taiwan. In 1988, Taiwan supplied

FIGURE 6–1

TAIWAN'S EXPORTS TO AND IMPORTS FROM THE MAINLAND, 1979–1994

(millions of U.S. dollars)

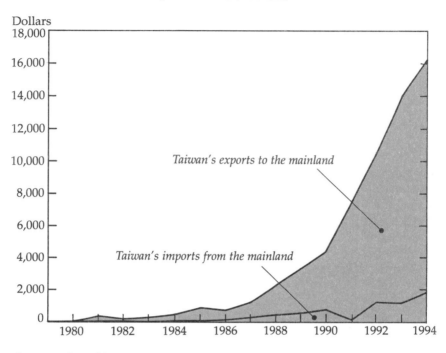

SOURCE: See table 6–5.

4.06 percent of the mainland's total imports. In 1992, Taiwan's share rose to 13.08 percent, and it reached 13.46 in 1993. The flow of Taiwan's products to the mainland market was not matched by trade in the opposite direction, however. Mainland China's exports to Taiwan grew roughly at the same rate as total exports, giving a low and stable export-dependence rate on the Taiwan market over the years (1.01 percent in 1988, 1.23 percent in 1990, and 1.20 percent in 1993). Taiwan's import dependence on the mainland correspondingly showed a slightly increasing rate (0.96 percent in 1987, 1.40 percent in 1990, and 1.43 percent in 1993). In short, over the years Taiwan's exports to the mainland have grown into a significant portion of Taiwan's total exports and the mainland's total imports, while mainland China's exports to Taiwan remained a minor phenomenon for both sides. In 1993, mainland China became the third largest trading partner for Taiwan, and Taiwan became the fourth largest trading partner for the mainland

160

FIGURE 6–2

PERCENTAGE OF TAIWAN'S EXPORTS FROM MAINLAND CHINA, JAPAN,
AND THE UNITED STATES, 1979–1994

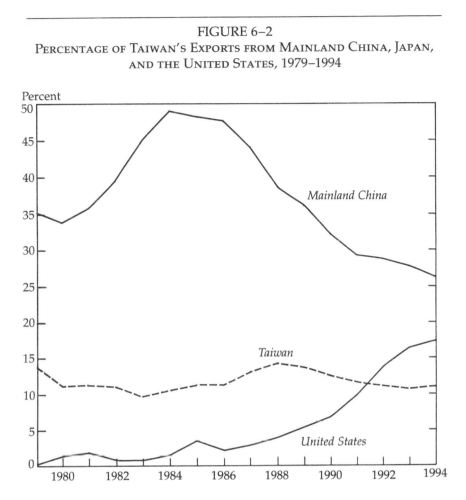

SOURCE: *Taiwan Statistical Data Book*, Council for Economic Planning and Development, 1992, p. 196; *Liang-an ching-chi t'ung-chi yueh-pao* (Mainland Affairs Council, Nov. 1995), p. 56, 57. *Taiwan chung-yao ching-chi pien-tung chih-piao* (Taipei: Chung-Hua Institution for Economic Research, April 1994), pp. 11, 12.

(Lee 1993). A full 92.7 percent of this booming economic relation, however, is accounted for by Taiwan's exports to mainland China. This imbalance is an apparent anomaly.[6]

If one compares the track record of the cross-strait trade with the general trade pattern of the Chinese mainland, the irregularity be-

---

6. No comparable imbalance can be found in the mainland's trade with major countries in the world.

comes even clearer. One typical case is the immediate post-Tiananmen development. From 1984 to 1989, the mainland registered a trade deficit for six consecutive years. Foreign indebtedness reached $41.3 billion at the end of 1989. The brutal suppression of the Tiananmen prodemocracy movement invited international sanctions against mainland China, which added to the economic recession that the mainland had been experiencing since the retrenchment policy *(zhili zhengdun)* was adopted in fall 1988. Foreign exchange reserves dropped to the 1987 level. Obviously, a contractionary policy was in order, and indeed it was taken with a vengeance. In 1990, Beijing slashed its total imports by 9.8 percent, which greatly contributed to the country's resumption of a surplus position that year. In that same year, however, the mainland's imports from Taiwan witnessed a 31.9 percent increase, clearly against the general trade pattern of the mainland and the current phase of the import cycle (in 1990, the mainland's imports from the United States dropped by 16 percent, that from Japan by 28 percent).

This strange phenomenon is explainable in terms of the nature of the cross-strait trade. This trade is investment driven; that is, to a great extent trade supports the investment activities of Taiwan's businessmen on the mainland (Lee 1993). The content of Taiwan's exports to the mainland, the bulk of the cross-strait trade, illustrates the point. From 1988 to 1993, Standard International Trade Classification (SITC) section 6 and 7 products (materials, parts and accessories, and machinery equipment) averaged around 70 percent of Taiwan's exports to mainland China. Many of these producer goods were imported by Taiwan-funded enterprises on the mainland. An estimated 54 to 78 percent of the materials and spare parts and 75 to 95 percent of the machinery and equipment needed by Taiwan businessmen (Taishang) were imported from Taiwan (Li 1993; Li Tsung-che 1994). These imports were necessary because Taiwan businessmen were required to provide for their own materials and semifinished products, so as not to disturb the mainland's domestic market. Because Taiwan's exports to the mainland were predominantly factors of production needed by the mainland's own export drive, it is only reasonable to expect a rising flow of goods from Taiwan to mainland China as the mainland's export industry booms. As these producer goods have high added value, they contributed greatly to Taiwan's trade surplus with the mainland.

Based on this theory, the 1990 rise in Taiwan's exports to the mainland against the background of general import reduction was not unusual. To tide over the unprecedented economic crisis the Communist regime was facing at the time, Beijing needed not just to cut imports but to expand exports. In 1990 the SITC section 6 and 7 commodities constituted 76.7 percent of the mainland's imports from Taiwan. These were producer goods used by Taiwan-funded and other mainland-based enterprises to export to the international market. Small wonder that the cross-strait trade ran against the general pattern of the time and that economic difficulties gave an additional boost to Taiwan-mainland trade relations.[7]

Other factors, having to do primarily with Taiwan's own political considerations, are at work to keep the mainland's deficit with Taiwan constantly growing. It has been thought prudent for Taiwan not to allow mainland investment on the island. The argument that capital endowment determines the direction of the flow of investment and that there are no economic incentives for mainland capital to come to Taiwan is untenable. The major reason for the absence of mainland investment on Taiwan is a political one. This being the case, it would be impossible to expect any investment-driven exports from mainland China to Taiwan. The other obstacle to increasing imports from the mainland is the limits that Taiwan's government sets on the permitted items of import. Mainland-produced consumer goods are prohibited from entering the Taiwan market altogether. Agricultural and industrial materials and semifinished products are regulated by a list of around 1,700 permitted items. These were allowed on Taiwan's market to cut production costs of local manufacturers. To import any products beyond these specified items is illegal. On the mainland side, the limited transportation capacity and growing domestic needs for materials and semifinished products also restrict the available products for the Taiwan market. It is only natural that exports from mainland China have been growing modestly compared with the leaps and bounds of the growth of Taiwan's exports to the mainland—hence the increasing trade imbalance.

Shifting Dependence

The cross-strait economic relations signify a great shift in Taiwan's growth pattern. Although Taiwan is still trade dependent, the direction of its foreign trade has changed. Taiwan still relies on Japanese imports for most of its producer goods, to such an extent that the rise of the yen has raised Taiwan's trade deficit with Japan to an unprecedented

---

7. Before the investment boom of the late 1980s, the cross-strait trade conformed to the mainland's general trade pattern. Thus one saw a decline in Taiwan's export to the mainland in 1982 (-49.38 percent) and 1986 (-17.8 percent), perfectly in sync with the mainland's import cycles. These fluctuations in trade were not to reappear in 1987–1993, a period characterized by uninterrupted growth in cross-strait trade (Chien 1994, 72).

FIGURE 6–3
PERCENTAGE OF TAIWAN'S IMPORTS FROM MAINLAND CHINA, JAPAN,
AND THE UNITED STATES, 1979–1994

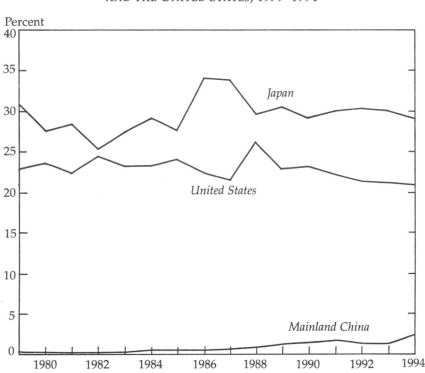

SOURCE: *Taiwan Statistical Data Book* (Council for Economic Planning and De-
velopment, 1992), p. 196; *Liang-an ching-chi t'ung-chi yueh-pao* (Mainland Affairs
Council, Nov. 1995), pp. 56, 57; *Taiwan chung-yao ching-chi pien-tung chih-piao*
(Taipei: Chung-Hua Institution for Economic Research, April 1994), pp. 11, 12.

high, and Japan's share in Taiwan's imports is sustained (figure 6–3).
The great shift occurred in the direction of Taiwan's exports. In the
past, Taiwan exported to the U.S. market labor-intensive products and
accumulated large trade surpluses. Since the late 1980s, with Taiwan's
exports gradually losing competitiveness on the U.S. market and Taiwan's firms rushing to transplant their manufacturing bases on the
Chinese mainland, the trade imbalance between the ROC and the
United States decreased. However, as Taiwanese investment on the
mainland accelerates and Taiwan-invested firms there maintain their
symbiotic relations with mid- and upstream producers on the island,
mainland China is in a position to replace gradually the United States

as the major outlet for Taiwan's exports. These exports are no longer labor-intensive manufactures but materials, parts, machinery, and equipment.

In the past, Taiwan accumulated a huge trade deficit with Japan but then gained a total trade surplus through aggressive exports to the U.S. market (Hokichi 1992, 178). Now with Taiwan's trade deficit with Japan on the rise and its trade surplus with the United States declining every year, Taiwan relies on the cross-strait trade to balance its trade account. As Taiwan's economy is still to a large extent fueled by the export drive, the mainland market now plays a crucial role in determining Taiwan's economic growth rate. Put in a nutshell, Taiwan still relies on Japan for imports but has been shifting its export dependence from the United States to the Chinese mainland.

Two problems arise from this major shift. The first one is economic; the second one, political. Taiwan's foreign exchange reserve, now standing at around $100 billion, is second only to Japan's. Taiwan's economy, however, cannot be properly characterized as advanced, on a par with OECD countries. And yet, as Taiwan's long-term capital outflow from 1986 to 1992 shows, Taiwan was the world's sixth largest overseas investor, after Japan, Germany, Switzerland, Britain, and the Netherlands, all well ahead of Taiwan in economic development and per capita income. That critical period was exactly when Taiwan needed to channel funds into developing new production technologies for its third import substitution.

Taiwan's outflow capital, however, went in pursuit of cheap labor in less-developed countries, particularly mainland China. The ratio of overseas to domestic investment for Taiwan was 21.4 percent in 1988, 33.9 percent in 1989, and 29.5 percent in 1990, four to six times as high as Japan's corresponding numbers. In 1991–1992, when Premier Hao Pei-tsun was in charge of the government, the ratio dropped to 9.2 percent and 6.6 percent. In 1993, with all the effort by the new Lien Chan cabinet to invigorate the economy, Taiwan's overseas investment grew by 87 percent. The trend continued through 1994. The government and the business community are both worried about a "hollowing up" of Taiwan's economy, that is, depleting of its industrial strength through capital outflow.

Accompanying accelerated overseas investment was a significant slowing down of Taiwan's economy. From 1980 to 1990, its annual growth averaged 8.25 percent, lower than the supergrowers mainland China (10.1 percent) and South Korea (9.9 percent) but higher than Hong Kong's 7.1 percent and Singapore's 6.3 percent (Barfield 1994, 59). But in the early 1990s Taiwan's economy slowed down to 5.02 percent in 1990, 7.24 percent in 1991, 6.02 percent in 1992, 5.87 percent in

TABLE 6–6
TAIWAN'S LABOR COST AND PER CAPITA GDP IN COMPARISON
WITH OTHER NICs, 1993 AND 1994
(U.S. dollars)

Country	Per Hour Labor Cost in Manufacturing, 1993	Per Hour Labor Cost[a]	Per Capita GDP, 1994	Per Capita GDP[a]	Per Capita GDP per Hour Labor Cost[a]
Taiwan	5.46	100	11,629	100	1.00
South Korea	4.93	90.29	8,470	72.84	0.81
Singapore	5.12	93.77	16,720	143.78	1.53
Hong Kong	4.21	77.11	20,050	172.41	2.24

a. Index: Taiwan = 100.
SOURCE: *United Daily*, March 22, 1995, p. 19.

1993, and 6.51 percent in 1994. At the root of the problem is the narrowing gap between labor productivity and wages, especially from an international perspective (table 6–6).

From 1990 to 1993, Premier Hau Pei-tsun counted on the ambitious six-year development plan to upgrade Taiwan's outmoded infrastructure and generate growth momentum by a huge infusion of government expenditures on hundreds of construction projects throughout the island. This stimulus proved of limited effect on economic growth, however, as there were serious underfulfillments caused by financial constraints and an eruption of scandals implicating high government officials (Wu 1994b, 50). Lien Chan, Hau's successor, was forced to slash government investment in mid-1993 and put the prospects of growth back onto the private sector. As has been demonstrated, counting on the private sector means relying on exports to mainland China as the growth engine. According to a survey made by the Ministry of Economic Affairs of 1,000 Taiwan firms in the mainland in 1994, however, Taiwan businessmen have tended to reduce their dependence on supplies from the island for materials, parts, and semifinished products (from 60–70 percent in 1992 to 55–61 percent in 1993). This trend shows that investment-driven exports may be on the decline. This being the case, Taiwan may very soon develop a trade deficit.

The second problem of Taiwan's dependence shift is the political risk involved in relying on the mainland market. Modern integration theories propose that economic exchanges are the optimal starting point to produce integrative momentum that may "spill over" to the political realm and achieve political amalgamation (Keohane and Nye 1975, 364, 396). Though economic interactions are usually beneficial to all the contracting parties and are less threatening to national sovereignty than any direct attempt at unification, political integration through economic interaction does not have to take a voluntary path as suggested by the integration theorists of the post–World War II era.

Adolf Hitler's strategy of creating a group of East European satellites through monopolies and monopsonies in the 1930s serves as a good example of how political dominance can be achieved through economic manipulation. As the cross-strait economic relations have developed into the most important link between Taiwan and the mainland, it seems only natural that Beijing will try to use economic ties to promote unification. Although the most immediate considerations of Beijing's Taiwan policy makers may be economic (Wu 1994c), that does not preclude the possibility that when push comes to shove, Beijing will not blackmail Taiwan through the growing economic link. That prospect haunts Taiwan's political leaders and forces them to take precautions.

Reorienting the Economy

Because of their understanding of Taiwan's increasing economic dependence on the Chinese mainland, economic planners in Taipei attempted to reorient the island's economy toward the international market in general and Southeast Asia in particular. In this context, bidding for membership in GATT and the WTO and building Taiwan into an Asia-Pacific operation center (*ya-t'ai ying-yun chung-hsin*) are aimed at expanding business opportunities for Taiwan as well as at diluting dependence on the mainland. The Southward Policy (*nan-chin cheng-ts'e*) championed by President Lee Teng-hui has an even sharper focus on directing Taiwan's overseas investment away from mainland China to Southeast Asian countries with abundant labor.

GATT and WTO membership and the Asian-Pacific operation center are mixed blessings in that, if realized, both will open a much broader arena for Taiwan's business activities, while making closer ties with mainland China inevitable. The World Trade Organization demands nondiscriminatory trade policies by members that would make Taiwan's constraints on cross-strait trade difficult to defend. The proposed Asia-Pacific operation center (which is basically an attempt to capture Hong Kong's position after 1997) is unthinkable for Taiwan if economic transactions across the Taiwan Strait are as restricted as they are now. In response to this situation, in May 1995 the ROC government appointed Kaohsiung Taiwan's "offshore shipping center," permitting the port to establish direct shipping links with mainland China. At the time of this writing, however, representatives from the two sides are still negotiating the terms of this limited opening.

Diluting Taiwan's economic dependence on the Chinese mainland through a greater degree of internationalization and liberalization is clearly an illusion, though, in the sense that mainland China has attracted such a volume of international business activities that opening up to the world market today means opening up to mainland China. This being said, it is still considered politically desirable to join international organizations and to facilitate international business transactions to reduce the political risks involved in cross-strait relations and to create bargaining chips for Taipei to deal with Beijing (Li Wen-chih 1994, 5). Whatever the merits of the two major internationalization plans, the Asia-Pacific operation center thus far remains basically a blueprint and a proposal, while the bid for membership in WTO has gone fairly far and may bear fruit soon, if the political pressure from Beijing can be effectively resisted by member states.

The other major government effort to reorient the economy is the Southward Policy championed by President Lee Teng-hui. Launched in the winter of 1993–1994, that policy aims to expand Taipei's political-economic influence into Southeast Asia, via President Lee's "vacation diplomacy," and to direct Taiwan's overseas investment toward Southeast Asian countries, away from mainland China. The government hopes that its signaling may tilt profitability toward the south and change the investment direction of private enterprises. It turned out, however, that only state enterprises and KMT corporations follow the lead of the government. Private investment continues to flow to mainland China.[8]

The bid for GATT-WTO membership, the attempt to build Taiwan into the Asia-Pacific operation center, and the Southward Policy are strategic moves to enhance Taiwan's economic position vis-à-vis mainland China in the context of Taiwan's increasing export dependence on

---

8. From January to July of 1994, 31.13 percent of Taiwan's overseas investment went to the mainland, totaling $467 million in 589 cases. The next largest receptor of Taiwan's outflowing capital was Hong Kong, with 27 cases and a sum of $113 million. Since most of Taiwan's investment in Hong Kong actually went to mainland China, a full 38.67 percent of Taiwan's overseas investment in this seven-month period was made across the Taiwan Strait. The Southward Policy did not produce any significant impact as none of the targeted countries were in the top nine receptors of Taiwan's capital in January–July 1994 (*United Daily* 1994, p. 19).

the mainland market. The shifting dependence from the United States to the Chinese mainland has its root in an outflow of massive capital from the island at a time when there is the greatest need for industrial upgrading. Taiwan's fundamental problem thus lies in its failure to conduct the third stage of import substitution. Without productivity gains comparable to increases in wages, it is only reasonable to expect continued capital outflow to the mainland and increasing dependence and vulnerabilities. Any offsetting strategies of internationalization and reorientation will have limited effect.

Compared with membership in the WTO, the Asia-Pacific operation center, and the southward policy, Taiwan's interest in the Asia-Pacific Economic Cooperation (APEC) forum is more political than economic. With the U.S. President Bill Clinton's strong support, APEC has rapidly evolved from a regional organization dedicated to creating "a community of Asia Pacific economies" at the Seattle summit to one committed to the goal of "free and open trade and investment" by 2010 for the industrial nations in the region and 2020 for the rest of the countries in the "Bogor Declaration." As one of the leading economies in the region, Taiwan believes it has every right to be included in the APEC activities and play an active role. Taipei is particularly keen on sending President Lee to the APEC summits that have been held in the United States, Indonesia, and Japan and will be sponsored by the Philippines at the end of this year. Each move, however, has been thwarted by Beijing, which insists on allowing only ministers from Taiwan to attend the APEC's summit meetings.

The 1995 APEC summit at Osaka proved disappointing not only to Taiwan for political reasons but also to the "Anglo-Saxons" (the United States, Australia, and New Zealand) for failing to fulfill the Bogor promises. Instead of opting for clear rules and targets to liberalize trade, the Osaka summit took into consideration the diverse circumstances in each economy and allowed member states to open their markets at the speed they chose, as long as they were done by the 2010 or 2020 deadlines. Even this last point was disputed by Malaysia, as reported in the *Far Eastern Economic Review* of November 30, 1995. Osaka was thus considered a triumph by the gradualist camp composed mainly of Asian countries, according to the *Economist* of November 11, 1995. During the meeting, Taiwan shared with other Asian countries, particularly Japan and South Korea, a deep concern over unchecked agricultural imports. Taipei was already busy dealing with the WTO's market-opening requirements and had no intention whatsoever of allowing a second-tier of trade liberalization to be imposed on it. Osaka's failure to produce a rule-based approach and fixed dates and targets thus did not worry Taiwan.

As Manila will host the fourth APEC summit, and Taiwan has developed massive economic clout in the Philippines, the chance for the Republic of China to send its newly elected president to the summit this time is greater than ever. Certainly, Beijing will resist the idea vehemently, putting Manila in a difficult position. At the summit, Taiwan will be much less concerned with the actual progress toward trade and investment liberalization than seeking an opportunity to break its international isolation and creating an impression that Taipei and Beijing are equals. With the PRC's missiles zooming across the Taiwan Strait on a regular basis, it is understandable that Taipei's leaders base economic policies on their political implications.

Two Trade Triangles

In an international context, Taiwan finds itself in two triangles that are particularly important. One such triangle is the United States-Japan-Taiwan. The other is the United States-the PRC-Taiwan. A common pattern is present in the two triangles. In both cases, an economically advanced exporter finds its export to the United States obstructed by large trade surpluses and resulting pressure from Washington; then it begins to circumvent that obstacle by selling producer goods to an economically backward exporter, using it as a manufacturing base for continued export to the U.S. market. In the first triangle, the advanced exporter is Japan; the backward one is Taiwan. In the second triangle, Taiwan is the advanced exporter, while mainland China is the backward.

Japan has long been in trade disputes with the United States, fueled by an ever-expanding trade deficit on the American side. Since 1985, the Japanese yen was forced to appreciate against the dollar, a tendency that has been accelerating recently. This long-term trend raised production costs in Japan to such a height that overseas investment became inevitable. Before the outward investment surge in the 1980s, however, Japan had already been extremely successful in establishing a manufacturing stronghold in Taiwan through "technical cooperation" with local businesses and by providing the largest portion of producer goods imports for Taiwan. As mentioned earlier in this chapter, this pattern was established in the 1960s. Thus, following our model, an economically advanced exporter, that is, Japan, circumvents trade obstacles by investing in an economically backward exporter, that is, Taiwan, selling Taiwan producer goods and directing it toward the North American market. In the 1980s, Taiwan's trade deficit with Japan and its trade surplus with the United States rose simultaneously to an unprecedented height. This phenomenon testifies to our observation.

This pattern has been repeated in the U.S.-PRC-Taiwan triangle. Here the advanced exporter is Taiwan. Since the 1980s, Taipei has been under tremendous pressure from Washington to reduce its trade surplus with the United States. The NT dollar began its abrupt appreciation against the greenback in 1987, a trend that continues into the 1990s. As a solution, Taiwan businesses began investing on the Chinese mainland to reduce their manufacturing costs. Whole industries were transplanted onto the mainland, including shoes, bicycles, and other products of which Taiwan was the world's leading exporter. Mainland-based Taiwan businessmen then purchased producer goods from Taiwan, where they have symbiotic relations with mid- and upstream manufacturers. The resultant investment-driven trade brought about huge surpluses for Taiwan, quite like the island's trade pattern with Japan, which provides producer goods for Taiwan's manufacturers and accumulates huge trade surpluses with Taiwan. Thus, in the 1990s the Chinese mainland has accumulated a huge trade deficit with Taiwan, at the same time replacing Taiwan as the country with the second largest trade surplus with the United States. This is exactly the same pattern that formed in the first trade triangle in the 1980s.

Circumventing trade obstacles by going through a downstream backward exporter does not necessarily mean a significant reduction of the advanced exporter's trade surplus with the United States. In this respect, Japan is likely to keep the largest trade surplus with the United States, even with Taiwan rapidly catching up and taking second place in the 1980s. The emergence of mainland China as Taiwan's downstream exporter, however, was indeed accompanied by a significant reduction of Taiwan's trade surplus with the United States. Now the PRC has taken Taiwan's position to accumulate the second largest trade surplus with the United States. The difference between the two triangles in this respect points out Taiwan's vulnerabilities. While Japan was able to move its low-tech manufacturing bases to backward exporters such as Taiwan and develop capital and technology-intensive exports for the U.S. market, thus keeping its trade surplus, Taiwan was merely doing horizontal investment, namely, shifting manufacturing resources to the Chinese mainland where labor and land prices are cheap but failing to develop products with high added value for export to the U.S. market. Another major difference is that Japan does not concentrate its investment in Taiwan or depend on Taiwan as its major export market for producer goods. Taiwan's investment concentration on mainland China is much greater, and its export dependence on the mainland market alarming.

The two triangles have evolved through pressure from across the Pacific. The Americans, by forcing one after another successful East

Asian exporter to change its mercantilist policies, brought about the circumventing strategy by the targeted country and created an opportunity for the emergence of a second group of aggressive exporters. As long as American protectionism is on the rise, there will be mounting pressure on Japan, Taiwan, and mainland China to redress the trade imbalance, a pressure that will most probably be met as the aggressive exporters shift their manufacturing bases to still more backward exporters. To be specific, the U.S. pressure on Japan to appreciate the yen further will force Japanese investors to expand their investment in Taiwan and other "tigers," thus increasing the export capacity of these second-tier exporters. The U.S. pressure on Taiwan to reduce its trade surplus will induce greater overseas investment with the Chinese mainland, the major recipient of Taiwan's outflowing capital. The result is more exports from Taiwan's businesses based on the mainland.

It would then be interesting to see how the PRC will receive the U.S. pressure and make adjustments. The Japanese response is to develop high production technology to offset partially the negative effects of high production cost. The Taiwanese response is horizontal investment in labor-abundant countries. Up to this point, Washington has been pressuring Beijing to open up its huge domestic market to redress the current trade imbalance through more exports to the Chinese mainland. Appreciation of the renminbi has not been tried. And yet, if that option is taken, the PRC will be ill equipped to adopt either the Japanese or the Taiwanese response: it lacks the necessary technological levels, or abundant capital, to adjust to rising production costs. The attraction of the Chinese market with a population of 1.2 billion who are rapidly getting rich remains the most powerful weapon in Beijing's hands to deal with pressure from the United States.

What then will be Taiwan's position in the two trade triangles? It is difficult to imagine Taiwan's shedding its bonds with Japan or reducing its engagement with the mainland. Taiwan is well situated in the second tier of East Asia's "flying geese formation," following Japan's lead. But it is exerting the same kind of influence on the third tier as Japan is exerting on itself. Its major danger is to "hollow up" by shifting its manufacturing and export capacities onto the Chinese mainland and to reduce its role in the two trade triangles to oblivion.

References

Baldwin, Robert E., Tain-jy Chen, and Douglas Nelson. *Political Economy of U.S.-Taiwan Trade*. Taipei: Chung-Hua Institution for Economic Research, 1992.

Barfield, Claude E. "U.S.-China Trade and Investment in the 1990s." In *Beyond MFN: Trade with China and American Interests*, edited by James R. Lilley and Wendell L. Willkie II. Washington, D.C.: AEI Press, 1994.

Chien Tse-yuan. *"Hsiang-kang tsai liang-an ching-chi chiao-liu te chung-chieh ti-wei: shih-cheng fen-hsi"* [An analysis of the intermediary role of Hong Kong in the economic exchanges between the two sides of the Taiwan Strait]. *Mainland China Studies* 36, no. 11 (1993): 69–81.

Hokichi, Yasuba. *"Ya-t'ai ching-chi te hui-ku yu chan-wang"* [The past and future of the Asian-Pacific economy]. In Li Ming, ed., *Chung-jih liang-kuo yu ya-t'ai ching-chi fa-chan* [China, Japan, and the economic development of the Asian-Pacific region]. Taipei: Institute of International Relations, 1992.

Johnson, Chalmers. "Political Institutions and Economic Performance: The Government-Business Relations in Japan, South Korea, and Taiwan." In *Asian Economic Development—Present and Future*, edited by Robert Scalapino, Seizaburo Sato, and Jusef Wanandi. Berkeley: University of California Press, 1985.

Keohane, Robert O., and Joseph S. Nye. "International Interdependence and Integration." In *Handbook of Political Science. Vol. 8, International Politics*, edited by Nelson W. Polsby. Menlo Park, Calif.: Addison-Wesley, 1975.

Lee, Ch'ing-p'ing. *"Liang-an ching-mao kuan-hsi chi tui ta-lu t'ou-tzu ying chu-i shih-hsiang"* [Cross-strait economic relations and important items for investing on the Chinese mainland]. Lecture to the Taiwan Chamber of Commerce, Vancouver, Canada, November 7, 1993.

Li Tsung-che. *"Chien-shih t'ai-shang tui-wai t'ou-tzi yu nan-hsiang cheng-ts'e"* [Review of overseas investment by Taiwan businessmen and the southward policy]. *Theory and Policy* 8, no. 3 (1994): 72–88.

Li Wen-chih. *"T'ai-wan fa-chan wei 'ya-t'ai ying-yun chung-hsin' te chan-lueh yi-i"* [The strategic importance for Taiwan to develop into the "Asian-Pacific operation center"]. *National Policy Dynamic Analysis* 91 (1994): 4–5.

Li Yu-ch'un. *Tui-wai t'ou-tzi tui wuo-kuo chih-tsao-yieh chih ying-hsiang yen-chiu pao-kao* [Research report on the impact of overseas investment on our manufacturing industry]. Taipei: Taiwan Institute of Economic Research, 1993.

Liang Kuo-shu and Hueh Ch'i. *"T'ai-wan tsai ya-t'ai ching-chi shih-tai suo pan-yen te chiao-se"* [Taiwan's role in the Asian-Pacific economic era]. In *Chan-wang tung-ya hsin-ch'ing-shih* [Looking ahead at the new East Asian situation], edited by Chang T'ai-lin. Taipei: Institute of International Relations, 1990.

Mainland Affairs Council. *Liang-an ching-chi t'ung-chi yueh-pao* [Monthly report on cross-strait economic relations]. Various issues.

Sah, Kung-ch'iang. *Chung-kung shih-nien ching-kai te li-lun yu shih-chien* [The theory and practice of the decade-old economic reform in mainland China]. Taipei: Institute of International Relations, 1991.

Ta-lu t'ou-tzu chih-nan [Guide to investment on the mainland]. Taipei: Chung-hua Institution for Economic Research, 1991.

United Daily, October 25, 1994.

Wu Jung-i and Ch'en Yen-huang. *Mei-shang t'ou-tzi te mao-i chi yi-chuan hsiao-kuo* [The trade and technology transfer effects of American investment]. Taipei: Institute of American Culture, Academia Sinica, 1988.

Wu Yu-Shan. *Comparative Economic Transformations: Mainland China, Hungary, the Soviet Union, and Taiwan*. Stanford: Stanford University Press, 1994a.

———. "Taiwan in 1993: Attempting a Diplomatic Breakthrough." *Asian Survey* 34, no. 1 (1994b): 46–54.

———. "Mainland China's Economic Policy toward Taiwan: Economic Needs or Political Scheme?" *Issues and Studies* 30, no. 9 (1994c): 29–49.

7
U.S.-ASEAN Trade and Investment in Pacific Perspective

Linda Y. C. Lim

The countries of ASEAN—the Association of Southeast Asian Nations comprising Brunei, Indonesia, Malaysia, the Philippines, Singapore, and Thailand—collectively constitute one of the largest and most rapidly growing economic regions of the developing world.[1] They have a combined population of 330 million, and most have enjoyed real growth of gross domestic product exceeding 6 percent a year for most of the past thirty years (table 7–1), including the early 1990s, when regional growth continued despite successive economic slowdowns in North America, Western Europe, and Japan. Real GDP in the region is projected to continue at a similar or even faster pace for the rest of the 1990s (Lim and Pang 1994; Lim 1995a).

The ASEAN countries have also been among the most open of developing economies in trade and foreign investment. Singapore, Malaysia, Thailand, and Indonesia rank among the top six developing countries in export shares of GDP and among the top ten in the value of their exports (table 7–2). Both exports and imports have been growing rapidly, and although most ASEAN countries run persistent current account deficits, they also have more than adequate foreign exchange reserves (table 7–3). In foreign direct investment inflows between 1988 and 1992, Singapore ranked second in the developing world (after China) with an average annual inflow of $4.3 billion, while Malaysia ranked fourth (after Mexico) with $2.7 billion, Thailand sixth (after Argentina) with $2 billion, and Indonesia tenth with $1.2 billion, as stated in the *Economist* of September 1994. Following three years of decline, foreign direct investment in Southeast Asia surged in 1994—

This chapter was prepared for the American Enterprise Institute project on U.S.-Asian trade. Thanks are due to Nathaniel Siddall for providing research assistance.

1. Vietnam joined ASEAN as its seventh member in July 1995 and is not considered here.

TABLE 7-1
BASIC INDICATORS OF THE ASEAN ECONOMIES, 1970–1996
(U.S. dollars)

Country	1993 Population (millions)	1993 GDP (billions of $)	GDP Growth per Year (%) 1970–80	1980–93	1994–96	1993 per Capita GNP ($)	GNP Growth per Capita 1980–93 (%)
Brunei	0.3	—	—	—	—	—	—
Indonesia	187.2	144.7	7.2	5.8	7.3	740	4.2
Malaysia	19.0	64.5	7.9	6.2	8.9	3,140	3.5
Philippines	64.8	54.1	6.0	1.4	5.9	850	−0.6
Singapore	2.8	55.2	8.3	6.9	8.4	19,850	6.1
Thailand	58.1	124.9	7.1	8.2	8.5	2,110	6.4

n.a. = not available.
SOURCE: World Bank, *World Development Report 1995*; Lim 1996.

TABLE 7–2

LARGEST EXPORTERS AMONG DEVELOPING ECONOMIES, 1993 AND 1994

Country	Exports, 1994		Exports/GDP, 1993	
	Billions of dollars	Rank	Percent	Rank
Hong Kong	151.4	1	143	2
China	120.8	2	24	8
Taiwan	93.7	3	40	4
Singapore	**96.4**	**4**	**168**	**1**
South Korea	96.0	5	29	6
Malaysia	**58.7**	**6**	**80**	**3**
Mexico	57.0	7	13	9
Brazil	44.5	8	8	10
Thailand	—	**9**	**37**	**5**
Indonesia	**36.8**	**10**	**28**	**7**

NOTE: ASEAN countries in bold.
SOURCE: International Monetary Fund, *Direction of Trade Statistics Yearbook 1995;* World Bank, *World Development Report 1995.*

when $24 billion went to Indonesia alone—and continued in 1995, leading to suggestions that the region might even be receiving "too much money" (Brauchli 1995).

As the world's largest trading nation, the United States has long been one of the two major external trade and investment partners of the ASEAN countries. The other is Japan, the world's second largest trading nation, which for additional reasons of geographical proximity (similar to that of the United States and Latin America) and resource complementarity (its dependence on energy and other raw material imports from ASEAN) has long outranked the United States as the largest single trade partner of the ASEAN region as a whole. In the 1980s, Japan's prominence on the world economic stage rose sharply as Japanese firms in many manufacturing industries posed an increasingly powerful competitive challenge to U.S. and European firms in global markets, running up persistent large bilateral merchandise trade surpluses with the United States in particular. At the same time, Japan's investment in ASEAN and other Asian countries grew dramatically in absolute terms, while U.S. investment shrank, beginning in the late 1980s.

Besides U.S. and Japanese firms, those from Western Europe have been trading with and investing in the region since early in the colonial era. More recently, the rapid economic development of the three East Asian newly industrialized economies (NIEs-3) South Korea, Taiwan,

TABLE 7-3

ASEAN EXPORTS, IMPORTS, CURRENT ACCOUNTS, AND FOREIGN RESERVES, 1993

(billions of U.S. dollars)

Country	1993 Exports		1993 Imports		1993 Current Account (billions of $)	1993 Foreign Reserves	
	Billions of $	Growth[a]	Billions of $	Growth[a]		Billions of $	Months of imports
Indonesia	33.8	6.7	28.1	4.5	−2.0	12.5	3.3
Malaysia	47.1	12.6	45.7	9.7	−2.1	28.2	4.5
Philippines	11.1	3.4	18.8	4.5	−3.3	5.9	3.3
Singapore	74.0	12.7	85.2	9.7	2.0	48.4	5.6
Thailand	36.8	15.5	46.1	13.8	−6.9	25.4	5.1

a. Percent per year, 1980–1993.
SOURCE: World Bank, *World Development Report 1995.*

and Hong Kong and the market-oriented economic reforms in China have increased the weight of these economies in world trade, and with it their trade with and investment in the ASEAN countries.

This chapter will examine and seek to explain the changing pattern and determinants of U.S. trade with and investment in the ASEAN countries, and their evolving bilateral trade relations, in the context of the broader Pacific regional trade and investment environment. It will draw on the scholarly as well as the popular business literature and on the latest descriptive statistics to focus particularly on the period since the late 1980s, with projections presented for the rest of the 1990s.

The United States, Japan, and ASEAN—A Pacific Trade Triangle?

The Issues. The U.S.-Japanese bilateral trade imbalance and resultant trade policy conflicts since the late 1980s have been and remain a matter of concern for the ASEAN countries. They fear that this conflict between their two largest external trade partners could affect them adversely—for example, through the raising of protectionist U.S. barriers to all nations, through U.S. targeting of Japanese exports originating in offshore plants in the ASEAN countries, or through special bilateral "managed trade" deals privileging U.S. exporters in the Japanese market. Although welcoming Japanese capital and technology, the ASEAN countries have also been concerned that, in the absence of counterbalancing flows from other countries, particularly the United States, those large inflows could make them more dependent on Japan with reduced choice and bargaining power in international trade, investment, and technology transfer. ASEAN's ballooning trade deficit with Japan since the late 1980s is also considered a problem.

At the same time, the United States has been concerned that Japan may be merely channeling its bilateral trade surplus with the United States through third countries by means of its manufacturing investments in ASEAN. It fears that Japan's massive capital investment in ASEAN since the late 1980s, together with its substantial aid to the region, well-known Japanese government-industry links, and transplantation of *keiretsu* business networks offshore, could signal an increasingly "monopolistic" domination by Japan of these large and fast-growing emerging economies. Their resulting close integration with the Japanese economy and Japanese international business networks might be prejudicial to U.S. competitors. To quote one analyst who has urged U.S. companies to invest more in Asia:

> The objective has to be to avoid or to pre-empt the de facto integration of Japanese capital, management and technology with the booming low-cost Asian economies. Otherwise [the

179

combination] would have stunning global competitive implications over the decade.[2]

A 1994 Carnegie Endowment for International Peace report also warned that inadequate investment was causing U.S. companies to be "marginalized in the world's fastest growing market," which could have "an adverse impact on U.S. growth, export and employment rates, and erode overall American influence in the region."[3]

Other observers take Japan's growing economic dominance in the Asian region as inevitable and by no means problematic (for example, Tokunaga 1992; Mourdoukoutas 1993; Abegglen 1994; Kwan 1994). According to one such observer, "There is no alternative. The position of Japan is one of economic dominance in the area, like it or not, and that position will not change significantly in this generation."[4]

The Evidence. Empirically, the first issue to consider is whether Japan has indeed increased its lead over the United States as ASEAN's major trade partner. The data in table 7–4 and figure 7–1 show that between 1980 and 1994 U.S.-ASEAN trade in dollar terms increased 4.2 times while Japan-ASEAN trade increased only 2.6 times, reducing the "excess" of Japan's total trade over U.S. total trade with the region from 84 percent in 1980 to a mere 14 percent in 1994.[5] The U.S. share of

---

2. Kenneth Courtis, first vice president of Deutsche Bank (Asia) based in Tokyo, quoted in Keatley (1994a). See also Encarnation (1992) and Dobson (1993) for more on the competitive dynamics of U.S.-Japan trade and investment in Asia.

3. Cited in Keatley (1994b).

4. Abegglen (1994), quoted in Lehner (1994). For a broader review of U.S.-Japan issues in Asia, see Cronin (1992).

5. The use of nominal dollar figures is problematic since exchange rates were far from stable during this period, when the yen appreciated by 40 percent against the dollar (see figure 7–6) and all ASEAN currencies that (except for Singapore) generally move with the dollar. A crude adjustment—converting the Japanese figures into local currency (yen) terms and deflating both U.S. and Japanese figures (with 1987 as the base year)—yields much smaller multiple increases all round, with the U.S.-ASEAN adjusted values being still much larger than the Japan-ASEAN adjusted values. Indeed, such an adjustment shows a significant (47 percent) decline in Japan's imports from ASEAN and a slight (14 percent) decline in its total trade with the region, in real yen terms. The general picture—reinforced by the share data reported in the text below—remains one of a much larger proportionate increase in U.S. than in Japanese trade with ASEAN over the period. Still, the data in these three paragraphs should be interpreted with the complex effects of the yen-dollar exchange rate in mind.

180

TABLE 7–4

U.S. AND JAPANESE TRADE WITH ASEAN, 1980 AND 1994

(billions of U.S. dollars)

	1980		1994	
	Billions of $	% share[a]	Billions of $	% share[a]
Japan				
Exports to ASEAN	13.2	10.1	60.4	15.3
Imports from ASEAN	24.6	17.4	37.8	13.8
Japan-ASEAN total trade	37.8	13.9	98.2	14.7
Trade balance	− 11.4	—	22.6	—
United States				
Exports to ASEAN	9.2	4.2	31.9	6.2
Imports from ASEAN	11.3	2.9	54.0	7.8
U.S.-ASEAN total trade	20.5	4.3	85.9	7.1
Trade balance	− 2.1	—	− 22.1	—
ASEAN				
Exports to Japan	24.6	34.6	37.8	15.1
Imports from Japan	13.2	20.7	60.4	22.2
ASEAN-Japan total trade	37.8	28.0	98.2	18.8
Exports to United States	11.3	15.9	54.0	21.6
Imports from United States	9.2	14.4	31.9	11.7
ASEAN-U.S. total trade	20.5	15.2	85.9	16.4

a. For Japan and United States, ASEAN share of their exports/imports/total trade. For ASEAN, Japan and U.S. shares of its exports/imports/total trade.
SOURCE: International Monetary Fund, *Direction of Trade Statistics Yearbook*, various years.

ASEAN's total trade increased slightly, from 15.2 percent in 1980 to 16.4 percent in 1994, while Japan's share actually fell, from 28 percent in 1980 to 18.8 percent in 1994 (figure 7–2). But both countries' shares of ASEAN's trade were greater than their respective shares of world trade, with the difference being particularly pronounced for Japan, which had only a 7.9 percent share of world trade but an 18.8 percent share of ASEAN's trade.

As shown by the exports and imports displayed in tables 7–5 and 7–6, the dollar value of Japan's exports to ASEAN increased 4.6 times between 1980 and 1994, whereas that of U.S. exports increased by only 3.5 times (table 7–4). In 1980, Japan's exports to ASEAN were 43 percent greater than U.S. exports to the region, but in 1994 the difference

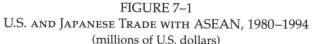

FIGURE 7–1
U.S. and Japanese Trade with ASEAN, 1980–1994
(millions of U.S. dollars)

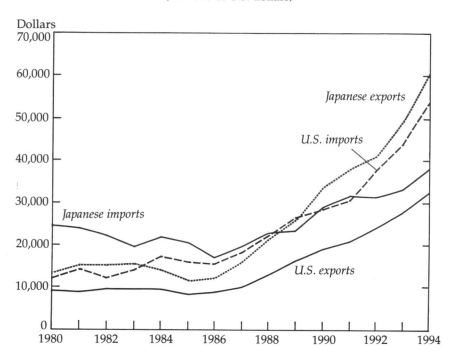

Source: International Monetary Fund, *Direction of Trade Statistics Yearbook,* 1987, 1995.

had widened to 89 percent (figure 7–1). While Japan's share of ASEAN's total imports increased slightly from 20.7 percent in 1980 to 22.2 percent in 1994, the U.S. share declined from 14.4 percent in 1980 (table 7–4 and figure 7–3), to 11.7 percent in 1994. At the same time, the share of both countries' exports to the ASEAN countries increased, with ASEAN accounting for a much higher share of Japan's exports (15.3 percent) than of the U.S. (6.2 percent) exports (table 7–4, figure 7–4).

As might be expected, imports present a different picture. Between 1980 and 1994, U.S. dollar imports from ASEAN increased 4.8 times while Japan's imports increased by only 54 percent. In 1980, Japan imported more than twice as much from the ASEAN countries as did the United States, but by 1994 it imported nearly one-third *less* than the United States. Japan's share of ASEAN's total exports fell by

182

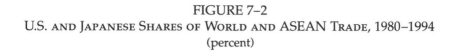

FIGURE 7–2
U.S. and Japanese Shares of World and ASEAN Trade, 1980–1994
(percent)

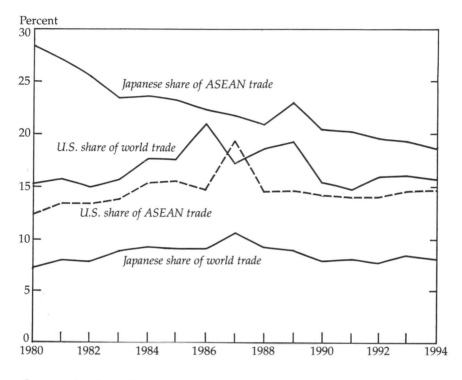

Source: See figure 7–1.

more than half, from 34.6 percent in 1980 to 15.3 percent in 1994, while the U.S. share of ASEAN's total exports rose from 15.9 percent to 21.6 percent (table 7–4 and figure 7–3). ASEAN's share of Japan's imports declined, while its share of U.S. imports increased (figure 7–4). ASEAN's trade surplus with the United States grew fifteen times between 1980 and 1994, while its $11.4 billion trade surplus with Japan in 1980 had turned into a $22.6 billion deficit by 1993—an amount 71 percent the size of ASEAN's surplus with the United States (table 7–4, figure 7–5).

Descriptive data like these would seem to support the argument that since the 1980s the ASEAN countries have increasingly imported machinery, equipment, and industrial raw materials from Japan, to which they sold little in return, processing these imports into finished

TABLE 7–5

ASEAN Exports by Destination Market, 1994

(billions of U.S. dollars)

From/To	United States	Japan	ASEAN	Other Asia	EU	World
Brunei	0.0	1.1	0.5	0.1	0.4	2.2
Indonesia	6.4	11.7	5.1	4.5	6.3	38.0
Malaysia	12.4	7.0	16.0	10.0	8.2	58.7
Philippines	5.2	2.0	1.2	1.9	2.3	13.4
Singapore	18.1	6.8	28.6[a]	21.0	12.5	98.2[a]
Thailand	9.7	7.5	5.7	6.5	6.6	41.8
ASEAN-6	51.8	36.1	57.1	44.0	36.3	252.3
Percent share to	20.5	14.3	22.6	17.4	14.4	100.0

a. Singapore does not publish data on its exports to Indonesia. This figure includes an estimate derived from Indonesia's data on its imports from Singapore, which is likely to be an understatement.
Source: International Monetary Fund, *Direction of Trade Statistics Yearbook 1995.*

TABLE 7–6

ASEAN Imports by Source Country, 1994

(billions of U.S. dollars)

To/From	United States	Japan	ASEAN	Other Asia	EU	World
Brunei	0.4	0.1	1.3	0.0	1.0	3.1
Indonesia	3.1	8.4	2.9	5.3	5.7	30.6
Malaysia	7.7	12.5	11.2	8.3	8.1	59.6
Philippines	4.2	5.4	2.6	4.2	2.3	22.5
Singapore	15.6	22.5	26.1[a]	12.4	12.4	105.6[a]
Thailand	6.1	16.5	6.0	9.0	7.8	54.3
ASEAN-6	37.1	65.4	50.1	39.2	37.3	275.7
Percent share from	13.5	23.7	14.2	14.2	13.5	100.0

a. Singapore does not publish data on its exports to Indonesia. This figure includes an estimate derived from Indonesia's data on its imports from Singapore, which is likely to be an understatement.
Source: International Monetary Fund, *Direction of Trade Statistics Yearbook 1995.*

FIGURE 7–3
U.S. AND JAPANESE SHARES OF ASEAN TOTAL EXPORTS AND IMPORTS,
1980–1994
(percent)

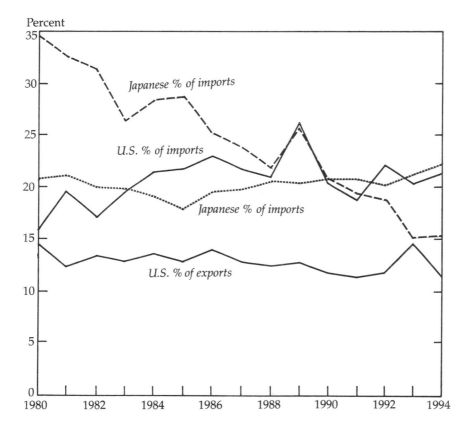

SOURCE: See figure 7–1.

manufactures that they then exported to the United States, from which they bought little in return. That is, in this "triangular trade" arrangement Japan has "diverted" its bilateral trade surplus with the United States through ASEAN. Figure 7–5 shows that as Japan's trade surplus with the United States declined in the late 1980s, its balance with ASEAN rose by a nearly equivalent amount, turning from deficit into surplus. This shift is all the more remarkable since the ASEAN currencies uniformly depreciated substantially against the yen.

There are, however, other possible explanations for the observed

185

FIGURE 7–4

ASEAN Shares of U.S. and Japanese Exports and Imports,
1980–1994
(percent)

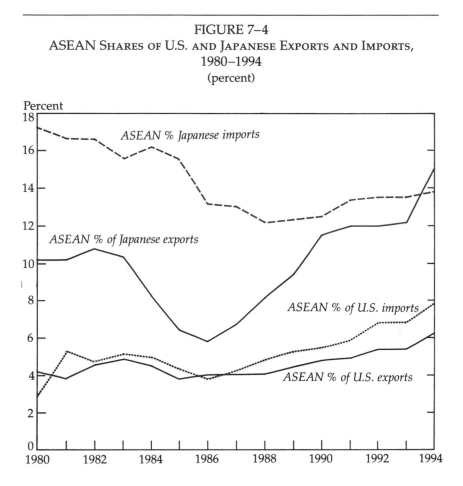

Source: See figure 7–1.

asymmetrical increase in ASEAN trade with the United States (concentrated in ASEAN exports) and with Japan (concentrated in ASEAN imports). Most important of these is the shifting commodity composition of trade,[6] based on the changing relative factor endowments and

6. The primary source for the information on commodity composition of U.S. and Japan trade with ASEAN countries presented below is the OECD Statistics Directorate, *Foreign Trade by Commodities*, Series C, Paris, France, various years. Individual country data from the following sources were also consulted: Economist Intelligence Unit, Country Reports on Indonesia, Malaysia, Philippines, Singapore, Thailand, 3rd Quarter, 1994; Department of Statistics, Malaysia, *External Trade Summary*, December 1993; Singapore Trade Develop-

FIGURE 7–5
ASEAN-U.S./JAPANESE BILATERAL TRADE BALANCES, 1980–1994
(millions of U.S. dollars)

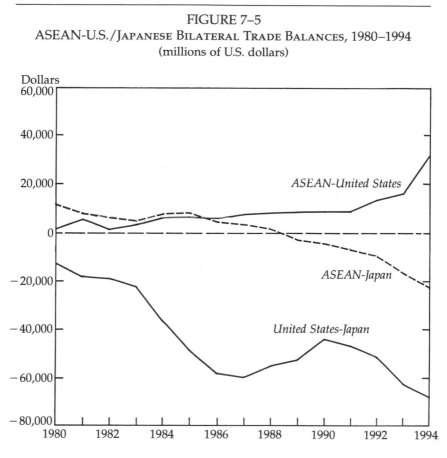

NOTE: First country's balance.
SOURCE: See figure 7–1.

different industrial structures of bilateral trade partners. Thus Japan's trade deficit with ASEAN in the early 1980s reflected the heavy concentration of its imports from ASEAN in oil, natural gas, and other raw materials in an era of high commodity prices. A decade later, commodity prices were much lower, and the composition of ASEAN exports had shifted significantly away from commodities (a disproportionate

ment Board, *Singapore Trade Statistics*, December 1993; Ministry of Commerce, Thailand, *Trade Statistics and Economic Indicators of Thailand 1992;* Central Statistics Bureau, Indonesia, *Indonesian Foreign Trade Statistics 1992;* National Statistics Office, Philippines, *Foreign Trade Statistics of the Philippines 1992.*

import for Japan) and into manufactures (a disproportionate import for the United States).

ASEAN imports from both the United States and Japan are remarkably similar, with machinery accounting for the largest commodity category by far, followed by other manufactured goods. Within these categories, however, there has been an asymmetry in the shares of U.S. and Japanese exporters by product. Thus, in the mid- to late 1980s Japan had a dominant share of ASEAN imports of products such as iron and steel, road vehicles, metals and metalworking, telecommunications, and general and specialized machinery. The United States had a dominant share in fertilizers, aircraft, and other transport equipment, and both countries had relatively equal shares of ASEAN imports of chemicals, office equipment, instruments, electrical machinery, and medical and pharmaceutical products (Gardner, Nie, and Mehta 1993).

This asymmetry reflects the influence of both the relative international competitiveness of U.S. and Japanese firms in particular commodity segments and the prevailing pattern of each country's industrial investments in ASEAN. Because Japanese firms are much more heavily and broadly invested in the ASEAN manufacturing sector and their subsidiaries here are more likely to import machinery and industrial materials from established suppliers in their home country—whether because of firm specificities or *keiretsu* networks—Japan ends up with a dominant share of ASEAN imports in these commodity segments. These are also the sectors likely to grow most rapidly as the ASEAN countries industrialize, resulting in the faster growth of their imports from Japan than from the United States. Tight linkages with Japanese supply sources also mean that ASEAN imports of capital and intermediate goods from Japan are relatively price inelastic. As a result, import values balloon as volumes adjust only marginally when the yen appreciates as it has since the mid-1980s (figure 7–6), deteriorating the terms of trade for ASEAN countries, whose currencies are more closely linked to the U.S. dollar.

Machinery is the most important U.S. import from ASEAN, with fuels second, whereas the "other" category is most important for Japan, followed closely by crude materials (table 7–7). This order reflects both Japan's dependence on imported raw materials (as compared with the more resource-abundant United States) and the heavy concentration of ASEAN exports to the United States in electrical and electronic "machinery" (including components and other intermediate inputs), much of it produced in wholly owned subsidiaries of U.S. high-tech multinationals in Singapore, Malaysia, Thailand, and the Philippines, thereby constituting intrafirm trade by U.S. companies.

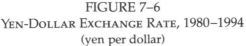

FIGURE 7–6
Yᴇɴ-Dᴏʟʟᴀʀ Exᴄʜᴀɴɢᴇ Rᴀᴛᴇ, 1980–1994
(yen per dollar)

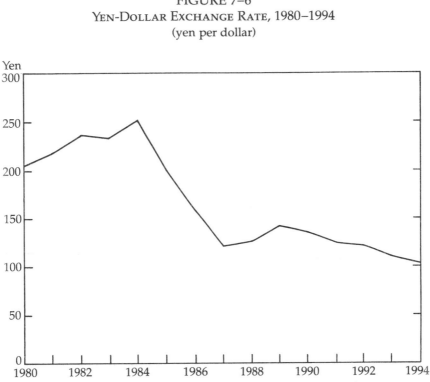

Sᴏᴜʀᴄᴇ: International Monetary Fund, *International Financial Statistics Yearbook 1995.*

Thus, the ASEAN case conforms to theoretical predictions and global empirical validation of a close relationship between trade and foreign direct investment (Naya and Imada 1990; Graham and Anzai 1994), which has been offered as an explanation for the persistence of the U.S.-Japan bilateral trade imbalance itself. In the ASEAN case, large and rapidly increasing imports of capital and intermediate goods from Japan beginning in the late 1980s are attributed to the "new wave" of Japanese manufacturing investment, which surged into the region following the appreciation of the yen since 1985 (Phongpaichit 1990; Holloway 1991; Lim and Pang 1991; Ramstetter 1991; Tokunaga 1992; Doner 1993; Craib 1994). This investment pattern established supply linkages not only between Japanese-owned subsidiaries in ASEAN, their parent companies, and *keiretsu* affiliates in Japan but also between

189

TABLE 7–7
COMMODITY SHARES OF U.S. AND JAPANESE TRADE
WITH ASEAN COUNTRIES, 1992
(percent)

SITC Code	U.S. Exports	U.S. Imports	Japan Exports	Japan Imports
0 Food	1	5	0	8
1 Beverages/tobacco	0	1	1	3
2 Crude materials	0	3	1	27
3 Fuels	1	28	1	7
4 Oils	0	0	1	1
5 Chemicals	5	7	7	5
6 Manufactures[a]	14	3	20	3
7 Machinery	70	39	51	11
8 Manufactures[a]	7	8	5	5
9 Other	3	5	15	31
Total	100	100	100	100

a. SITC Code 6 classifies manufactures by raw material, for example, leather, plastics, and the like. Code 8 is miscellaneous manufactures.
SOURCE: OECD Statistics Directorate, *Foreign Trade by Commodities*, Series C, 1992.

other Asian-owned firms in the region and Japanese suppliers (Doherty 1995).

This wave of Japanese investment in ASEAN induced by the high yen of the late 1980s tapered off in the early 1990s for several reasons, including consolidation of the new investments, economic recession and financial downturn in Japan, and competition from new low-cost investment sites in China, Vietnam, and India. In contrast, U.S. investment in ASEAN, after declining precipitously in the late 1980s (LeCraw 1991; Lim 1991a), increased in the early 1990s until it matched new Japanese investment in the region in 1993 (figure 7–7). Breakdowns by host country are provided in tables 7–8 and 7–9.[7] If this increase is sustained, U.S. exports to ASEAN—which also took off during this period, though not quite as rapidly as exports from Japan (figure 7–1)— should grow even more rapidly, aided by the fall of the dollar against such ASEAN currencies as the Singapore dollar and the Malaysian

7. Note, however, that U.S. and Japanese FDI data are not readily comparable. See also Graham and Anzai (1994), who show a rising ratio of U.S. to Japanese FDI flows in East Asia (not just ASEAN) from 23 percent in 1987 to 63 percent in 1992.

FIGURE 7–7
U.S. AND JAPANESE DIRECT INVESTMENT IN ASEAN, 1989–1993
(billions of U.S. dollars)

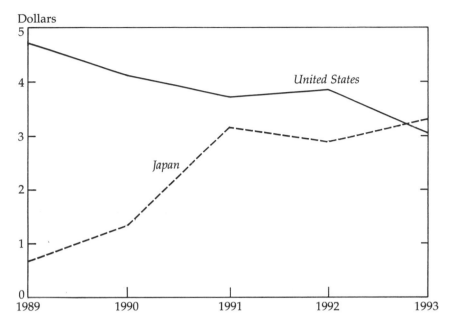

SOURCE: Ministry of Finance, Japan, and U.S. Department of Commerce, various years.

TABLE 7–8
JAPAN'S DIRECT INVESTMENT IN ASEAN, 1989–1993
(billions of U.S. dollars)

Host Country	1989	1990	1991	1992	1993	1989–93
Indonesia	0.6	1.1	1.2	1.7	0.8	5.4
Malaysia	0.7	0.7	0.9	0.7	0.8	3.8
Philippines	0.2	0.3	0.2	0.2	0.2	1.1
Singapore	1.9	0.8	0.6	0.7	0.6	4.6
Thailand	1.3	1.2	0.8	0.7	0.6	4.6
ASEAN-5	4.7	4.1	3.7	4.0	3.0	19.5

SOURCE: Ministry of Finance, Japan.

TABLE 7–9
U.S. Direct Investment in ASEAN, 1989–1993
(billions of U.S. dollars)

Host Country	1989	1990	1991	1992	1993	1989–93
Indonesia	−0.1	0.7	0.4	0.8	0.6	2.4
Malaysia	0.1	0.2	0.3	−0.1	0.3	0.8
Philippines	0.0	0.2	0.0	0.1	0.1	0.4
Singapore	0.2	0.6	1.1	1.3	1.8	5.0
Thailand	0.4	0.3	0.2	0.5	0.2	1.6
ASEAN-5	0.7	2.0	2.0	2.6	3.0	10.2

Source: U.S. Department of Commerce, *Survey of Current Business,* various issues.

ringgit. Note that the high-value "machinery" category accounts for a higher proportion of U.S. (70 percent) than of Japan's (51 percent) exports to ASEAN (table 7–7).

Stimulated by Japan's economic recovery and the continued relentless record appreciation of the yen against the dollar, a "fourth wave" of new Japanese investment into ASEAN has already begun (Craib 1994)[8] and may be expected to add to the boom in exports of Japanese capital goods to the region in years to come. But unlike past waves, the target markets for exports produced by new and expanded Japanese factories in ASEAN are less likely to be in the United States and other Western countries and more likely to be within Asia at large, including Japan itself and especially China, the East Asian NIEs, India, and the whole of Southeast Asia as their respective domestic markets develop.

As more of established and future Japanese industrial capacity is transplanted to Southeast Asia in line with shifting comparative advantage and the high yen, the question arises whether the "flying geese" model of Japan's economic integration with its developing Asian neighbors will become at least partially realized. This model views Japan as the technological leader of a flock of industrializing Asian nations, progressively transferring to them industries and tech-

---

8. See also "The Great Escape," *Far Eastern Economic Review,* March 30, 1995, pp. 54–56; "Surviving Yen Fever," *Asiaweek,* April 21, 1995, pp. 50–53. The Japanese Finance Ministry reported in May 1995 that Japan's direct investment in Asia as a whole swelled by 47 percent in fiscal 1994, reaching a record $9.7 billion, which accounted for the largest (24 percent) share of Japan's total overseas direct investment (Reuters Business Report, May 16, 1995).

nologies that are no longer competitive in Japan itself. It is the thinking behind such comments as:

> Companies like Hitachi or Toshiba will go from being assemblers to being parts makers. In assembly, Japan has no value-added; but parts and materials like ceramic composites are still black boxes; there, the Japanese still have power because they can't be imitated—yet.[9]

> Japan has no option but to carve out a new niche—probably services or high-tech like the information industry.[10]

The flying-geese model is not popular among other Asians. They prefer to see their economies as independent players on the world stage, with access to technology from other countries as well and with the prospect of overtaking (rather than always following behind) Japan in such sectors or product niches as shipbuilding and DRAM chips (South Korea), computer parts and peripherals (Taiwan), and financial services (Hong Kong and Singapore). Indeed, the continued relevance of the flying-geese model is challenged by observations such as these:

> Some very good, efficient companies in Korea, Taiwan, Hong Kong and Southeast Asia are giving the Japanese a pretty hard time. These guys are now exporting to Japan and . . . . they seem to be doing very well.[11]

> Other East Asian companies are slowly eating away the market share of Japanese companies, in the rest of the world as well as Japan.[12]

> Companies are starting to shift high value-added production offshore. Hitachi, for example, recently said it would open a factory in the Philippines to make computer disk drives. . . . Product design is moving abroad too. Companies like Matsushita are carrying out increasingly sophisticated research and development work in their laboratories in Malaysia and Singapore at a fraction of what it would cost at home.[13]

Thus, even as Japan loses its "monopoly" of high value-added activities, their transfer to ASEAN and other Asian developing countries will serve to integrate these economies closer with each other and with Japan itself.

---

9. Tadahiko Abe of the LTCB Research Institute, quoted in "Surviving Yen Fever" (1995).

10. C. H. Kwan, Nomura Research Institute, quoted in ibid.

11. Andrew Shipley of Lehman Brothers, Tokyo, quoted in ibid.

12. C. H. Kwan, quoted in ibid.

13. Quoted in "The Great Escape" (1995).

The Policy Implications. To date, the ASEAN countries appear to have been beneficiaries of the U.S.-Japan bilateral trade conflict and its policy consequences. The exchange rate realignment favored (or at least approved) by the United States as a means of reducing its trade deficit with Japan has encouraged a massive outflow of investment capital from Japan to ASEAN and other Asian countries as the strong yen has made producing in Japan for world markets too costly, while investing overseas became cheap for Japanese firms.[14] This effect of the strong yen was felt in the late 1980s and more recently in the mid-1990s. Financial liberalization in Japan, pushed by the United States, has also encouraged the outflow of capital to ASEAN (Frankel 1993).

U.S. government pressure on Japan to open its domestic markets has also benefited the ASEAN countries—most notably Thailand in the case of rice—but also increasingly in manufactures as well. U.S. pressure on Japan to liberalize domestic distribution restrictions, for example, has created new outlets for low-price, labor-intensive, mass consumer goods manufactured in ASEAN and China, as in the case of the U.S. chain store Toys-R-Us. Even market-share agreements foisted on Japan by the United States could benefit the ASEAN countries, since many U.S. high-tech multinationals have subsidiaries there producing semiconductors, other electronic components, telecommunications and computer parts, and equipment that could be exported to Japan to fill these quotas. In sectors like glass and automobiles, where transport costs are heavy, U.S. companies may be induced by the opening of the Japanese market to invest in production in the ASEAN countries for export to Japan. Already, pressures from both the high yen and aggressive U.S. market-opening policies in the automotive sector are likely to encourage more Japanese imports of parts from Japanese subsidiaries and *keiretsu* suppliers in ASEAN. Even retaliatory restrictions on Japanese exports to the United States may divert U.S. purchases to Japanese or other multinational subsidiaries based in ASEAN. Investment liberalization in Japan is also likely to benefit ASEAN, since U.S. companies that invest there may be more likely than Japanese companies to import parts and components from abroad, including those from the competitive ASEAN economies nearby.

Thus, U.S. trade policy toward Japan has had the effect of increasing Japanese investment in, exports to, and imports from the ASEAN countries, thereby stimulating their economic growth and continued integration with the Japanese economy, in the financial as well as the

---

14. Note that for some ASEAN countries the high yen also imposes costs, particularly by increasing the debt service burden for countries like Indonesia, which have been large recipients of Japanese aid and loan capital.

real goods sectors. By improving cost competitiveness, deepening industrial structures, and raising incomes in the ASEAN countries, this process also increases ASEAN exports to and imports from the United States. More U.S. investments are then attracted to the ASEAN countries to supply both Japan and the rest of the Asian regional market, and that investment in turn increases U.S. exports to the greater number of U.S. affiliates here. The descriptive data do indeed suggest such a "circular" as distinct from "triangular" relationship, with both the U.S. and Japan's two-way trade with and investment in ASEAN growing in tandem.

Conflicts exist among the three trading partners—the United States, Japan, and ASEAN—but they tend to be bilateral rather than trilateral in origin and expression. Much like the United States, for example, the ASEAN countries are vexed by their persistent and enlarging bilateral trade deficits with Japan, which they believe is "not buying enough" from them, especially in manufactures. Until very recently, the ASEAN countries have also been disappointed with what they see as inadequate levels of U.S. investment as compared with Japan's, with its attendant trade implications. Since the ASEAN countries' domestic firms generally lack the technological and marketing capability to penetrate Japanese markets and Japanese firms in ASEAN have not always been eager to do so, ASEAN must arguably rely on U.S. and other Western firms with more sophisticated technology to produce there for export to Japan, thereby helping to reduce the ASEAN trade deficit with that country.

At the same time, various U.S. trade policies toward developing countries have caused friction between the United States and its ASEAN trade partners—most notably the U.S. multilateral promotion (through the WTO) and bilateral practice (through its own GSP program) of linking market access with achievement in such social policy areas as human rights, labor rights, democracy, and the environment (as well as in the more familiar arena of intellectual property rights). The ASEAN countries tend to see such a trade linkage as unwarranted political interference in their domestic affairs, as "disguised protectionism," and as disregard of the effect of different cultural standards and stages of development on social policy performance. They have been more receptive to U.S. pressures to protect intellectual property rights. In Singapore, Malaysia, and the Philippines, this protection is facilitated by established British and American legal systems and heavier dependence on high-tech multinationals, and in the first two cases by higher income and technological levels as well. Protection of intellectual property rights is more a problem in U.S. trade relations with Indonesia and especially Thailand.

195

Japan, however, is under pressure by the ASEAN countries to localize the supplier base, technological capacity, and management of its industrial investments in these countries, and many of its multinationals are apparently making major efforts in this direction (Biers 1994). If successful, such efforts may well eventually reduce the bilateral ASEAN-Japan trade deficit but not necessarily the bilateral ASEAN-U.S. surplus. Reducing that surplus will require U.S. companies to expend more investment and marketing efforts in ASEAN, mirroring those of the Japanese. In this effort, the boost the strong yen has given to their competitiveness in this region is already a help.[15]

Both the United States and Japan have on occasion called on ASEAN and the other Asian countries to support them in their trade conflicts with each other (Davis 1994). ASEAN's loyalties are divided in this regard. On the one hand, Japan is their largest aid donor, foreign investor, and trade partner (twice as important as the United States in the case of Indonesia, for example). Like Japan, the ASEAN countries also run trade surpluses with the United States, and they share its fears of U.S. protectionism, which might well be directed to them at a later date. As previously mentioned, the ASEAN countries also have their own bilateral trade conflicts with the United States, for which they need Japan as a willing and supportive champion. On the other hand, the United States is a very important aid donor, foreign investor, and trade partner (second only to Japan, which it overtakes in some sectors and countries in some years) that is valued as a counterweight to overdependence on Japan. The ASEAN countries share U.S. frustration with Japan for its persistent bilateral trade surpluses with them, and as discussed earlier, they often stand to benefit from the success of U.S. market-opening pressures on Japan.

The United States has also been encouraging the ASEAN countries themselves to liberalize their markets, and in this context it needs to be wary of alienating them by any move to restrict their access to its own market—whether through social policy linkage or other protectionist measures. For both the United States and Japan, the ASEAN market for their respective exports is growing much more rapidly than each

---

15. In 1994, for example, the sales of U.S. auto companies in Asia increased dramatically from a very low base, because of the "yen umbrella," as the prices of auto parts and vehicle imports into ASEAN from Japan rose relative to those of similar imports from U.S.-owned companies in Europe, North America, and Australia. U.S. auto companies like General Motors and Chrysler are also actively investing in new assembly plants in the ASEAN countries. In other industries, the United States is also a likely beneficiary of machinery purchases diverted from Japan because of the high yen.

other's (albeit larger) market and will provide an important source of growth for their economies in the future. Both economic superpowers therefore need to be aware of and sensitive to the effects of their bilateral conflicts over trade policy on ASEAN (and other nations). Both will also find ASEAN a valuable ally in their conflicts with each other and in their support for global trade liberalization through the WTO. Both can aid in the ASEAN countries' continuing unilateral trade and investment liberalizations (motivated by domestic political and economic pressures) by the example of their own. And the United States in particular can advance its trade and economic self-interest in ASEAN by promoting more investment and participation by U.S. firms—especially small and medium-sized firms, which lag behind their Japanese counterparts—in the booming ASEAN regional market.

Japan's accelerating economic integration with ASEAN and other newly industrializing and developing economies in Asia—fostered in part by U.S. trade and exchange-rate policy—poses some potential challenges for the United States as it seeks to correct its bilateral trade deficits with all countries in the region. U.S. companies will face more competition in the opening Japanese home market from the exports of Japanese subsidiaries in Asia, which have the advantage of combining high-tech with low cost as well as established cross-border customer-supplier relationships. Sourcing cheap components from Asia will also give Japan's home exports a new competitive edge in world markets, helping them to avoid the effects of the high yen. Increased Japanese manufacturing in Asia may make those markets less penetrable to U.S. companies, given the transplantation of *keiretsu* networks and the Japanese head start in developing local relationships and other first-comer advantages. The Japanese position may hold back U.S. export and market share increases in the region despite the price competitiveness imparted by the weak dollar. Japan may also become more resistant to U.S. trade pressure since it has access to an alternative market that (taking all of Asia together) is already larger and growing much more rapidly than the U.S. market.[16]

---

16. Economic developments are arguably accompanied by political-psychological changes, causing Japan to see itself increasingly as "part of Asia" rather than as part of the Western-dominated community of advanced industrial nations. (See "Japan's New Identity," *Business Week*, April 10, 1995, pp. 108–19; and "Coming Home," *Asiaweek*, April 28, 1995, pp. 22–27.) For example, much has been made of Japan's embrace of Malaysian Prime Minister Mahathir Mohamed and former Singapore prime minister Lee Kuan Yew for their vociferously articulated views of "standing up against the West," particularly the United States. Mahathir—who in the 1980s embarked on a "Look East" policy that sought to emulate Japan's development and deepen Malaysia's economic

Finally, several related developments may impede the recovery of the U.S. dollar from its long and sharp decline against the yen. They include the heavier flow of Japanese and U.S. portfolio and direct investment in Asia, reducing capital inflows to and enlarging capital outflows from the United States itself; the increasing switch of Asian central bank currency reserves out of the dollar and into the yen as their economic links with Japan grow;[17] and the maintenance of U.S. bilateral and regional current account deficits with Asia as Japanese industrial relocation makes it more difficult for U.S. companies to increase home exports to Japan and Asia.

These developments do not, however, mean that Japan's progressive economic integration with the ASEAN countries is an unmitigated gain to Japan and a threat to the United States:

• Integration does not mean domination—Japan is only one, albeit the largest, of ASEAN's external economic partners, all of whose combined trade and investment is dwarfed by domestic production and investment in the region (with the exception of Singapore).

• U.S. trade and investment in the region are also increasing, though not always as rapidly as Japan's.

• Japan's trade and investment with Western industrial nations, which are its developmental peers, will continue growing in absolute terms,[18] though again not as rapidly as its trade and investment with Asian developing countries.

• Closer Japan-ASEAN economic integration carries with it the potential for heightened bilateral conflict, as well as for mutual benefit.

• Many Japanese themselves fear that the relocation of Japanese industry to ASEAN and other developing Asian countries will mean a "hollowing out" of their home industrial base with consequent job and income losses.[19]

But for both the United States and Japan in ASEAN, regional growth is likely to mitigate if not overwhelm any negative displacement effects.

ASEAN, the NIEs, and China

The past decade has seen an increase in ASEAN's trade with other Asian countries besides Japan—most notably with the three northeast

---

ties with that country—has even cowritten with Ishihara Shintaro a book entitled *The Asia That Can Say No*.

17. See "Passing the Buck," *Asiaweek*, May 5, 1995, p. 48.

18. See, for example, the argument in "A Question of Balance," *Economist*, April 22, 1995, pp. 21–23.

19. For a skeptical evaluation of this concern as it relates to Asian countries in general, see Graham and Anzai (1994).

TABLE 7–10
ASEAN Trade with Hong Kong, Taiwan, South Korea,
and China, 1983 and 1994
(billions of U.S. dollars)

	ASEAN Exports To		ASEAN Imports From	
	1983	1994	1983	1994
Hong Kong	2.2	—	2.4	7.7
Taiwan	1.3	8.6	2.1	12.4
China	0.7	6.6	1.1	8.2
South Korea	2.1	7.6	1.4	11.8
Greater China[a]	4.2	30.3	5.6	28.3
Hong Kong, Taiwan, S. Korea	5.6	31.3	5.9	31.9
Hong Kong, Taiwan, S. Korea, China	6.3	37.9	7.0	40.1

a. Hong Kong, Taiwan, and China.
Source: International Monetary Fund, *Direction of Trade Statistics Yearbook,* 1990 and 1995.

Asian newly industrialized economies of South Korea, Taiwan, and Hong Kong and with China. By 1993, the collective share of these trading partners in ASEAN's total trade has risen to 80 percent that of Japan's, with exports and imports rising 6 and 5.7 times respectively between 1983 and 1994 (table 7–10). While ASEAN's trade with Hong Kong is in surplus, trade with Taiwan and Korea favors the NIEs, with Taiwan enjoying a particularly large surplus. Trade with China (the smallest of these four partners) turned from surplus to deficit in 1994.

Primary commodities dominate ASEAN exports to these economies, especially food and raw materials, and petroleum products to Hong Kong, while their imports (except for China) are concentrated in manufactures and, increasingly, machinery and equipment. As in the case of Japan, this pattern reflects the wave of NIE investments, which surged into the ASEAN countries in the late 1980s and 1990s in response to (U.S.-encouraged) currency appreciation in Korea and Taiwan, the loss of U.S. Generalized System of Preferences (GSP) privileges for the NIEs, and rising labor costs in their home countries (associated with both labor scarcity and stronger labor movements following U.S.-supported political democratization in Korea and Taiwan after 1987). These developments caused a serious loss of cost competitiveness in NIE-based labor-intensive export manufacturing industries, which were consequently relocated to lower-cost ASEAN countries (Wells 1993; Stoltenberg and Lim 1994). In some years, NIE investments in ASEAN, if Singapore is included, exceeded those of Japan.

NIE investments in the ASEAN countries have generated corresponding trade flows. For example, ASEAN-manufactured exports to the United States have grown, especially in previously NIE-dominated labor-intensive product lines like textiles, garments, footwear, toys, housewares, electrical and electronic components and consumer products, and miscellaneous manufactures—artificial flowers, Christmas tree lights, and the like. In addition, ASEAN imports of machinery and equipment from both the investing NIEs and Japan, which is still a major supplier of machinery and equipment to the NIEs themselves, have increased. This industrial relocation did not, however, result in substantially more ASEAN-manufactured exports to the NIE home markets, since they are small consumers of the manufactures produced relative to their productive capacity for the global market. ASEAN exports to the NIEs did increase, but largely as a function of rising demand and trade liberalization in the NIEs, particularly in agriculture.

By the early 1990s, NIE investment of this type in the ASEAN countries had slowed dramatically, reflecting both slackening world market demand as the industrial countries rolled into recession and the diversion of "footloose" NIE labor-intensive investment into newly opened, lower-cost locations in China, Vietnam, and elsewhere. NIE investors are currently experiencing a renewal of interest in the ASEAN countries, particularly Indonesia and the Philippines, for both political and economic reasons as difficulties emerge, for Taiwan firms especially, with respect to concentrating investments in China and as continued investment liberalization makes the ASEAN countries more attractive in their own right. At the same time, industrial country markets are recovering, and the ASEAN and wider Asian developing-country markets themselves are booming. This recovery makes it more likely that NIE investments in the production of low-priced consumer goods and industrial components in the ASEAN countries will increase the exports of those manufactures to a wider range of markets, with the regional market taking an ever-increasing share.

Besides the NIEs, China is rapidly developing as both a supplier of imports for and a destination market for exports of the ASEAN countries, in both food and raw materials and, increasingly, manufactures. Investment and other business links between China and the ASEAN countries are also considerable and growing rapidly. ASEAN-based Overseas Chinese companies and some government-linked companies (particularly from Singapore) are investing in agribusiness, services, real estate, infrastructure, and manufacturing in China. The single largest foreign investor in China, for example, is the Charoen Pokphand group of Thailand, which is involved in activities as diverse as chicken farming, fast-food restaurants, motorcycle assembly, and telecommunications, often with foreign partners (both Western and Japanese) providing the technology. The second largest foreign investor in China is the Malaysian tycoon Robert Kuok, whose Kerry Group has large holdings in real estate (the Beijing World Trade Center), hotels (the Shangri-la Group), soft drinks (Coca-Cola), and telecommunications, again with both Western and Japanese partners. The Salim and Lippo Groups of Indonesia and various Chinese-Filipino conglomerates are also major foreign investors in China.[20]

Meanwhile, Chinese companies, particularly in the trade and banking sectors, are beginning to establish footholds in the ASEAN countries themselves. These links should eventually generate related trade flows, though the composition and direction of these are likely to be complex and their magnitude difficult to predict.

Unlike the United States, Japan, and the NIEs, for example, the ASEAN countries are not at a stage of development where they can provide indigenous technology to China on a significant scale, though some exceptions are likely, notably in construction, agribusiness, and raw material extraction and processing. The ASEAN-based facilities of multinationals from all over the world, however, may become sources of supply to China of international-standard machinery, equipment, and technology already adapted to developing-country circumstances. Products manufactured in multinational subsidiaries in ASEAN may also be exported to China as they already are to other industrialized and developing countries. Examples here would include Matsushita room air-conditioners made in Malaysia, Motorola telecommunications equipment made in Singapore, and Otis elevators made in Thailand. Multinationals that invest in production facilities in China may also seek to supply the ASEAN market from there. And Chinese companies themselves may eventually produce in the ASEAN countries for export as well as for the domestic market. Political considerations may be involved here, as in the reported case of a Chinese state enterprise that plans to produce military equipment in Malaysia for export to "other developing countries" (including the Middle East).

In general, ASEAN trade with the NIEs, China, and other emerging Asian economies—most notably Indochina, Myanmar (formerly

---

20. Some securities analysts even advise that the best way for foreign portfolio investors to benefit from China's economic boom is to buy stock in overseas Chinese-owned companies in the ASEAN countries, where economic fundamentals are much stronger and political risk much lower than in China itself.

TABLE 7–11
SHARES OF ASEAN TOTAL TRADE, 1983 AND 1994
(percent)

Country or Group	1983	1994
United States	16.0	16.4
European Union	10.8	14.1
Japan	23.5	18.8
China	1.2	2.8
Taiwan	2.2	4.0
Hong Kong	3.1	4.4
Greater China	6.5	11.2
Korea	2.3	3.7
Hong Kong, Taiwan, S. Korea	7.6	12.6
ASEAN	23.5	18.2

SOURCE: International Monetary Fund, *Direction of Trade Statistics Yearbook*, 1990, 1995.

Burma), and India—is expected to continue growing more rapidly than its trade with the mature Japanese, North American, and Western European economies (table 7–11). This trend simply reflects the more rapid growth of these economies and their openness to international trade and investment. The emerging regional division of labor is likely to be both more complex and more diverse than the "neocolonial" pattern observed with the United States and Japan (in which the ASEAN countries essentially exchange low-tech products for high-tech products) and to become more completely integrated into ASEAN's global trade with Japanese and non-Asian trade partners.

Regional Preferential Trade Arrangements

The increase in intraregional trade and investment in Asia since the 1980s is by now a well-established and well-recognized phenomenon, as indicated by the larger share of the region's international trade and investment now accounted for by Asian countries rather than by non-Asian partners. Rather than resulting from regional bureaucratic policies, most of this increase in intraregional economic links has been led by the private sector and motivated by market forces as individual countries liberalized their trade and investment regimes. Rapid developments are also occurring at the subregional level where new forms of private-sector–public-sector collaboration linking trade and investment are moving across national boundaries (Toh and Low 1993; Lim 1994).

AFTA. At the regional level, the most significant development for the ASEAN countries is the ASEAN Free Trade Area (AFTA) (Park 1993). AFTA was first inaugurated on January 1, 1993 (partly in response to fears of trade diversion resulting from NAFTA and European single-market integration), with a target completion date of 2008 (or fifteen years). In late 1994 the timetable for achieving tariff-free regional free trade was accelerated by five years, to 2003, and in late 1995, to 2000, with a three-year extension for Vietnam and, later, Cambodia, Laos, and Myanmar, which are expected to join ASEAN by the year 2000. The announced acceleration is in part a reaction to aggressive U.S.-led moves to turn the seventeen-member Asia-Pacific Economic Cooperation (APEC) forum into a much larger regional free trade area, which would subsume AFTA and within which the ASEAN countries would have a much less influential role than they do now as the only formal regional trade grouping within Asia.

Motivation aside, the current low level of intra-ASEAN trade,[21] continuing national-level trade liberalization in individual ASEAN countries, and the high and rising level of ASEAN economic integration with non-ASEAN trade partners suggest that even if it is successfully implemented, AFTA is unlikely to make a major difference in ASEAN trade patterns. Where it will have an effect is in boosting the competitiveness—through competition and scale effects—of particular industrial sectors that are currently heavily protected and in making ASEAN countries more attractive as investment locations for multinationals seeking to produce there to supply the entire large and rapidly expanding regional market (Lim 1993).

Much of the new trade flows generated by AFTA will reflect underlying patterns of comparative advantage among the ASEAN countries that national-level trade liberalizations will also achieve. Differences in comparative advantage also underlie the division of labor and resultant trade flows between the ASEAN countries on the one hand and Japan and the NIEs on the other. The agreed-upon eventual expansion of ASEAN to include Vietnam, Cambodia, Laos, and Myanmar will significantly heighten comparative advantage differences and hence trade within the enlarged regional grouping. Particular institutional developments within ASEAN—in both the public and

---

21. The share of intra-ASEAN trade in ASEAN's total trade has remained at less than 20 percent for over twenty years. Most of this is accounted for by trade between free-trading Singapore (which accounts for 40 percent of ASEAN's total trade) and its neighbors, especially Malaysia, which has relatively low tariffs and many free trade or export processing zones, and Indonesia.

TABLE 7–12
SHARES OF ASEAN EXPORTS TO VARIOUS COUNTRIES, 1993
(percent)

From or To	ASEAN	EAEC	APEC	World Total (billions of $)
Indonesia	13.0	60.9	76.3	26.8
Malaysia	27.8	56.7	78.8	47.1
Philippines	7.0	38.1	77.9	11.3
Singapore	24.4	54.7	75.4	75.9
Thailand	12.7	45.6	68.5	37.1
ASEAN-6	20.7	53.9	75.8	208.2

SOURCE: International Monetary Fund, *Direction of Trade Statistics Yearbook 1994.*

the private sectors and in collaborations between the two—will also facilitate intragroup trade (Lim 1994, 1995b).

The existence of strong complementarities between the ASEAN economies and their industrial country trade partners makes it unlikely that the partners will suffer from trade diversion as a consequence of AFTA. On the contrary, given the region's rapid growth prospects and openness to foreign investment, positive dynamic growth effects are likely to outweigh any negative static redistributive effects of the preferential trading bloc on nonmember countries, which will have an added incentive to participate in the enlarged regional market through direct investment. The NIEs' and China's trade with ASEAN may be more subject to trade diversion, as AFTA favors Singapore (and possibly Malaysia) over the other NIEs in medium-technology sectors, and Indonesia and (when admitted) Indochina and Myanmar over China in labor-intensive low-technology sectors.

Among non-ASEAN members, initially Japanese companies may be expected to benefit the most from AFTA, as they increase efficiency by reallocating production among facilities that they have already established in the different ASEAN countries. But U.S. companies previously discouraged by the small size and fragmentation of the ASEAN market will also benefit if they respond to AFTA by investing there. Companies of all nationalities can better benefit from scale economies and efficient regional divisions of labor within the grouping.

APEC. Unlike AFTA, preferential free trade at the APEC level will affect a very large share—about three-quarters (see tables 7–12 and

TABLE 7–13
SHARES OF ASEAN IMPORTS TO VARIOUS COUNTRIES, 1993
(percent)

To/From	ASEAN	EAEC	APEC	World Total (billions of $)
Indonesia	9.2	49.1	62.5	28.3
Malaysia	19.7	61.6	79.6	45.6
Philippines	10.6	51.7	72.2	18.0
Singapore	24.4	59.6	75.8	88.8
Thailand	11.9	57.0	69.6	46.1
ASEAN-6	18.2	57.4	73.7	229.4

SOURCE: International Monetary Fund, *Direction of Trade Statistics Yearbook 1994*.

7–13)—of ASEAN's total trade. Both trade creation and trade diversion will be greater for individual ASEAN countries. For example, Indonesia will face more competition from China and Malaysia will face more competition from Mexico and Taiwan for both foreign investment and export markets within the region. At the same time, the ASEAN countries will obtain freer access to a much larger regional market than can be provided by ASEAN members alone. By the same token, they will account for a much smaller share of the total APEC market, and their influence on group decision making will be correspondingly less.

Despite the agreement at the November 1994 Bogor summit to establish APEC-wide regional free trade by the year 2020, it is likely that the ASEAN countries (except for Singapore) will prefer to go slow on APEC free trade, since they need the growth promised by the resulting trade creation less than they fear the competition from the accompanying trade and investment diversion and the loss of influence from submergence in a much larger regional grouping. Both multilateral free trade under the World Trade Organization and regional free trade under AFTA are also more important to ASEAN than APEC-wide free trade. ASEAN's own history suggests that it will be inclined to resist the institutionalization of APEC along the lines of either the European Union or the North American Free Trade Agreement, both of which are seen as too bureaucratic and inflexible. As in the case of AFTA, the ASEAN countries' main positive interest in APEC is in its policies to encourage intraregional investment—through, for example, the proposed harmonization of investment standards and regulations—since the grouping includes the chief source and host countries for ASEAN foreign direct investment. The noncommittal outcome of the November 1995 Osaka APEC summit would appear to be exactly to ASEAN's taste.

EAEC. Malaysia's proposal for an East Asian Economic Caucus (EAEC) that will function as an "informal forum" within APEC, involving all its Asian members only, is interesting here for several reasons. A smaller group (EAEC), within which ASEAN forms the only organized subregional grouping, would increase ASEAN's decision-making influence within the larger group (APEC), if prior support could be obtained—by "consensus"—from other members within the EAEC. Certainly, the ASEAN grouping's relative importance to its other Asian trade partners would be greater within EAEC than within APEC.

Thus, EAEC could be used to slow down APEC moves toward a trans-Pacific free trade area, since its most aggressive proponent, the United States, would be excluded, and many EAEC countries themselves (including Japan, China, and Korea) are not eager for rapid trade liberalization of their national economies. At the same time, the EAEC countries could move informally toward freer trade among themselves that would reduce the added value of further free trade with the already relatively barrier-free non-EAEC APEC members. This arrangement would reduce the threat of investment as well as trade diversion from ASEAN to Mexico and other potential future Latin American members of APEC, particularly from the United States. EAEC support could also be invaluable in strengthening ASEAN's bargaining power vis-à-vis the United States in remaining bilateral trade disputes such as the social links issue, on which EAEC members are united against the U.S. position.

Whereas the other ASEAN countries and China have supported Malaysia's EAEC proposal—albeit with varying degrees of enthusiasm—Japan and Korea were, until recently, opposed to the idea. This hesitancy reflected their continued heavier reliance on the U.S. market and the importance of the United States to each of them as a counterweight to the respective influence of (for Japan) China and (for Korea) Japan. But in 1994, Japan in particular softened its stand against the EAEC. This change reflected both its frustration with the United States in their bilateral trade conflicts and the decisive shift in Japan's own export market dependence from North America to Asia. For both Japan and Korea, their economic future arguably lies much more with the booming markets in China and Southeast Asia than with the United States.

For ASEAN, the putative initiator of the EAEC proposal, the pri-

206

mary challenge to regional trade policy is arguably to ready its own economies for free trade on a step-by-step basis. ASEAN is already likely to be a major beneficiary of the Uruguay Round of the General Agreement on Tariffs and Trade, which liberalized trade in agriculture and textiles in which ASEAN is highly competitive but limited liberalization of trade in services in which (except for Singapore) it is not. Meanwhile, individual ASEAN members are already proceeding with national-level trade-barrier reductions unilaterally. Free trade under AFTA would further liberalize a relatively modest proportion of ASEAN's total trade, whereas free trade under APEC would subject a much larger share of these very open and still developing economies to broader and more intense global competition (tables 7–12 and 7–13). The EAEC—which was once strongly opposed, and is still not favored, by the United States—may be a useful institutional means for ASEAN both to build closer economic relations with its increasingly important Asian trade and investment partners and to restrain the pace of APEC-wide free trade if it ever gets off the ground.

Growth Triangles. Intraregional trade and investment within East Asia and ASEAN itself are already growing rapidly, mostly as the result of private enterprise and market forces rather than of any regional preferential trade arrangements (Lim 1994). Several subregional "growth triangles" have also appeared within ASEAN: the original Singapore-Johor (Malaysia)-Riau (Indonesia) triangle; the Northern Triangle encompassing Penang (Malaysia), north Sumatra (Indonesia), and southern Thailand; the East ASEAN Growth Area, involving Sabah (east Malaysia), eastern Indonesia, and the southern Philippines; and the Golden Quadrangle, which will link eastern Burma, northern Thailand, northern Laos, and adjacent southwestern provinces of China. These novel institutional arrangements have already contributed to the increased movement of people, goods, and capital between contiguous provinces in different countries, without the need for national-level or regionwide liberalization (Toh and Low 1993; Lim 1994).

U.S.-ASEAN Trade Relations in Pacific Perspective

This chapter has argued the following main points.

- U.S. trade with ASEAN has been expanding fast and will continue to do so in the foreseeable future. Factors underlying this growth include rapid growth and industrial deepening of the ASEAN economies, continuing multilateral and national-level trade liberalization, increased international competitiveness of both the ASEAN and the

U.S. economies, and increased U.S. investment in ASEAN.

• U.S.-ASEAN trade growth has exceeded the pace of Japan-ASEAN trade growth, with a rising U.S. and a falling Japanese share of total ASEAN trade. ASEAN exports to the United States have increased much more rapidly than ASEAN exports to Japan, while the reverse is true for ASEAN imports. ASEAN now accounts for a higher share of U.S. exports, U.S. imports, and Japan's exports, but a lower share of Japan's imports, than in the 1980s. Factors underlying this development include changes in the commodity composition of ASEAN trade, commodity price and exchange-rate changes, and trade flows and institutional networks generated by Japanese investments. The decline in ASEAN's share of Japan's imports should eventually be reversed by the currently accelerated yen-driven relocation of Japanese industrial production to ASEAN, including in more sophisticated components.

• The ASEAN countries have generally benefited from U.S.-Japan trade policy conflicts, the results of which have often contributed to opening the Japanese market for ASEAN exports while diverting Japanese investments to ASEAN. ASEAN still has bilateral trade policy problems with Japan—over its persistent and growing bilateral trade deficit—and with the United States—over intellectual property rights and the linkage of social policy to market access.

• ASEAN trade with the East Asian NIEs and China has grown more rapidly than its trade with Japan or the United States, reflecting the more rapid growth and liberalization of these economies and trade flows generated by increased investments from the NIEs in ASEAN and from the NIEs and ASEAN in China. Burgeoning intraregional trade flows are highly complex and dynamic and are related to extraregional as well as other intraregional trade relationships.

• The expansion of intraregional trade in the Asia-Pacific, including ASEAN, reflects private sector actions and market forces based on shifting and complementary comparative advantages among neighboring Asian countries. In addition, ASEAN countries have initiated an ASEAN Free Trade Area among themselves and are members of APEC, a much larger trans-Pacific regional grouping that also seeks to achieve regional free trade and investment links. The ASEAN countries prefer a slower move to APEC-wide free trade than does the United States and have proposed an alternative East Asian Economic Caucus within APEC that might help them influence this process.

Trade and investment within the ASEAN region involving all their external partners are increasingly linked and increasingly determined by market forces as national policies continue to be liberalized. Thus, future U.S.-ASEAN trade patterns and relations will be more and more influenced by U.S. private investments in the region, which need to be diversified beyond the extractive and high-tech sectors where they are now concentrated into a broader range of industrial and consumer products. This expansion will enable the United States to increase its exports to ASEAN and will generate closer competition with Japanese and other Asian companies. Because of the rapid rates of growth anticipated for the regional market, heightened competition will not involve zero-sum outcomes but is likely to include new partnerships between the United States and its Asian competitors on an eventual global as well as regional scale.

For example, some U.S. companies like 3M and Dana are already leveraging relationships with Japanese customers, partners, and suppliers, developed in the U.S. and Japanese home markets in the 1980s and 1990s, to enter the ASEAN market where those same Japanese companies have well-established operations.

For the ASEAN countries, the recent spurt in U.S. trade and investment is very welcome, not only for the stimulus it gives to regional growth but also for the opportunities it presents for a more diversified dependence on external sources of capital, technology, and markets even as the region itself develops greater technological and market self-sufficiency. A continued strong U.S. economic presence in Asia at large also helps encourage continued regionwide economic liberalization and more transparent business practices that will benefit the ASEAN countries and their home companies as well. Opportunities for private sector collaboration between ASEAN and U.S. companies—for example, in the emerging markets of China, India, and Vietnam as well as in established ASEAN markets—will expand. ASEAN companies can partner with U.S. companies to learn the technology that they require to compete with more technologically advanced Japanese and NIE firms (with which such partnerships are already common), while U.S. firms can partner with ASEAN companies to benefit from their established business networks and knowledge of local markets and cultures. The resulting two-way trade—and investment as well—flows will be complex but mutually beneficial.

In short, U.S. fears that growing ASEAN trade and investment links with other Asian countries, especially Japan, will result in the progressive exclusion of U.S. companies from this large and dynamic regional growth market appear to me to be overstated. Like U.S. fears, claims from the Japanese side that ASEAN and other developing countries' integration into Japanese regional business networks will be both inevitable and complete may be unfounded. Other scholars have shown statistically that to date there is no such "regional" or "Japan" bias to evolving patterns of intraregional trade and investment within

Asia (Frankel and Kahler 1993; Frankel and Wei 1994). The Japanese have some historical and institutional advantages that parallel disadvantages that U.S. firms face in operating in ASEAN (Doner 1993). But these barriers to the entry of U.S. firms are by no means absolute or immutable, as already suggested by the increase in U.S. trade and investment in the region since 1990.

Rather, any institutional and historical barriers appear to be readily overwhelmed by global and regional macroeconomic developments and by trade and investment liberalization in individual countries, including in Japan itself. At the same time, firms in the ASEAN countries—whose private sectors are heavily dominated by overseas Chinese companies[22]—are maturing and internationalizing their operations and have both the incentive and the wherewithal to diversify their dependence on external trade and investment partners. Like enterprises from the NIEs, they provide new elements of diversity and competition within the Asian regional economy even as it becomes progressively integrated by intraregional trade and investment. The resultant broadening and deepening diversification, increased competitiveness, and expanding Asian regional links of the already large and fast-growing ASEAN market enhance both its attractiveness to U.S. firms and their ability to participate effectively there. Japanese economic domination and the evolution of exclusionary business practices by other Asian actors are, if anything, on the wane, though the continued market-driven expansion of Japanese business networks in ASEAN does increase their competitive presence in Asia.

Needless to say, even more active and widespread U.S. participation in the region's trade and investment is necessary and welcomed by both U.S. and ASEAN governments and businesses—to preserve and enhance the global competitiveness and market share of U.S. corporations, to expand and improve Asian production systems and technology, and to increase competition and consumer choice in Asian markets. In a region and a world where falling trade and investment barriers, market-oriented economic reforms, and the expanding internationalization of firms are inextricably intertwining the fortunes not only of different countries but also of firms of different nationalities in those countries, the "us versus them" mentality that previously often colored U.S. and Japanese views on their respective relations with third countries has become obsolete.

---

22. For more on the overseas Chinese and their role in economic regionalization in Southeast Asia, see Lim 1991, 1992, 1994; Lim and Gosling 1995.

References

Abegglen, James C. *Sea Change: Pacific Asia as the New World Industrial Center.* New York: Free Press, 1994.

Biers, Dan. "Japanese Investors in Asia Face Pressure to Localize." *Asian Wall Street Journal Weekly,* August 15, 1994.

Brauchli, Marcus. "Foreign Capital Holds Key in Southeast Asia." *Wall Street Journal,* January 23, 1995.

Craib, Anne. "Japan and the United States in Southeast Asia in the 1990s." *JEI Reporter* no. 32A. Washington, D.C.: Japan Economic Institute, August 19, 1994.

Cronin, Richard P. *Japan, the United States, and Prospects for the Pacific Century.* Singapore: Institute of Southeast Asian Studies, 1992.

Davis, Bob. "U.S. Seeks Other Asian Nations' Support during Testy Trade Battle with Japan." *Wall Street Journal,* February 22, 1994.

Dobson, Wendy. *Japan and East Asia: Trading and Investment Strategies.* Singapore: Institute of Southeast Asian Studies, 1993.

Doherty, Eileen M., ed. *"Japanese Investment in Asia: International Production Strategies in a Rapidly Changing World."* Conference report. Asia Foundation and the Berkeley Roundtable on the International Economy, San Francisco, 1995.

Doner, Richard F. "Japanese Foreign Investment and the Creation of a Pacific Asian Region." In *Regionalism and Rivalry: Japan and the United States in Pacific Asia,* edited by Jeffrey A. Frankel and Miles Kahler. Chicago: University of Chicago Press, 1993, pp. 159–216.

Encarnation, Dennis J. *Rivals beyond Trade: America versus Japan in Global Competition.* Ithaca, N.Y.: Cornell University Press, 1992.

Frankel, Jeffrey A. "Is Japan Creating a Yen Bloc in East Asia and the Pacific?" In *Regionalism and Rivalry: Japan and the United States in Pacific Asia,* edited by Jeffrey A. Frankel and Miles Kahler. Chicago: University of Chicago Press, 1993, pp. 53–88.

Frankel, Jeffrey A., and Miles Kahler, eds. *Regionalism and Rivalry: Japan and the United States in Pacific Asia.* Chicago: University of Chicago Press, 1993.

Frankel, Jeffrey A., and Shang-Jin Wei. "Is a Yen Bloc Emerging?" In *Economic Cooperation and Challenges in the Pacific: Japan, Korea, China, the United States and the Economies of East Asia,* edited by Robert Rich. Washington, D.C.: Korea Economic Institute of America (forthcoming).

Gardner, James, Winter Nie, and Raj Mehta. "An Exploratory Study of U.S. and Japan Export Patterns in Industrializing Asian Countries." *Journal of Asian Business* 9, no. 3 (summer 1993): 1–16.

211

Graham, Edward M., and Naoko T. Anzai. "The Myth of an Asian Economic Bloc: Japan's Foreign Direct Investment in East Asia." *Columbia Journal of World Business* 29, no. 3 (1994): 6–15.

"The Great Escape." *Far Eastern Economic Review*, March 30, 1995, 54–56.

Holloway, Nigel, ed. *Japan in Asia.* Hong Kong: Review Publishing Company, 1991.

International Monetary Fund. *Direction of Trade Statistics Yearbook.* Washington, D.C.: IMF, various years.

Keatley, Robert. "U.S. Diplomats, on an Unusual Mission, Urge American Firms to Give Asia a Try." *Wall Street Journal,* June 24, 1994a.

———. "Many U.S. Companies Still Shun Asia, Raising Doubts about America's Growth." *Wall Street Journal,* September 30, 1994b.

Kwan, C. H. *Economic Interdependence in the Asia-Pacific Region.* New York: Routledge, 1994.

Lecraw, Donald J. "Trading Blocs in Southeast Asia and the Pacific Rim." *Journal of Southeast Asia Business* 7, no. 2 (spring 1991): 36–52.

Lehner, Urban C. "Asia's Banker and Big Brother." *Wall Street Journal,* 1994.

Lim, Linda Y. C. "Explaining the Decline of U.S. Investment in Southeast Asia." *Journal of Southeast Asia Business* 7, no. 2 (spring 1991a): 90–93.

———. "The New Ascendancy of Chinese Business in Southeast Asia." Paper presented at the 43rd annual meeting of the Association for Asian Studies, The Changing Dynamics of Dominance, April 14, 1991b, New Orleans.

———. "The Emergence of a Chinese Economic Zone in Asia?" *Journal of Southeast Asia Business* 8, no. 1 (winter 1992): 41–46.

———. "Engines of Regional Integration in Asia." In *AFTA after NAFTA.* Washington, D.C.: Korea Economic Institute of America, 1993, pp. 145–59.

———. "The Role of the Private Sector in ASEAN Regional Economic Cooperation." In *South-South Co-operation in a Global Perspective,* edited by Lynn K. Mytelka. Paris: OECD Development Centre, 1994, pp. 125–68.

———. "Economic Outlook: ASEAN 1995–1996." In *Regional Outlook: Southeast Asia 1995–1996.* Singapore: Institute of Southeast Asian Studies, 1995a, pp. 34–50.

———. "Models and Partners: Malaysia and Singapore in Vietnam's Economic Reforms." In *Marketization in Southeast Asia,* edited by Scott Christensen and Manuel Montes. Stanford University and East-West Center Press (forthcoming).

Lim, Linda Y. C., and L. A. Peter Gosling. "Economic Growth, Liberalization and Ethnic Relations: The Chinese in Southeast Asia." In *En-*

trepreneurial Minorities and Modern Nationalism, edited by Anthony Reid and Daniel Chirot (forthcoming).

Lim, Linda Y. C., and Pang Eng Fong. *Foreign Investment and Industrialization in Malaysia, Singapore, Thailand and Taiwan.* Paris: OECD Development Centre, 1991.

———. "The Southeast Asian Economies: Resilient Growth and Expanding Linkages." In *Southeast Asian Affairs 1994.* Singapore: Institute of Southeast Asian Studies, 1994, pp. 22–33.

Mourdoukoutas, Panos. *Japan's Turn: The Interchange in Economic Leadership.* Lanham, Md.: University Press of America, 1993.

Naya, Seiji, and Pearl Imada. "Trade and Foreign Investment Linkages in ASEAN Countries." In *Foreign Direct Investment in ASEAN,* edited by Soon Lee Ying. Kuala Lumpur: Malaysian Economic Association, 1990, pp. 30–58.

OECD Statistics Directorate. *Foreign Trade by Commodities.* Series C.: Paris: OECD, various years.

Park, Chin Kuen. "The ASEAN Free Trade Area: Concepts, Problems and Prospects." In *AFTA after NAFTA.* Washington, D.C.: Korea Economic Institute of America, 1993, pp. 127–42.

Phongpaichit, Pasuk. *The New Wave of Japanese Investment in ASEAN.* Singapore: Institute of Southeast Asian Studies, 1990.

Ramstetter, Eric D., ed. *Direct Foreign Investment in Asia's Developing Economies and Structural Change in the Asia-Pacific Region.* Boulder, Colo.: Westview Press, 1991.

Stoltenberg, Clyde D., and Linda Y. C. Lim. "Investment in South-east Asia." In *Taiwan Trade and Investment Law,* edited by Mitchell Silk. Hong Kong: Oxford University Press, 1994, pp. 247–68.

"Surviving Yen Fever." *Asiaweek,* April 21, 1995, pp. 50–52.

Toh, Mun Heng, and Linda Low, eds. *Regional Cooperation and Growth Triangles in ASEAN.* Singapore: Times Academic Press, 1993.

Tokunaga, Shojiro, ed. *Japan's Foreign Investment and Asian Economic Interdependence.* Tokyo, Japan: University of Tokyo Press, 1992.

U.S. Department of Commerce. *Survey of Current Business,* various issues.

Wells, Louis T., Jr. "Mobile Exporters: New Foreign Investors in East Asia." In *Foreign Direct Investment,* edited by Kenneth A. Froot. Chicago: University of Chicago Press, 1993, pp. 173–98.

World Bank. *World Development Report 1994.* Washington, D.C.: World Bank, 1995.

Index

Abe, Tadahiko, 193n
Abegglen, James C., 180n
Admiral Co., 12, 147
Aerospace sector, 136
Agency for International Development, 116
Agriculture and food, 169
  ASEAN trade, 15, 199, 200, 207
  China, sector growth, 110
  China trade, 90, 91, 95, 105
  East Asia-Japan trade, 5, 57, 64, 67
  Korea-U.S. trade, 122–23
  Taiwan, 11, 12, 150
Aircraft industry, 93, 188
Anam Co., 137
Andean Pact, 45, 46
Anderson, Kim, 24
Antidumping laws, 37, 41, 120, 122
Anzai, Naoko T., 190n
Apparel. *See* Textiles and apparel trade
Appliances, 5, 60–64, 69, 70
Argentina, 27, 46, 47, 51, 120n
Asia-Pacific Economic Cooperation (APEC) forum, 36
  ASEAN views, 15–16, 204–8
  Asian perspective, 4, 40–45, 49
  China policy, 8, 101, 106
  establishment, 2, 39
  Korea view, 10–11, 132–35, 142, 143
  policy recommendations, 6, 50, 82–86
  Taiwan policy, 13, 168–70
  U.S. policy, 2–3, 11, 31, 33, 34, 38–40, 169, 203, 206
Association of South East Asian Nations (ASEAN), 99, 103, 105
  ASEAN Free Trade Agreement (AFTA), 15, 16, 203–5, 207, 208

ASEAN-Japan-U.S. trade triangle, 14, 179–98, 208
  China and NIEs trade, 14–15, 198–202, 208
  countries comprising, 13, 175
  economic growth, 13–14, 175–79
  EU trade relations, 48
  foreign direct investment figures, 42
  income per capita, 18
  Japan trade structure, 5, 57, 67
  Korea trade relations, 10, 128
  population, 14, 175
  regional preferential trade arrangements, 15–16, 202–7
  U.S. trade relations, 16, 120n, 177, 207–10
Audiovisual equipment, 57
Australia, 3, 6, 39, 40, 85, 169
Automotive trade
  ASEAN-Japan-U.S. trade triangle, 70, 188, 194, 196n
  China-United States, 93
  East Asia patterns, 57
  Japan-U.S. negotiations, 16, 50, 141
  Korea, 10, 99, 122, 136
  rules of origin, 37

Baker, James, 32
Baldwin, Robert, 52
Banking sector, 89, 94–95
Bank of China, 91
Bank of Japan, 101
Bark, Tae Ho, 9–11
Bayard, Thomas O., 140n
Beijing World Trade Center, 201
Bergsten, C. Fred, 40, 47
Bhagwati, Jagdish, 35–37, 140n
Big emerging markets (BEMs) policy, 2, 10, 120

215

A NOTE ON THE BOOK

*This book was edited by
Ann Petty, Dana Lane, and Cheryl Weissman
of the staff of the AEI Press.
The index was prepared by Nancy Rosenberg,
and the figures were drawn by Hördur Karlsson.
The text was set in Palatino, a typeface
designed by the twentieth-century Swiss designer
Hermann Zapf. Coghill Composition Company,
of Richmond, Virginia, set the type,
and Edwards Brothers of Lillington, North Carolina,
printed and bound the book,
using permanent acid-free paper.*

The AEI PRESS is the publisher for the American Enterprise Institute for Public Policy Research, 1150 17th Street, N.W., Washington, D.C. 20036; *Christopher DeMuth*, publisher; *Dana Lane*, director; *Ann Petty*, editor; *Leigh Tripoli*, editor; *Cheryl Weissman*, editor; *Jennifer Lesiak*, editorial assistant (rights and permissions).